Y0-BRW-358

Gymnastics for Men

Nik Stuart

Gymnastics for Men

Stanley Paul, London

Stanley Paul & Co Ltd
3 Fitzroy Square, London W1P 6JD

An imprint of the Hutchinson Publishing Group

London Melbourne Sydney Auckland
Wellington Johannesburg and agencies
throughout the world

First published 1978
© Nik Stuart 1978
Drawings © Stanley Paul & Co Ltd 1978

Set in Univers Light by Print Origination Ltd
Printed in Great Britain by The Anchor Press Ltd
and bound by Wm Brendon & Son Ltd, both
of Tiptree, Essex

ISBN 0 09 131280 9 (cased)
        0 09 131281 7 (paper)

to E.C.

All the photographs in this book have
been provided by Elanpics International
photo library

Contents

Acknowledgements

Mr Franklyn Edmonds OBE, President BAGA: For understanding
Yuri Titov, President FIG: For continued support
George Whiteley: For continued rationale
Helmut Bantz: For all his help unselfishly given
Adelbert Dickhut: For counsel
Tom Slaven: Motivator
Jim Pearson: Best team manager
Ray Taylor: Organizer *par excellence*
Dick Gradley: The essential element in training
Jack Srivener: Ethical excellence
Jim & Pauline Prestiege: Example for all
Prof. Abe Grossfeld, USA Champion: For knowing the value of humour
Eizio Kenmotsu: Sock brother
Boris Schaklin: Inspiration
Eugene Wettstone: Whose centre of gravity is correctly placed
Frank Bare, US Gym Federation: Evolutionary accomplishment
Television sports commentators: For trying harder
B.T. Belyakov, USSR: Art inspiration and sowing the seed
Prof. Ukran: For laying the foundations
Bill McLaughton: For mechanics and statistics
John Atkinson: Accuracy and detail
Eric Hughes, USA: For method and prolific output
Evan Tuck: For the captions
Alan Burrows: For the best photographs in the world
Bill Cosgrave: For industry and end-product
Roddy Bloomfield: For patience and tolerance

Foreword

Nik Stuart

The reason for my sudden plunge into print is my growing recognition – the longer and more deeply I examine the contemporary gymnastic scene – that gymnastics is an art. This book is intended to emphasize and encourage an artistic form of movement using the human body.

Art and artistic activities are the result of an early discipline in an art form – such as painting, mathematics, sculpture, dress design. No one achieves freedom from the discipline until he has subjected himself to the discipline. The sequences I have described will help the gymnast to develop his essential discipline and to move correctly and coordinate arms and legs, to enhance and extend the aesthetic appeal of the movement (and yet eliminate any hint of effeminacy from male gymnastic movement). The lesson plans will help the gymnast – and his coach – to prepare his body to work correctly and efficiently towards the competitive form of artistic gymnastics which enjoys world-wide popularity today.

Let's look first at Standard One, Lesson 1: floor exercises. These movements would excite neither an international gymnastic nor circus-orientated public. Accurately performed, however, they will help the gymnast to move rapidly to more advanced exercises and he will know that the structure of each movement is sound. The arm positions

7

(illustrated later in the book), the forward horizontal stand, the front support, the roll, walking with co-ordinated arm movements and turning and standing correctly are basic skills which must be accurately learned if the gymnast is to perform smoothly and easily without undue concentration to the exact position. When he can do this, his mind is free to concentrate on more complex types of movement.

The vaulting section is broken down to very simple jumps and vaults to encourage the gymnast to learn to take off properly, to learn to run properly, to learn to thrust from the horse correctly, to learn to stand exactly, accurately and correctly. Even the first lesson on the pommelled horse demonstrates that movement up and down the pommelled horse is required; movements on all three sections of the horse are therefore included. Circling the legs is extremely important, and getting the hips in the right position for the double leg circle is essential. By following the exercises prescribed in Lesson 1, the gymnast will realize that there is a high point and a low point to each leg circle.

In this way, the lessons are extremely functional in their contents.

You may detect a difference in difficulty between Lesson 1 and later lessons in any standard. This 'downhill' method is calculated to ease the work load at critical times in the learning process. Gymnastics can be fun and the commitment can rise to dedication but, whatever the level, deviation from progressive increase in skill and understanding should be minimal. There is nothing in this book to waste your time or take you from the direct route to competitor status.

I began gymnastics at the age of twenty-five – by which time it was essential that my programme was streamlined and free from irrelevancies: this system was the main reason for my success. I feel that publication of the system is vital – especially when the dominant school of contemporary thought implies that, unless you begin before birth almost, you will never be a top-class gymnast.

Introduction

One of the major difficulties which confronts the older beginner is starting this apparently endless process of learning gymnastics techniques. A prime aim of this book is to remove the guesswork and substitute a positive plan.

However enthusiastic the novice gymnast, it is most embarrassing to join a class of children in order to obtain the necessary basic coaching – and totally unsafe for his small colleagues. I was a very late starter myself and know something of the difficulties – by reflecting on my own experience, I can probably offer some positive help to those in a similar situation – people (such as college students, youth-club members, servicemen and the ordinary club member) who want not only a recreational connection with the sport but also the knowledge that behind the recreational activity lies a plan which will eventually lead to competition – whatever the age-group and level.

Success depends on the rapidity with which the gymnast can learn enough to assemble a routine. The scheme in this book consists of a series of simple routines which move from one set of necessary elements to the next. The common denominators of gymnastic proficiency are gradually included to educate the gymnast positively towards an accurate understanding of the fundamentals. The gymnast has chosen an interesting and often very attractive sport/art-form – now best described in English as 'Olympic gymnastics'.

I make no claim to originality in this scheme. I have described a tried and proven method which has worked successfully for thousands both in Britain and in the USSR. This method still forms the basis of gymnastic teaching in the Army Physical Training Corps and is particularly adaptable to the needs of older teenagers and those who begin even later.

We have in Great Britain a tremendous wealth of talent and enthusiasm. Undoubtedly our greatest need is for coaches. These can only be drawn from the older age groups, where there has been a great lack of understanding about the modern sport. I hope that this book will help to overcome that bewilderment. Two million or more children are now interested in the activity and this number is growing fast. It is vital that we offer them creative and positive guidance.

This book certainly will help exploit and enlarge the capacity of those who are sufficiently attracted to gymnastics to begin at Standard One, Lesson 1...

The development of British gymnastics

In the field of gymnastics Britain got off to a slow start – however, the sport has gained in popularity and proficiency steadily since the end of the Second World War.

More recently there has been a tremendous surge of enthusiasm for gymnastics especially amongst school children. This acceleration in interest may be attributed in part to the emergence of such figures as Olga Korbut and Nadia Comaneci and the initiation of the British Amateur Gymnastics Association/*Sunday Times* scheme which has made over two million awards for gymnastics since it started six years ago.

This increased interest in gymnastics in Britain has inevitably resulted in a tremendously improved competition standard. British juniors are now recognized as among the best in the world. In 1976 they achieved first place in the under-seventeens world championships for girls and second place in the same competition for boys. At Montreal two British girls were awarded the World-Class Gymnast badge. This award is made only to gymnasts who average 9.00 points or more in top-class competitions such as the world championships or the Olympic Games and this must be over the whole competition.

One of the factors that has delayed the progress of gymnastics in Britain is the fact that it has seldom been incorporated into training college programmes. This means the school teacher who leaves college with little or no understanding of the sport must then commit himself to an expensive series of courses run by the British Amateur Gymnastics Association or by local authorities. Fortunately this situation is now changing and several colleges now actively encourage the sport. Nevertheless even now Olympic gymnastics is rarely taught in schools as part of the sports programme. Classes are run outside school hours in clubs run, in many cases, by teachers who devote long hours and dedication to the sport.

I offer this book as a means to a practical understanding of gymnastics especially for teachers who wish to follow a progressive scheme of work for the further understanding and enjoyment of this truly great sport.

Ten commandments for gymnasts

Resolution and perseverance are necessary to the gymnast who aims for the summit.

As he progresses, he often experiences a crisis of morale. Morale even fluctuates periodically but its role can become positive and very important in the development of technique. Even so the gymnast is advised to avoid all self-complacency.

1   The gymnast must not approach training until he has established a programme that specifies the types of exercise to be learnt and the objective of his efforts for that session.

2   When the gymnast plans to train, he must see that he is suitably dressed for the purpose. He must present himself at the gym, or wherever he trains, even if he is not in the mood for practice. In the extreme case, he will observe his colleagues. This is the practice in judo, a sport in which the observation of others is highly valued.

3   The gymnast must keep and regularly update his training notebook to remind him easily of the details of the actions which he has accomplished each day. He can then consider and evaluate them readily.

4   The gymnast must regard his apparatus as a part of himself. The greatest violin virtuoso would take extreme care of his instrument to learn to play even better. The gymnast who aims for championship must use his equipment with an equivalent respect.

5   The gymnast must not shy from any effort to coax, help, or advise his associates. His active and spontaneous participation is useful not just for a single mutual friendship, but also contributes to the conscious assessment of gymnastic material.

6   No matter how unskilled and awkward another person might be, the gymnast must not ever, under any circumstances, make fun of him. On the contrary he should help. He should attentively observe the clumsily performed version in order to cultivate his own ability to demonstrate the movement so that the awkward performer can understand quickly and with accuracy the necessary technique for a successful performance.

The road to excellence has no end. The strong gymnast will meet one who is even stronger. Brilliance has only a relative value. The ambitious gymnast must continually pursue the search for greater technical skill. Before criticizing the clumsy efforts of others he should direct his attentions towards his own ability.

7   In training, the gymnast must not compare his own performance with that of anyone else. The competition is the only place where this type of comparison is valid. The gymnast must only apply to himself a standard or absolute value based on past or present performance assessed either by himself or by his coach or trainer. If, during the training, the gymnast is unduly

The scene at Varna – 1974 world championship arena.

influenced by the showing of others and compares their performance with his own technical ability he may feel disconsolate or even suffer a deep disappointment evoked by his own mistakes. In other words, his satisfaction or disappointment will depend on whether the *other* performer has excelled or worked badly. *The real champion does not compete with the others for high status but with himself to achieve his goal.* This applies not only to training but also and above all to competition.

8   The gymnast must not feel discouraged or impatient if he sometimes cannot complete movements which he has accomplished on a previous occasion. This technical trouble in the development of an exercise is common and is a quick way to discover an inherent weakness in technique. It is favourable to the improvement of skill on condition that the gymnast persists in efforts to overcome the obstacle and is not discouraged. Such trouble could help to eradicate a badly perceived yet persisting defect in the performance. If the gymnast can abolish this technical trouble, then he will accomplish the exercise more skilfully and more safely than before. Above all, he will acquire a very firm will – an important factor for success in training.

9   The gymnast must take the responsibility for assimilating the various exercises spontaneously without other assistance. As soon as the new movement is assimilated, the gymnast will directly compare his

performance to his standard and will relate it to his own abilities as a whole. Not even the best trainers should interfere with this delicate reciprocal relationship. If the trainer wishes to teach the gymnast a new movement, he must not merely show him, but must support him with extreme care. In competition the gymnast is on his own. Therefore it is important that the gymnast always sustains the mental attitude necessary to overcome obstacles in his everyday training programme on his own. A traditional ancient Japanese proverb reads: 'You should learn your own way without a teacher.'

10   During exercises at his usual training time, the gymnast must always perform with the utmost possible seriousness in accordance with the psychological pattern which is the competition norm. At training, the gymnast never exercises at 100-per-cent stress; otherwise under the tension of actual competition, he may possibly do less well.

The mental attitudes described here by no means exhaust the issue but it is still vital, however briefly, to emphasize their importance because of their key role in the technical improvement of the devotee and of the novice.

The six Olympic disciplines

Both body and mind must be fully conditioned to accept the full six disciplines as one competitive unit. For body and mind to achieve this, it is necessary to examine and understand the order of working the apparatus. There is an accepted order of working the apparatus established by the International Gymnastics Federation. The order is both logical and physically acceptable. The order of working in all major competitions is as follows:

1   Floor (free) exercises
2   Pommelled horse
3   Rings
4   Vaulting horse
5   Parallel bars
6   Horizontal bar

This order is normally followed in all competitions. It is best from the very beginning to become accustomed to this fixed situation. If, for some reason, you take part in a competition with a large entry of teams, then you may find that you start on the rings (for instance), but from that point you will follow the normal order. The specific order for you or your team will run: 3, 4, 5, 6, 1, 2.

Investigate your next competition and discover your exact starting point in the performing order. Then your subsequent training can be geared to the precise competition running order. It is quite startling and disruptive to begin on the rings after training beforehand on the normal 1, 2, 3, 4, 5, 6 order. To the unprepared gymnast, working on the floor exercises last can prove a real disaster. All competition and preparation training should resemble the competition conditions as closely as possible. If you are lucky, your order will be the normal one. A few points about the normal competition order follow.

Floor exercises

The thorough warm-up produced by this discipline is like a solid kick in the nervous system. You will be aquiver with the physical well-being which the violent activity will generate. This well-being can lead you to over-confidence on the pommelled horse. Here the slightest deviation from accurate form can spell failure. You must, therefore, discipline your mind and your body to remain cool and steady. Gymnastics demands discipline; self-control is largely mental and physical discipline. After enjoying the large open-type movements of the floor exercises, you must regain emotional stability. The floor exercises may have disappointed or pleased you but depression or elation are disturbing factors which must be recognized and dealt with before the next apparatus. One emotional fluctuation from the norm can affect the whole competition.

Dimensions

The work in this scheme does not demand the use of a measured floor area. The very nature of the compulsory exercises, however, determines that they conform to a pattern. The gymnast will grasp from this the importance of working within prescribed limits. The floor dimensions specified by the International Gymnastics Federation in the Code of Points (which all gymnasts follow) is illustrated.

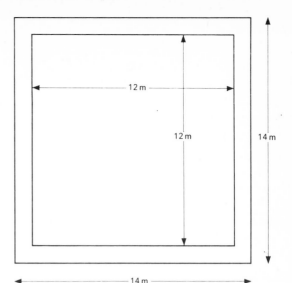

Description of the work

The exercise must form a continuous whole, harmonious and rhythmical, alternating (among other movements): balance, hold parts, strength parts, leaps, 'kips', handsprings and tumbling movements. The gymnast must move around the available floor space in all directions to give the different

The 12 metre floor square. The modern 'System Reuther' area is standard for top international events. It consists of panels of elastically joined plywood layers on a rubber base. Inserts with shock absorbent foam are bonded to the boards and covered with nylon carpet.

movements personal and postural expression.

All elementary arm, trunk, leg, hand, foot and head movements must be performed in a technically correct manner. Too long a run before leaps, handsprings and saltos should be avoided. The duration of the floor exercise is one minute, with an allowance of 10 seconds either way. An audible signal will be given at 50 seconds and again at 70 seconds.

Pommelled Horse

This is the first of the apparatus in the normal competition order and it can be the most disturbing. Fresh from the freedom of the floor exercises, you must now take into account the most precise movements. There is no possibility of a free swing to regain any lost momentum and the 'rest' position does not occur at all on the horse. It is on this apparatus that condition shows through most clearly. If the previous discipline has taken too much out of the gymnast, then the necessary accuracy will not be there, correct body tension will be lost and the results most discouraging over the whole competition.

The pommelled horse. Miroslav Cerar (Yugoslavia). A great World, European and Olympic Champion. Forerunner of the modern techniques in 'circling', 'combination' and 'shears elevation'.

Condition is vital to success

Sit down quietly for a few minutes before the pommelled horse and let matters settle in your mind. Relax; remember that the horse is not half the effort of the floor exercises; take it easy. You do not compete to learn how to do the exercise – just to demonstrate the exercises for assessment by the judges under competition conditions. This is definitely not the time to worry and fret about your big movement in the routine. Worry will certainly ensure a lack of overall concentration and probably cause a major fault in the routine at some very easy point. Try to be composed and quiet of mind. Proceed in the way you did a hundred times in training. Feel the leather of the horse and the wooden handles. It is as important that you obtain the right grasp at the right time as it is that the violinist should hit the right note – by an absolute understanding of the shape and feel of the thing. If the base of the sternum is always over the centre line of the horse, then you really cannot go far wrong. The badge in the centre of your leotard can be used as a guide.

Rings

They say the rings separate the men from the boys. In the figurative sense this is true but not in the literal sense. There are now many good ring workers in their early teens amongst the Russians, Chinese and Japanese. Tension is important here. Although you may feel tired when you move from the pommelled horse, remember that the rings will be operated by different sets of muscles. The rings are a hanging apparatus and your body will respond to the old adage that 'a change is as good as a rest' in no uncertain way. Strength–weight ratio is more important here than on any of the other apparatus. Maximum bodyweight, sometimes in still positions, is an integral part of the work. Timing is important. You cannot balance unless the weight is over the base of support: this is true in any gymnastic event, but on the rings, the base is generally on the move; understanding this movement or oscillation is essential to accurate execution of the routine.

Vaulting Horse

You must now relax. As the stress moves from the arms and shoulders after the rings, this is a good place to settle and to establish that the physically tough events are over. Finesse will now pay off. You have worked on one hanging and one supporting apparatus and there's only two to go after this one. Get rid of your frustrations explosively on the vault. Really make the vault count is the attitude necessary: a good vault can get you out of a psychological hole.

The rings. Modern equipment is to the highest safety standards. With the forces exerted by a gymnast, only the best will do for International events.

The vaulting apparatus. Yamashita (now Matsuda) (Japan) shows the movement which he first introduced to the international scene.

Parallel Bars

Normally the fourth apparatus and, for some reason, concentration can go a little haywire at this stage. Give extra attention to the settings of width and height; make sure that the bars are adjusted inwards or outwards an equal amount at each side to ensure symmetrical recoil through movements like the swinging turns and back rolls; give amplitude to the swinging elements; give poise to the slow or static movements.

Horizontal Bar

Even at this last event, you must still be looking sharp and clean in execution. The last element may well be mentally the toughest for you to perform. You will be tired but this will give you a chance to exploit the swing. Take care, when passing through handstand, that the abdominals do not cause 'Opening Time' to occur between sternum and pelvis. Tension through extended swings is the key: check handstraps, bandages and all elastic fastenings.

Parallel bars. Stan Wild (Great Britain), double Olympian, shows 'half lever' position.

The horizontal bar. Zoltan Magyar (Hungary) shows an 'ordinary grasp Stalder shoot', a movement named after the famous Swiss Olympian of the early fifties.

Competition podium: men and women

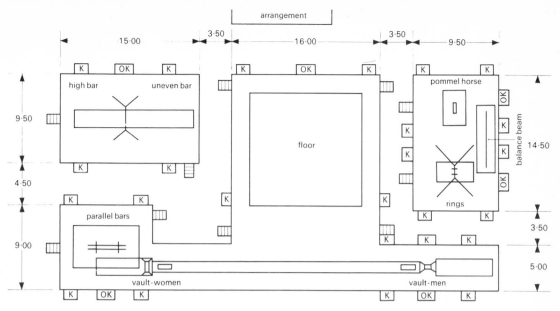

arrangement

15·00 3·50 16·00 3·50 9·50

9·50

| K | OK | K |
high bar   uneven bar

floor

K | OK | K

pommel horse

OK

balance beam

14·50

rings

K | OK | K

4·50

parallel bars

K

K

9·00

vault-women

vault-men

3·50

5·00

K | OK | K

K | OK | K

Abbreviations K Judge
OK Superior Judge

Height of Podium 0·90–1·10 m

The layout of a hall for a full international competition is included here to assist both coach and gymnast to understand the facilities with which they will be provided at the stage when they are proficient enough to participate in international competitions or full national competitions. The podium is arranged to meet requirements of both men's and women's work. The positions of the judges and officials are clearly marked. Dimensions are most important and they are followed precisely as set down here. This is currently the official layout recommended by the International Gymnastics Federation. It can also be used as a guide for your own competitions and can be adjusted to suit the apparatus available.

The International Podium, Wembley Stadium, Empire Pool. The scene of many world and European events presented by the BAGA, who have an international reputation for top organization of the meetings.

General conditioning

If you are not in good general condition, it is not possible to obtain any degree of specific condition. Good physical health is the first step to top-class physical condition.

Boris Shaklin, Russia's top gymnast for several years, wrote that his daily habit of personal exercises in the morning significantly helped him become and remain one of the world's best gymnasts. His self-discipline included a daily rub-down with water at room temperature and he followed that by pouring water over himself to complete the job of toning up mind and body. Room temperature in Russia is something best left to the imagination. Shaklin established the principle of daily body-conditioning by this routine. An advantage of good personal conditioning is that you can direct the routines at any weakness whether in range of movement or in strength. The time spent in this individual style of improving physical fitness can vary considerably. At the beginning, ten minutes is sufficient; then gradually extend the time and build up to half an hour. At peak efficiency, you would require a maximum of forty minutes.

The exercises in this book are of two kinds: one group is intended to improve the strength and the other to improve the range of movement. These are the two areas in which you will most probably need to strive for greater depth.

Unless you perform the exercises with sufficient effort and concentration to produce perspiration, then your efforts are fruitless. Perspiration keeps the skin healthy and indicates that the body's chemical functions are correctly tuned.

The well-known rules for personal health and hygiene must be followed. You will be amazed at the improvement in your state of mind and in your ability to cope generally. A short walk after supper and before retiring brings better sleep and greater recovery benefits in training the next day. Alcohol and similar contemporary 'benefits' must be taken, if at all, in moderation. Later the value of not partaking in these vices will become clearer to you. 'They allow me to unwind', you may maintain, but they have nothing but a harmful effect on the athlete.

Daily conditioning, then, is vital to the success of every sportsman. For the gymnast, it is doubly important. Miss one day's training and you know it yourself; miss two days' and the judge knows it; miss three days' training and the audience knows it. The fine edge goes from your work and the attack is absent. I led a most frugal existence when preparing for the competition season and abstained from just about everything that had no positive bearing on my attempts to produce a condition in every respect better than that of my rival gymnasts.

Here the basic splits, folding, shoulder and
spine extending positions are shown. These
should be practised at every training session.
The hip and shoulder girdles must be strong and
elastic for Olympic gymnastics.

1 Programme for general conditioning over a five-week period – to improve cardio-respiratory condition

Week	Monday	Wednesday	Friday
1	10 × 15m dashes (30 seconds between dashes) 4 stair-climbs	10 × 55m dashes (30 seconds between dashes) 4 stair-climbs	15 × 55m dashes (30 seconds between dashes) 4 stair-climbs
2	15 × 55m dashes (30 seconds between dashes) 6 stair-climbs	8 × 250m dashes (3 minutes between runs) 8 stair-climbs	2 × 1 000m runs (8 minutes between runs) 8 stair-climbs
3	4 × 500m dashes (3 minutes between dashes)	4 × 500m dashes (3 minutes between dashes) 4 × 750m dashes (30 seconds between dashes) 8 stair-climbs	1 × 2 000m run (under 6 minutes)
4	15 × 100m dashes (30 seconds between each 5 dashes) 8 stair-climbs	5 × 500m dashes 3 × 100m dashes (3 minutes between all dashes) 8 stair-climbs	1 × 4 000m run (under 15 minutes) 20 stair-climbs
5	15 × 100m dashes (1 minute between dashes) 1 × 500m dash 1 × 250m dash 10 stair-climbs	1 × 6 000m run (under 25 minutes)	No activity

Allow 3 minutes between running and beginning of stair-climbing.

2 For shoulder strength (twice daily)

1 Heaving, 6
2 Low squat jumps, 6
3 Sit-ups, 5 × 10 (20 seconds rest)
4 Skipping, 30 × 5 (20 seconds rest)
5 Heaving, 5 × 3
6 High jumps, maximum 20
7 Handstands, maximum 3 attempts (45 seconds rest)
8 Push-ups, maximum 3 (45 seconds rest)
9 Trunk circling, 5 each way
10 Jumps with arms circling, 20

3 For shoulder suppling (twice daily)

1 Heaving, 6
2 Low squat jumps, 6
3 Leg raising, 3 × 8 all round
4 Dislocations with stick, 8
5 Splits practice, 10 bouncing
6 Shoot-outs in back support, 10
7 Back bends rocking, 10
8 Flat side lunge, right and left, 4
9 Back bends against the wall in handstand, 5
10 Jumps with arms circling, 20

General Conditioning

For shoulder strength Twice daily		For shoulder suppling Twice daily	
1 6	2 6	1 6	2 6
3 5 x 10 (20 sec rest)	4 30 x 5 (20 sec rest)	3 3 x 8 all round	4 8 dislocates
5 5 x 3 (20 sec rest)	6 20 max height	5 10	6 10
7 max (time) 3 attempts (45 sec rest)	8 max x 3 (45 sec rest)	7 10	8 R and L x 4
9 5 each way	10 20	9 5	10 20

23

Specific conditioning

The specific conditioning exercises here will enable you to do something positive towards achieving your gymnastic aims quickly. If you follow them correctly, they will provide better balance, strength where and when needed, and suppleness as specifically required. The specific conditioning exercises will enable you to save time on those really intended for general conditioning. 'We exercise to become fit enough to do more exercises' is a false philosophy. We do exercises in order to reach our gymnastic aims. The more specific the aims, the more specific the exercises must be. The exercises presented here are a distillation of the rest of the world's ideas on specific conditioning (about which much has been written). Some exercises are 'old-fashioned', some are new. Each one is included because it offers more benefit than any other. The exercises are not spectacular and require little space or equipment. They do, however, form the most important part of your gymnastic preparation and will help you to avoid the sticking point in those levers and presses which you thought beyond your capacity.

Make your own hand bars and carry them with you in your training bag.

Shigeru Kasamatsu (Japan) shows a perfect 'top change' on the horizontal bar. Conditioning the body to produce a perfect line in handstand is important since the gymnast uses the handstand on all apparatus except the pommelled horse.

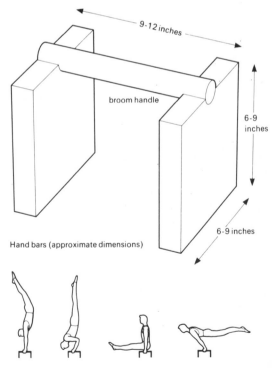

9-12 inches

broom handle

6-9 inches

6-9 inches

Hand bars (approximate dimensions)

Exercises for specific conditioning

Start with six repetitions and gradually increase according to condition.

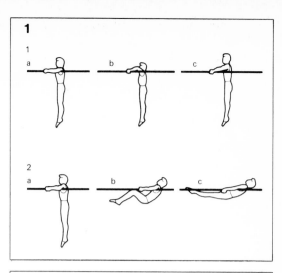

1/1 (a)(b)(c) Shoulder shrugging in upper-arm support.
1/2 (a)(b)(c) Body extending forwards in upper-arm support.

2/1 (a)(b) Heaving in overgrasp.
2/2 (a)(b)(c)(d)(e)(f) From hanging with body backwards forwards and upwards to front support.

3/1 (a)(b)(c) Hips raising legs extending forwards.
3/2 (a)(b)(c) Hips raising and extending legs backwards to front support.
3/3 (a)(b)(c)(d) Combining the first exercise and the last exercise, legs snapping through forwards backwards.

4/1 (a) (b)   From long sitting between small bars pressed to half lever.

4/2 (a) (b) (c)   From half lever fall slowly to the rear with straight legs.

4/3 (a) (b)   Lean forwards in support with bent legs, raise legs from ground bend arms.

4/4 (a) (b)   On straight arms with straight body lean forwards to attempt front planche.

4/5   Handstanding.

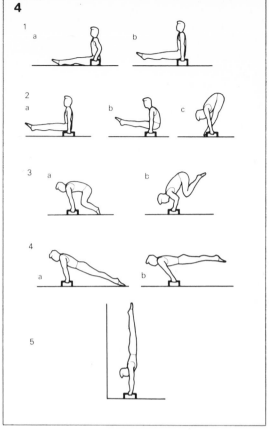

5/1 (a) (b) (c)   From handstand fall against wall draw shoulders back until balance is reassumed.

5/2 (a) (b) (c) (d) (e)   Kick to handstand shoulder weaving, rearranging shoulders and legs around the line of equilibrium without losing balance.

5/3 (a) (b)   In leaning support against wall bend and stretch arms.

26

5/4 (a) (b) (d) (e)   From half lever draw with straight legs and straight arms to handstand.

5/5 (a) (b) (c) (d)   From free straddle support elevate to handstand.

5/6 (a) (b)   From prone lying with arms extended arch back strongly as possible, return to lying.

5/7 (a) (b)   From back lying arms extended raised saucer position hold return to lying.

6/1 (a) (b) (c)   From kneeling on box support on rings, push rings forwards extend body as far as possible.

6/2 (a) (b)   Reverse the action.

6/3 (a) (b)   From kneeling support on box top lower until rings are parallel with ground and body is on box.

6/4 (a) (b)   From half lever with leg supported lower backwards to cross.

6/5 (a) (b)   Using rubber strands hooked from rings round feet front planche and back planche below rings.

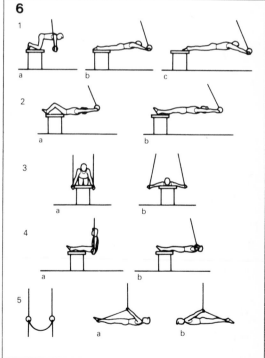

7/1 (a) (b) Standing 1 m from the wall with strands touching the wall press arms forwards.

7/2 (a) (b) Reverse the procedure.

7/3 (a) (b) Press strands behind with arms in downward position.

7/4 (a) (b) Kneeling facing wall bars pull strands backwards.

7/5 (a) (b) Reverse the procedure.

7/6 (a) (b) With strands over parallel bar press arms downwards in sitting position.

7/7 (a) (b) With strands under seat lift arms strongly.

7/8 (a) (b) With strands under feet raise arms forwards.

7/9 (a) (b) With strands under feet raise arms backwards.

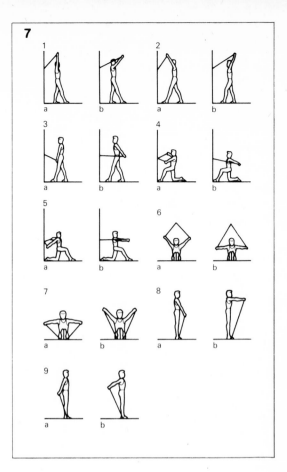

Applying the lessons

Warming-up

Each training session must start with a warm-up to ensure that body and mind are attuned to accept the physical activities encountered in the lessons. The warm-up need not be complex. Its aims are as follows:

to increase respiration
to increase circulation
to improve muscular reaction
to improve and to maintain a range of
    movement

At least 10 minutes should be spent on the warm-up. You should spend longer in cold weather or when your condition has improved to the point where a longer warm-up is really necessary. The following examples may be used as a guide:

running around the gym (on toes, with
    high knee raise, with legs straight,
    skipping)
arm exercises (arm circling and
    swinging, wrist and finger exercises)
trunk exercises (forward, side and
    backward bending and circling)
leg exercises (leg raising, forwards,
    sideways and backwards)
back suppling (from back lying raise to
    back bend, forward bending in
    sitting)
simple agilities (rolls, cartwheels,
    handstands, handsprings)

Your first session for Standard One, Lesson 1, should proceed in the following way:

1   Place the equipment in position as soon as you arrive in the gym.
2   Dress warmly (a track suit and even a woollen hat and gloves may be necessary).
3   Warm up for 10 minutes or so.
4   Floor exercises (15 minutes): perform the first element, then the second element. Next the first, and the second element. Proceed with the third element. Then the first, second and third elements. Then the fourth element. Then proceed through from first to the fourth and so on – until the whole lesson is learnt or time runs out.
5   Pommelled horse (15 minutes): proceed as for the floor exercises.
6   Rings (15 minutes): proceed as for the floor exercises.
7   Vaulting (15 minutes): proceed as for the floor exercises.
8   Parallel bars (15 minutes): proceed as for the floor exercises.
9   Horizontal bar (15 minutes): proceed as for the floor exercises.
10 Conditioning (15 minutes): specific conditioning practice.
11 Leave gym as you would wish to find it (5 minutes).

Total time 2 hours

Henri Boerio (France), the second ranked gymnast of the western world, finalist on the horizontal bars in Montreal, shows here a perfect 'crucifix' on the rings. The movement must be performed with a straight body and shoulders in line with the hands.

The lesson guide

This lesson guide will enable you to find your place in the programme at a glance.

Standard	Discipline	Lesson	Pages
One	Floor Exercises	1 2 3	40 – 47
	Pommelled Horse	1 2 3 4 5 6	48 – 53
	Rings	1 2 3	54 – 55
	Vaulting	1 2 3 4	56 – 57
	Parallel Bars	1 2 3 4 5 6	58 – 63
	Horizontal Bar	1 2 3 4 5 6	64 – 73
Two	Floor Exercises	1 2	74 – 81
	Pommelled Horse	1 2 3 4 5 6	82 – 87
	Rings	1 2 3	88 – 91
	Vaulting	1 2 3 4 5	92 – 95
	Parallel Bars	1 2 3 4 5 6	96 – 101
	Horizontal Bar	1 2 3 4 5 6	102 – 107
Three	Floor Exercises	1 2 3 4	108 – 121
	Pommelled Horse	1 2 3 4 5 6	122 – 127
	Rings	1 2 3	128 – 131
	Vaulting	1 2 3 4 5 6	132 – 135
	Parallel Bars	1 2 3 4 5 6	136 – 143
	Horizontal Bar	1 2 3 4 5 6	144 – 155
Four	Floor Exercises	1 2 3 4	156 – 165
	Pommelled Horse	1 2 3 4 5 6	166 – 171
	Rings	1 2 3 4	172 – 179
	Vaulting	1 2 3 4 5 6	180 – 183
	Parallel Bars	1 2 3 4 5 6	184 – 189
	Horizontal Bar	1 2 3 4 5 6	190 – 199
Summary:	Floor Exercises	13 lessons	
	Pommelled Horse	24 lessons	
	Rings	13 lessons	
	Vaulting	21 lessons	
	Parallel Bars	24 lessons	
	Horizontal Bar	24 lessons	

The lesson check-sheet

Standard	1			2		3				4			
Lesson	1	2	3	1	2	1	2	3	4	1	2	3	4
10													
9													
8													
7													
6													
5													
4													
3													
2													
1													
0													

FLOOR EXERCISES

Standard	1						2						3						4					
Lesson	1	2	3	4	5	6	1	2	3	4	5	6	1	2	3	4	5	6	1	2	3	4	5	6
10																								
9																								
8																								
7																								
6																								
5																								
4																								
3																								
2																								
1																								
0																								

POMMELLED HORSE

Standard	1			2			3			4			
Lesson	1	2	3	1	2	3	1	2	3	1	2	3	4
10													
9													
8													
7													
6													
5													
4													
3													
2													
1													
0													

RINGS

Standard	1				2					3						4					
Lesson	1	2	3	4	1	2	3	4	5	1	2	3	4	5	6	1	2	3	4	5	6
10																					
9																					
8																					
7																					
6																					
5																					
4																					
3																					
2																					
1																					
0																					

VAULTING

Standard	1						2						3						4					
Lesson	1	2	3	4	5	6	1	2	3	4	5	6	1	2	3	4	5	6	1	2	3	4	5	6
10																								
9																								
8																								
7																								
6																								
5																								
4																								
3																								
2																								
1																								
0																								

PARALLEL BARS

Standard	1						2						3						4					
Lesson	1	2	3	4	5	6	1	2	3	4	5	6	1	2	3	4	5	6	1	2	3	4	5	6
10																								
9																								
8																								
7																								
6																								
5																								
4																								
3																								
2																								
1																								
0																								

HORIZONTAL BAR

Using the lesson check-sheet

The check-sheet shows your level of progress throughout the lessons. It can be used for a quick indication of what you have done and of what is left to be done – and also provides a graphical account of your progress. Indicate your score with a dot and join the dots with a straight line.

You may find that Standard One, Lesson 2, Floor Exercises takes six sessions to master but Standard One, Lesson 2, Pommelled Horse takes only three sessions to accomplish. The material is planned to help you adjust to the different learning loads involved. For example, the total Floor Exercises lessons in Standard One occupy roughly the same time as the Pommelled Horse in Standard One.

Aim for pass level of:

Standard One: 5 points out of 10
Standard Two: 6 points   "
Standard Three: 7 points   "
Standard Four: 8 points   "

These levels are by no means easy to achieve and over-lenient marking by anyone judging your attempts does you a bad turn. Remember that flattery will get you nowhere; patience, determination, study and courage must be the key factors in your gymnastics.

The training cycle

The Training Cycles run annually and are divided into three basic phases:

Preparation Phase
Main Training Phase
Competition Phase

The cycle given in the attached chart should be used as a guide for the second and subsequent cycles. Adjustments will be made by the coach in accordance with the success or shortcomings of the first cycle.

Strength

General strength training as it suggests is aimed at overall improvement of the physical reserves through a wide programme of movements. Specific strength training consists of using strength movements to improve specific needs – these would be different, for instance, for the shot putter and the gymnast.

Acrobatics

The agility or acrobatic movements are often practised separately. Handsprings and somersaults are therefore classed as the acrobatic parts of the floor exercise routine. To practise them only in the full context of the routine would give little time for real concentration on what the Russian System describes as the 'acrobatic jumps'. Therefore separate sections of the programme must be made available for improving these movements.

Games

As a relaxation and a form of respiratory training you cannot afford to overlook the value of games such as basket ball, soccer, volley ball and other active ball games. These should be included in the overall programme.

Ballet

Ballet exercises are valuable for they encourage a positive range of movement. For example, the ability to swing the leg high to the side is in no way as valuable as the ability to hold the leg static at the highest point of the swing. To be able to drop into the splits is fine but to jump into the air and perform the splits at the peak of the jump is infinitely more valuable. Ballet exercises encourage poise, body tension spring and range of movement. However, to achieve real progress, it is advisable to spend some time with a qualified ballet teacher. More harm than good can come from ballet training without guidance.

Training Cycle for Gymnasts

		T'	1	2	3	4	5	6	7	8	9	10	11	12	13	14	15	16	17	18	19	20	21	22	23	24	25
Suppling	(General &) Formal	25	X	X	X	X	X	X	X	X	X	X	X	X	X	X	X	X	X	X	X	X	X	X	X	X	X
	Shoulders	5	X	X	X	X	X																				
	Trunk	5			X	X	X	X	X																		
	Hips	5					X	X	X	X	X																
	Strength	9		X		X		X		X		X			X			X			X			X			
Olympic disciplines (6)	Floor	10																X	X	X	X	X	X	X	X	X	X
	P. horse	12			X		X		X		X		X				X	X	X		X		X		X		X
	Rings	11		X		X		X		X		X		X		X		X		X		X		X			
	Vault	20	X	X	X	X	X	X	X	X			X		X			X	X	X		X	X	X	X	X	X
	P. bars	12	X	X		X		X		X		X		X		X		X		X		X		X		X	
	H. bar	13	X		X		X		X		X		X		X		X		X		X		X		X		X
	Acrobatics	13	X		X		X		X			X		X	X	X				X		X	X		X	X	X
	Ballet	25	X	X	X	X	X	X	X	X	X	X	X	X	X	X	X	X	X	X	X	X	X	X	X	X	X
	Games	4	X	X	X	X																					
	Tactics	3																							X	X	X
	Total daily activities		8	8	9	9	9	8	8	7	5	6	5	5	6	6	5	8	6	7	6	7	7	7	8	7	8

T' = Activities Total in the Cycle

✗ = 10/20/30 mins; adjusted to intensity required

The training plan

First variation (for national standard gymnasts)

Month	Period	Contents
August (first half)	Preparation period	General conditioning
August (second half) September October (first half)	Main period	Specific conditioning
October (second half) November December	Competition period	Competition preparation (routines)
January	Preparation period	General conditioning
February March April	Main period	Specific conditioning
May June July	Competition period	Competition preparation (routines)

The above plan is in use by the current men's British national Senior Squad

Second variation

Month	Period	Contents
September (first half)	Preparation period	General conditioning
September (second half) October	Main period	Specific conditioning
November December	Competition period	Competition preparation (routines)
January (first half)	Preparation period	General conditioning
January (second half) February	Main period	Specific conditioning
March April	Competition period	Competition preparation (routines)
May (first half)	Preparation period	General conditioning
May (second half) June	Main period	Specific conditioning
July August	Competition period	Competition preparation (routines)

The above plan can be varied to suit your own requirements.

These illustrations show 'forward and backward swings' on the rings. It is not enough for most gymnasts to just practise the movement. The majority must do specific conditioning related to the exercise.

The lessons

Standard One
Floor Exercises
Lesson 1

This exercise is marked out of 10

I
1 From standing at attention, raise right arm sideways and step to the rear with the right foot.
2 Raise left arm sideways and step to the rear with the left foot.
  Bring right foot back to join left and place arms forwards.
3 Circle arms forwards, downwards, backwards, bending and straightening the legs to arms upwards.
4 Circle arms inwards to sideways.   1.5 points

II
1 Raising right leg to the side lunge to the right side.
2 Arms upwards.
3 Transfer weight and lunge left.
4 Lower arms pushing from left leg with quarter turn to stand erect on right leg.   1.0 points

III
1 2 3 4 Forward horizontal stand on right leg.   2.0 points

IV
1 Swedish fall left leg raised.
2 Lower left leg and straighten arms to front support, raise left arm and transfer weight to right arm.
3 To back support.
4 Bend hips to long sitting.   0.5 points

V
1 Bend forwards and reach forwards past the feet, roll backwards.
2 3 4 Roll and extend to shoulder balance with hip and elbow support.   0.5 points

VI
1 Roll forwards to crouch, stand legs crossed.
2 Continue to turn and rise. Half turn dive forwards and   2.0 points
3 4 Roll forwards to crouch.

VII
1 Swing right arm forwards and left leg with half turn of upper body continuing to extend arms sideways, swing arms downwards and turn body back to face forwards.
2 Continuing to turn to the right extend arms to the side. Swing arms downwards and continue to turn to the right.
3 Turning the upper trunk to the right and extending the arms sideways.
4 Bring right foot to the attention position and raise arms upwards.   1.5 points

VIII
1 Lower the arms and crossing the wrists to the rear open legs to astride, close legs and raise arms to the side.
2 Raise arms upwards to touch above head and open legs to astride, lower arms to sideways and bend legs, knees outwards.
3 Stretch legs.
4 Lower arms to attention.   1.0 points

40

Standard One
Floor Exercises
Lesson 2

This exercise is marked out of 10

I
1 From attention bend knees and raise arms sideways.
2 Stretch legs and raise arms overhead.
3 Bend to crouch position.
4 Stand opening legs to astride and raising arms sideways.   1.0 points

II
1 Bend knees, place hands on knees bending body forwards and downwards.
2 Stand erect opening legs to astride and raising arms sideways.
3 Arms across bend and arms stretch forwards.
4 Bend trunk forwards and raise arms sideways.   0.5 points

III
1 Turn trunk to left extending left arm upwards.
2 Turn trunk to right extending right arm upwards.
3 Return to arms sideways, trunk forward-bend position.
4 Raise trunk and lower arms to sides and bend trunk forwards downwards and place hands on ground.   0.5 points

IV
1 Raise trunk and lower arms to sides. Fall forwards to prone position, arms bent.
2 Straighten arms and close legs to front support.
3 Push backwards reaching arms forwards to kneeling.

4 Spring, stretching right leg to side and bring left bent knee between hands.   1.0 points

V
1 2 Complete leg circle of right leg to extend right leg sideways.
3 Hop and extend left leg sideways rising and passing weight from right leg to left leg return to –
4 Right leg extended sideways turn, standing on left leg rise to lunge.   1.5 points

VI
1 2 Hold lunge.
3 Lower leg and stand erect.
4 Lower arms to sides and raise left leg forwards.   1.0 points

VII
1 Lunge forwards arms remaining overhead.
2 Extend left leg, turning to right and lowering arms to side, and circle arms downwards inwards to –
3 4 Arms sideways.   0.5 points

VIII
1 Place left hand on hip, stretch right hand overhead, balance lunge right.
2 Extend arms sideways straightening legs.
3 Balance lunge left.
4 Return arms to sideways position.   0.5 points

IX
1 Turn trunk to right bending right leg and reaching forwards with right hand.
2 Swing left leg forwards to touch right hand.
3 Return to starting position.
4 Turn left to astride stand with arms sideways.   0.5 points

continued

X

1 Turn to left bending left leg.
2 Swing right leg forward to touch left hand.
3 Return to original position.
4 Bring left arm forward to join right arm.   0.5 points

XI

1 Raise arms overhead and bring right leg to join left standing erect.
2 3 4 Bend forward to crouch and roll forwards to crouch.   1.0 points

XII

1 Spring upwards extending hips and swinging arms to rear, land with legs bent and arms raised forwards and jump with quarter turn right raising arms overhead.
2 Land with knees bent and open and arms moving to the side.
3 Extend legs raising arms sideways. Lower arms to attention.   1.5 points

Sawao Kato (Japan) performing here a 'double back somersault' with great style and courage. He is an all-round Gold medallist (Mexico 1968 and Munich 1972), and Silver medallist and team Gold medallist in Montreal.

'Front horizontal half stand'. This movement is frequently included in set and optional work from beginner to Olympic level.

44

Standard One
Floor Exercises
Lesson 3

This exercise is marked out of 10

I
1 From attention raise arms sideways.
2 Bend knees and fold arms fully.
3 Stand with legs astride and arms raising sideways.
4 Bend forwards swinging arms inwards and across.   1.5 points

II
1 Swing arms to sideways position.
2 Swing arms downwards and upwards bending left leg.
3 Return to original position.
4 Bend forwards and swing arms downwards across.   1.5 points

III
1 Raise trunk erect and arms sideways.
2 Bend right knee and lunge sideways raising arms upwards.
3 Push from right leg lower arms sideways to balance on left leg.
4 Bend left leg and place hands round.   1.0 points

IV
1 Hop change to extend left leg sideways.
2 3 Circle left leg clockwise underneath right leg to extend left leg sideways.
4 Quarter turn right.   1.0 points

V
1 Place right leg alongside left leg and bend arms.
2 Straighten arms and raise left leg.
3 Lower left leg to front support.
4 Push backwards from hands to kneeling.   1.0 points

VI
1 2 Push forwards from lower leg and roll forwards crossing legs.
3 4 Stand erect with half turn to attention.   1.5 points

VII
1 Step forwards with left leg raising arms sideways.
2 Swing arms forwards and right leg forwards to touch both hands.
3 Swing right leg to the right with quarter turn raising arms sideways.   1.0 points

VIII
1 Place legs together and bend forwards.
2 Stand erect raising arms sideways upwards with quarter turn to right, balance lunge to the left with arms raised overhead, push from left leg to join legs and lower arms sideways.
3 Swing arms downwards returning them upwards whilst bending and stretching the legs, and jumping with legs astride and arms sideways upwards and land with legs bent and arms sideways downwards.
4 Recover to attention.   1.5 points

Standard One
Pommelled Horse
Lesson 1

This exercise is marked out of 10

1	Right circle of right leg	2.5 points
2	Half right circle of left leg	0.5 points
3	Full left circle of right leg with three quarter turn of body to straddle sit	2.5 points
4	Half left circle of left leg to squat stand	0.5 points
5	Right circle of right leg grasp pommel with right hand	2.0 points
6	Circle right leg to rear and rear dismount	2.0 points

Wolfgang Thune (West Germany). Shears from the rearward view. Note the strong 'squeezing' grip and locked support arm. Compare the head position with the other pommelled horse photographs. Only on a finish is the head lifted high.

Standard One
Pommelled Horse
Lesson 2

This exercise is marked out of 10

1	One and a half left circle of right leg to feint right	2.5 points
2	Right leg in crouch, full circle of left leg with half right turn of body, carry both legs to front rest	2.5 points
3	Right leg half right circle	1.0 points
4	Left leg half right circle to feint left	1.0 points
5	Rear vault to ground to right	3.0 points

Zoltan Magyar (Hungary). 'Shears movement'. The World, European and Olympic Champion on the pommelled horse shows high leg lift, good separation, with excellent hip extension and shoulder displacement.

Standard One   Pommelled Horse   Lesson 1

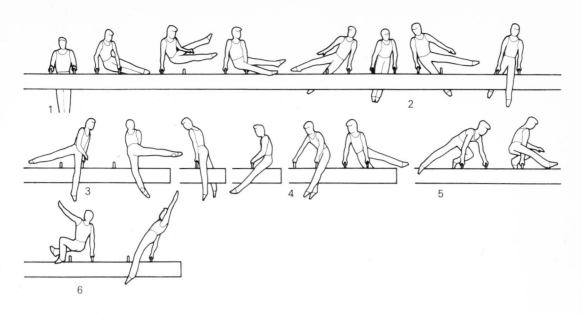

Standard One   Pommelled Horse   Lesson 2

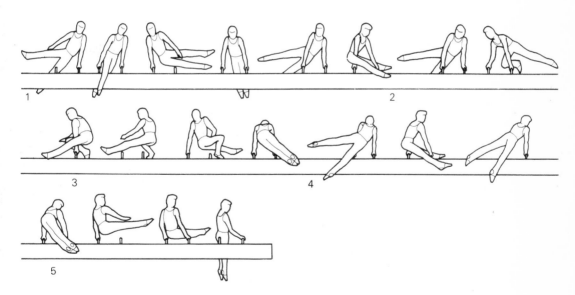

Standard One
Pommelled Horse
Lesson 3

This exercise is marked out of 10

1 Circle right leg with half turn
  left to feint on right arm   2.5 points
2 Return legs to front rest as
  shown   1.5 points
3 Right circle of right leg   3.0 points
4 Half circle of left and right
  legs to back rest   1.0 points
5 Half left circle of left leg,
  half turn of body and placing
  right hand on end of horse
  remove left leg and with
  further half turn, dismount   2.0 points

Standard One
Pommelled Horse
Lesson 4

This exercise is marked out of 10

1 Full left circle of left leg   2.5 points
2 Half left circle of right leg
  swing to left   0.5 points
3 Half right circle of right leg   1.0 points
4 Left leg half right circle, feint
  right   1.0 points
5 Left leg half left circle   1.0 points
6 Right leg half right circle   0.5 points
7 Flank vault right   3.5 points

Standard One Pommelled Horse Lesson 3

Standard One Pommelled Horse Lesson 4

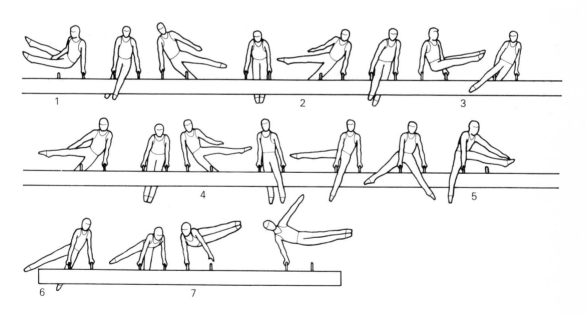

**Standard One
Pommelled Horse
Lesson 5**

This exercise is marked out of 10

1 One and a half right circles
 of left leg   2.5 points
2 Swing to right left leg half
 left to front rest   1.5 points
3 Right half left   0.5 points
4 Left leg half left feint   0.5 points
5 Right half right   1.0 points
6 Left leg half left   0.5 points
7 Flank vault left   3.5 points

**Standard One
Pommelled Horse
Lesson 6**

This exercise is marked out of 10

1 Half left circle of left leg   1.5 points
2 Half right circle of left leg to
 stand   1.5 points
3 Crouch right circle of left leg
 continue to feint right of
 right arm   3.0 points
4 Remove feint leg to rear half
 right circle left leg   0.5 points
5 Swing right and left half left
 to front rest   1.5 points
6 Right leg half right, swing to
 left swing right leg to rear
 and dismount   2.0 points

Standard One   Pommelled Horse   Lesson 5

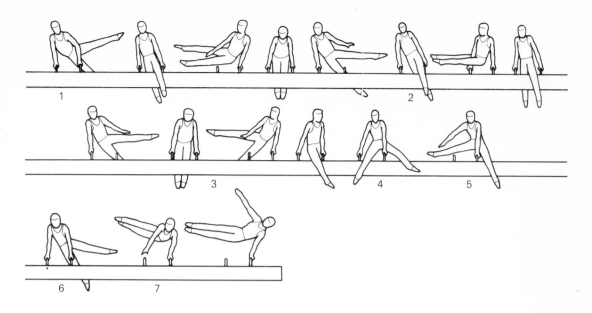

Standard One   Pommelled Horse   Lesson 6

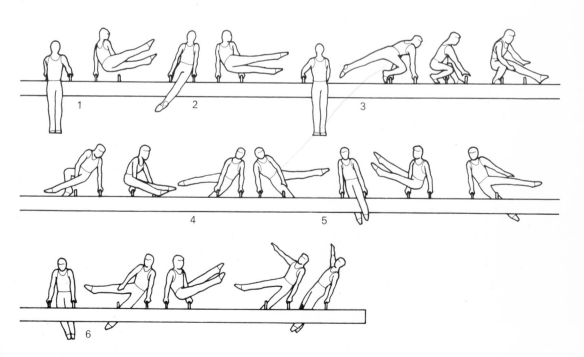

Sawao Kato (Japan) shows a 'straddle lever' on the rings. Compare the photograph with the performance of Klimenko. Note the better hand and arm positions, together with higher leg elevation which makes Kato's position more artistic.

Victor Klimenko (USSR)—the 'straddle lever' is a position which demands strength as well as flexibility.

**Standard One
Rings
Lesson 1**

This exercise is marked out of 10

1 Rise to straight-arm rest	3.0 points
2 Raise legs to half lever	1.5 points
3 Roll forwards to half inverted hang	1.0 points
4 Swing backwards in bent-arm hang	0.5 points
5 Swing forwards in straight-arm hang	0.5 points
6 Raise to half inverted hang change to inverted hang	1.0 points
7 Swing down to rear and dismount	2.5 points

**Standard One
Rings
Lesson 2**

This exercise is marked out of 10

1 Uprise to bent-arm hang	1.0 points
2 Front lever with arms bent	3.0 points
3 Inlocate to inverted hang	4.5 points
4 Dismount to rear	1.5 points

**Standard One
Rings
Lesson 3**

This exercise is marked out of 10

1 Swing to inverted hang, legs astride	2.5 points
2 Bring rear leg forwards and leg assisting upstart	3.5 points
3 Return to half inverted hang	0.5 points
4 Heave	2.0 points
5 Swing back and lower to straight-arm hang	0.5 points
6 Swing forward and dismount	1.0 points

54

Standard One   Rings   Lesson 1

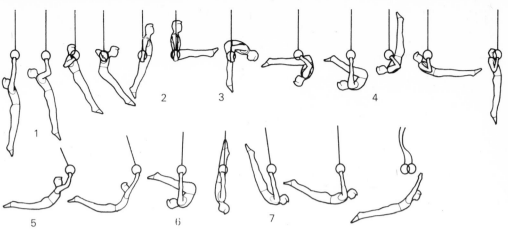

1   2   3   4

5   6   7

Standard One   Rings   Lesson 2

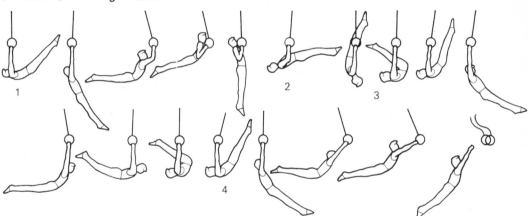

1   2   3

4

Standard One   Rings   Lesson 3

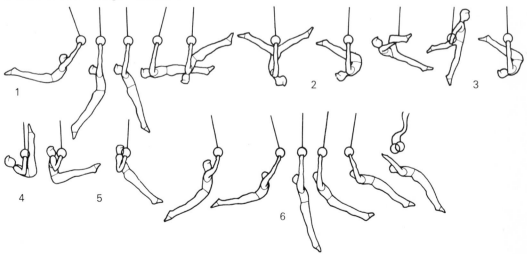

1   2   3

4   5   6

Haruhiro Matsuda (Japan), the inventor of the 'Yamashita' vault, shows spectacular flight onto the horse in this 'cartwheel vault'.

Standard One
Vaulting
Lesson 1

This exercise is marked out of 10

1.20m	10 points
1.15m	8 points
1.10m	6 points
1.05m	4 points
1.00m	2 points

Running forward high jump over rope or lath to improve landing practice and flight awareness. (Lean backwards at take-off and keep weight forwards until landing – land with feet together. Co-ordinate arm swing to assist with elevation at take off.)

Standard One
Vaulting
Lesson 2

Straddle vault over buck set at 1.30m. (Open the legs only after the hands strike the horse top. Stay extended in the hips throughout until landing.)

Standard One
Vaulting
Lesson 3

Squat vault over buck set at 1.30m and placed sideways.
(Without lay out but with full squat and with maximum flight after leaving horse. Extend fully before landing.)

Standard One
Vaulting
Lesson 4

Side vault over buck set at 1.30m.
(Show extended flank position on straight arm, inside leg leading up into vault followed by hip thrust to obtain correct position passing over horse.)

Standard One   Vaulting   Lesson 1

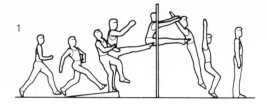

Standard One   Vaulting   Lesson 2

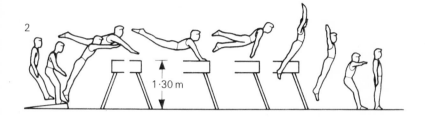

Standard One   Vaulting   Lesson 3

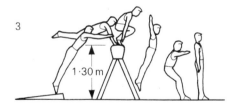

Standard One   Vaulting   Lesson 4

Standard One
Parallel Bars
Lesson 1

This exercise is marked out of 10

1 Straddle over right bar and return to 1	1.5 points
2 Straddle over right bar and return to 1	1.5 points
3 Roll to cross riding seat hands in front	1.5 points
4 Grasp in forearm rest uprise forwards	1.0 points
5 Swing to shoulderstand (straight body)	2.5 points
6 Swing down and place left leg on bar	0.5 points
7 Swing leg to rear and flank dismount	1.5 points

Nikolai Andrianov (USSR) terminates the under somersault with the straddle into the 'half lever' position. It is used before the strength press, which is an obligatory part of every top-class routine. (The preparation for this exercise is contained in Standard Four.)

Standard One
Parallel Bars
Lesson 2

This exercise is marked out of 10

1 Jump to forearm rest, swing forwards, backwards into shoulderstand	3.0 points
2 Swing down forwards	0.5 points
3 Upstart from upper arms, swing backwards	3.5 points
4 Place left leg on left bar, swing right leg backwards and return to commence forward swing	0.5 points
5 Swing forwards and flank vault dismount	2.5 points

58

Standard One   Parallel Bars   Lesson 1

Standard One   Parallel Bars   Lesson 2

Standard One
Parallel Bars
Lesson 3

This exercise is marked out of 10

1	Run in, uprise forwards	3.5 points
2	Swing back, cross legs, turn to cross riding seat hands behind	1.0 points
3	Place hands in front, lift to shoulderstand	1.5 points
4	Roll forwards and beat to cross riding seat	0.5 points
5	Grasp forwards in forearm rest, remove legs and uprise forwards	1.0 points
6	Swing backwards straddle forwards to ground	2.5 points

Standard One
Parallel Bars
Lesson 4

This exercise is marked out of 10

1	Back uprise to front rest	3.5 points
2	Swing forwards, place left leg on bar and turn to cross riding seat hands behind	2.0 points
3	Remove legs and swing to shoulderstand	2.5 points
4	Swing down and rear vault dismount	2.0 points

'A perfect handstand'—elbows locked, shoulders extended, body straight, leg muscles locked— toes and ankles extended. A lot of work for the beginner. Even the champions train every day for perfection in this position. (See Standard Four, Lesson 6, Element 3.)

Standard One   Parallel Bars   Lesson 3

Standard One   Parallel Bars   Lesson 4

Standard One
Parallel Bars
Lesson 5

This exercise is marked out of 10

1	Forward grasp, running long underswing, upstart to upper arms, swing back in upper arms	3.5 points
2	Uprise forwards to cross riding seat hands behind	1.5 points
3	Remove legs and hold half lever for 3 seconds	2.0 points
4	Swing back, swing forwards through bent-arm rest to straight-arm rest	1.5 points
5	Swing to rear and front vault dismount right (or left)	1.5 points

Standard One
Parallel Bars
Lesson 6

This exercise is marked out of 10

1	Alternate grasp, circle up with half turn to front rest (straddled)	1.5 points
2	Remove legs, swing forwards, upstart from upper arms	3.0 points
3	Swing to rear with straight arms	1.0 points
4	Swing forwards, place right leg on right bar swing left leg rear and straddle sit on left bar after turning	1.5 points
5	Remove right leg and turn to outside riding seat	1.0 points
6	Rear vault with quarter turn to face bars	2.0 points

Standard One   Parallel Bars   Lesson 5

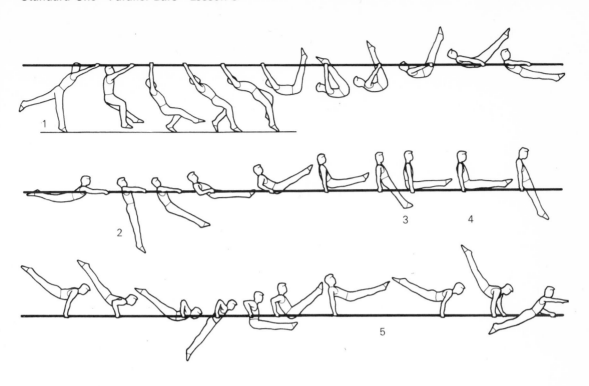

Standard One   Parallel Bars   Lesson 6

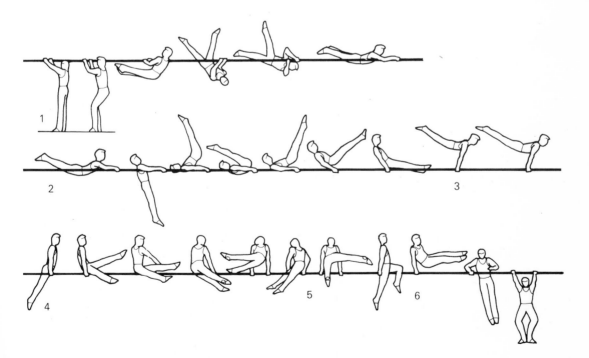

Standard One
Horizontal Bar
Lesson 1

This exercise is marked out of 10

1 Mill circle to raise above bar   3.0 points
2 Change grasp and knee
    circle forwards to mill rest   2.0 points
3 Remove leg and turn to front
    rest   1.5 points
4 Place foot between hands
    and leap forwards to land on
    ground   3.5 points

*Nikolai Andrianov (USSR). This is a similar
position for beginners and experts. This
movement was part of the 1976 Montreal
Olympic sets.*

Standard One
Horizontal Bar
Lesson 2

This exercise is marked out of 10

1 Long underswing to front,
    upstart to front rest   4.0 points
2 Place leg outside hands and
    knee circle backwards   2.0 points
3 Half knee circle backwards,
    half knee circle forwards   0.5 points
4 Remove leg and dismount to
    ground at rear of bar, high
    underswing forwards to
    stand   3.5 points

*Gennadi Kryssin (USSR) demonstrates the first
phase of the reverse upstart on the horizontal
bar.*

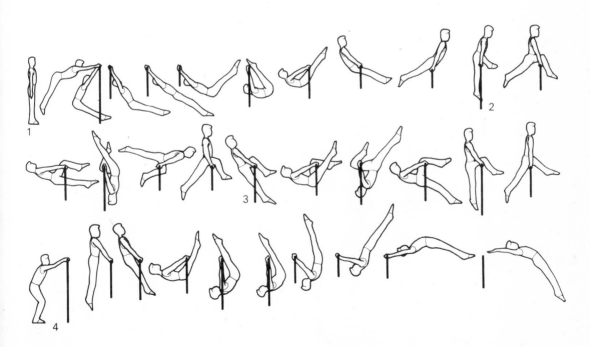

Standard One
Horizontal Bar
Lesson 3

This exercise is marked out of 10

1	Overgrasp, leg acting between hands to mill rest	2.0 points
2	Change to undergrasp and mill circle forwards to rest	2.5 points
3	Turn forwards to front rest	1.5 points
4	Lay out forwards	1.0 points
5	Swing backwards and cross hands, swing forwards and execute half turn with release and regrasp	1.5 points
6	Swing forwards and dismount forwards	1.5 points

The Finish – for every gymnast the competition is the moment of truth. Twisting, turning and spinning to land from sixteen feet in the air is the finality of those moments. As the gymnast lands he will know from experience the result of his efforts – the crowd and judges merely endorse the fact. The photograph shows Andrianov in a triple somersault from high bar.

Standard One
Horizontal Bar
Lesson 4

This exercise is marked out of 10

1	Upward circle to rest	1.5 points
2	Lay out forward	1.0 points
3	Swing back cross right over left, swing forward turn and overgrasp	1.0 points
4	Swing forward, half hook forward, full hook back to mill rest	2.0 points
5	Underswing and return above, half mill circle	2.5 points
6	Remove leg and dismount with half turn	2.0 points

Paata Shamugia (USSR) performs an 'inlocate swing'. A complete spatial awareness is needed for top high bar work. Also a strongly developed grip and forearm strength is needed to counteract strong 'G forces' at the bottom of a swing. Note the strong handguards made of highest quality leather, designed to help grip and prevent hand soreness.

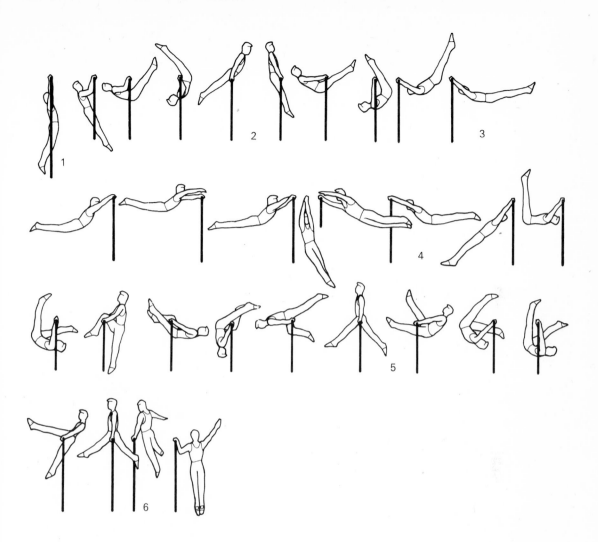

Standard One
Horizontal Bar
Lesson 5

This exercise is marked out of 10

1	Lay out swing back, swing forward	0.5 points
2	Half mill circle forwards to mill rest	3.5 points
3	Turn about	0.5 points
4	Mill circle backwards to rest, remove leg	2.5 points
5	Lay out forwards	1.5 points
6	Swing back, place hands close together	0.5 points
7	Kick! Chest! And dismount forwards	1.0 points

Wolfgang Thune (West Germany) shows a perfect dislocate on the horizontal bar.

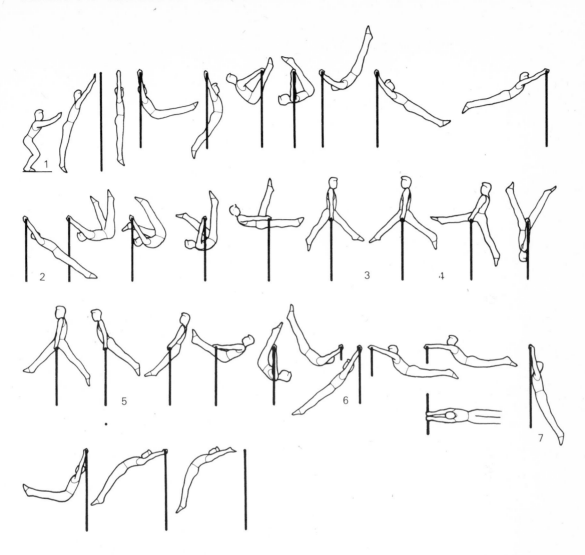

Standard One
Horizontal Bar
Lesson 6

This exercise is marked out of 10

'The forward seat circle' shown here, is a preparation for 'the dislocation' and 'rotated grasp giant swings'. It requires good 'lumbar folding' and well-stretched hamstrings.

1	Lay out forwards	0.5 points
2	Swing forwards and upstart	4.0 points
3	Short circle to rear	2.5 points
4	Lay out forwards	1.0 points
5	Swing to rear and dismount	2.0 points

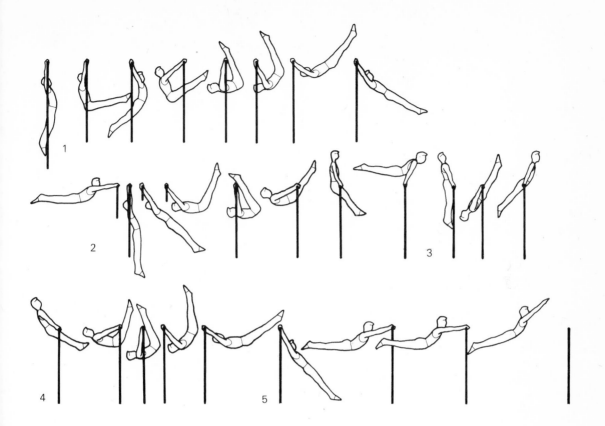

**Standard Two
Floor Exercises
Lesson 1**

This exercise is marked out of 10

I
1 From attention bend knees and straighten swinging arms backwards.
2 Continuing to circle the arms to sideways upwards extend right leg to the rear.
3 Circle arms inwards bending left leg and jumping with change of leg to land on right leg, left leg forwards, arms sideways. Place left leg on ground and bend.   1.0 points

II
1 Swing right leg to right extending left arm upwards.
2 Side lunge to right on right leg, arms upwards.
3 Passing through astride position side lunge to left arms upwards. Push from left leg with quarter left turn to stand on right leg, left leg raised forwards arms upwards.   0.5 points

III
1 2 3 4 Step forward on right leg to forward horizontal stand.   1.0 points

IV
1 Fall to Swedish fall position.
2 Lower leg and straighten arms.
3 4 Squat, legs between hands to back support, one leg bent.   0.5 points

V
1 Lower to long sitting, raise arms upwards.
2 Bend forwards to touch toes, head on knees, roll backwards over left shoulder to –
3 4 Front support, thighs on ground, push back to kneeling.   0.5 points

VI
1 2 From kneeling rise erect and extend body backwards, arms upwards.
3 4 Return to deep kneeling.   0.5 points

VII
1 2 Extend legs placing head on ground, elevate legs.
3 4 Hold headstand for two counts.   1.0 points

VIII
1 Fall to front support left leg bent, stand erect stretching arms high stepping forwards with right leg.
2 Lower arms stepping forwards with left leg bending legs standing erect swinging arms to rear, swing arms forwards with quarter right turn to stand with legs astride arms upwards.
3 Continuing to turn bring both legs together and arms upwards.
4 Bend legs swinging arms to rear with legs straightening.   0.5 points

IX
1 Bend legs and roll forwards.
2 Continue to roll, stand erect.
3 Step forwards and kick to handstand changing legs and immediately placing right leg on ground left leg straight behind.   0.5 points

continued

'Double twist'. Height and form by a Russian team member. Note the close 'wrap' of the arms to aid acceleration of the twist. At the top level a floor routine lasts 50-70 seconds and has to contain a variety of movements. These include strength, balance and acrobatic parts, linked with flowing joining movements. Before attempting the spectacular 'stunts' of the champions, the beginner should master the most basic tumbling, balancing and joining movements.

X

1 Stand erect on right leg cartwheel left.

2 3 Continue cartwheel.

4 To side lunge left arms sideways.   1.5 points

XI

1 Circle right arm upwards downwards to join left arm, transferring weight from left leg to right leg passing both hands close to the left foot, place them in support with left leg extended sideways, hop change to right leg extended sideways.

2 Circle right leg with half turn to extend right leg sideways continuing to turn another half turn swing left leg to right to astride stand with hands on ground.

3 Raise arms sideways.   1.5 points

XII

1 Swing arms inwards, downwards, upwards to jump to attention arms upwards.

2 Bend legs swinging arms down and backwards, extend legs and jump landing with legs bent.

3 Spring high with arms circling and legs opening sideways, land with legs bent, knees outwards, arms sideways upwards.

4 Lower arms, extend legs to attention.   1.0 points

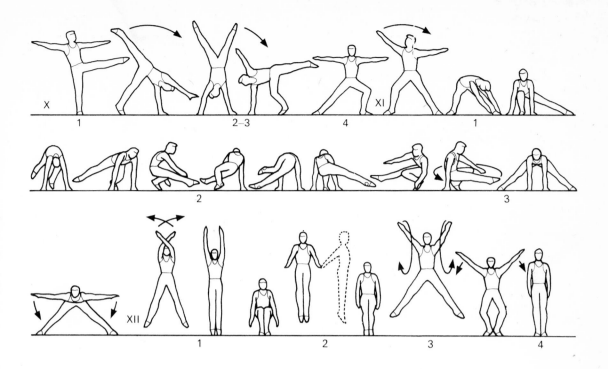

Standard Two
Floor Exercises
Lesson 2

This exercise is marked out of 10

I

1 From attention raise both arms forwards, step backwards with right foot.   0.5 points
2 Sweep left arm to left and bend right arm across chest, stepping backwards with left foot.
3 Stepping backwards with right foot, sweep right arm to right.
4 Bringing left foot to right foot, circle both arms to left, bending left arm until arms are extended to the left and parallel.

II

1 Sweep both arms down to the right, kicking high to the left with right leg.
2 Close legs and raise arms by swinging to the right upwards.
3 Circle arms downwards to the left, swinging left leg to the right.
4 Swing arms to the right to upwards.   0.5 points

III

1 2 Bend legs to crouch, extend arms sideways to span as wide as possible, head lowered.
3 Raise head.
4 Lower head, stand erect to attention.   0.5 points

IV

1 Arms upward bend.
2 Arms extend sideways upwards, head forwards.
3 Raise head upwards.
4 Raise right leg to right.   0.5 points

V

1 Place right leg on ground, bending right leg and placing hands on ground with left leg extended to the side, leg circle to the right.
2 Continue circling leg to extend left leg to the left.
3 Hop change to extend right leg to the right and extend left leg and place weight on bent right leg, hands on ground, left leg extended to side.
4 Circling arms outward, rise erect on right leg with left leg extended to the left.   1.0 points

VI

1 2 Cartwheel left, to stand erect with quarter left turn.
3 Bend forwards with legs straight and arms straight.
4 Bend legs and arms to crouch.   1.0 points

VII

1 2 Raise right leg to the rear, extending to forward horizontal stand.
3 Forward horizontal stand with arm raised sideways upwards.
4 Bend left leg, placing right leg to rear with arms forwards.   0.5 points

continued

79

VIII

1 Bend forward as deeply as possible swinging arms downwards to the rear with legs straight.
2 Stand with quarter right turn raising right leg to the right and arms to shoulder height.
3 Circling arms downwards, inwards and upwards, hop to land on right leg with left leg extended to the right, arms sideways.
4 Place left leg on ground to astride and bend forwards with arms sideways.   0.5 points

IX

1 2 Hold straddle stand with arms sideways body parallel with ground.
3 4 Place hands on ground and roll forwards to crouch.   0.5 points

X

1 Spring carrying legs to rear landing in prone lie with arms bent.
2 Straighten arms opening legs to astride.
3 Close legs and return to bent-arm prone lie.
4 Push back to crouch extending arms sideways.   0.5 points

XI

1 2 Roll with quarter left turn extending legs to long sitting.
3 4 Elevate hips to back support.   0.5 points

XII

1 2 Bend hip to back support with legs and hips bent.

3 Push back to long sitting.
4 Circle arms forwards, bending trunk to deep pike sitting.   0.5 points

XIII

1 2 Balance rock backwards with legs straight and arms sideways.
3 4 Continue to roll backwards balance on upper arms and head, with body straight.   0.5 points

XIV

1 2 Hold the position attained with hips straight.
3 4 Roll down bending left leg reaching forwards with arms.   1.0 points

XV

1 Straighten left leg swinging right leg backwards to the rear, quarter right turn to stand with legs astride and arms sideways.
2 Step to right with left leg circling arms downwards and inwards to upwards.
3 Swing right leg to right, lunge to the right.   1.0 points

XVI

1 Turn trunk to face forward leg, bending right arm and extending left arm to the side.
2 Push backwards from left leg, placing left leg to the rear, right arm sideways, left arm across bend.
3 Continue pushing backwards extend up and sideways, close legs.
4 Lower arms to attention.   0.5 points

VIII

1   2   3   4

IX   1–2

3–4   X   1   2

3   4   XI   1–2   3–4   XII   1–2

3   4   XIII   1–2   3–4   XIV   1–2   3–4

XV   1   2   3   4   XVI   1

2   3   4

Standard Two
Pommelled Horse
Lesson 1

This exercise is marked out of 10

1	Left circle of left leg	2.0 points
2	Place left leg on horse one and a half left circles of right leg to front rest	2.0 points
3	One circle left of right leg	2.5 points
4	Half left of right and half of left legs to back rest	0.5 points
5	Rear vault right to ground	3.0 points

Nikolai Andrianov (USSR). 'High front vault finish' on pommelled horse. Note the head and shoulder position and locked arms. The legs are extended and pressed together in a perfect position.

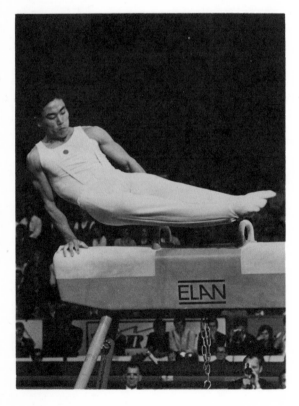

Standard Two
Pommelled Horse
Lesson 2

This exercise is marked out of 10

1	Right circle of left leg	2.5 points
2	Half right circle of left leg, half left circle of right leg	0.5 points
3	Full left circle of right leg	3.5 points
4	Full left circle of left leg, half turn of body placing right hand on end of horse	2.0 points
5	Half left circle of right leg and flank vault right with quarter turn	1.5 points

Eizio Kenmotsu (Japan), Silver medallist on the pommelled horse at Montreal. Here Kenmotsu demonstrates a superior circling method.

Standard Two   Pommelled Horse   Lesson 1

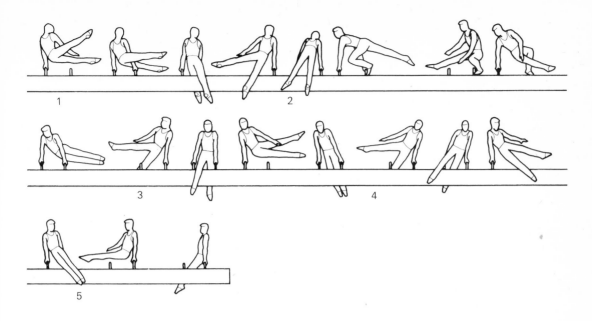

Standard Two   Pommelled Horse   Lesson 2

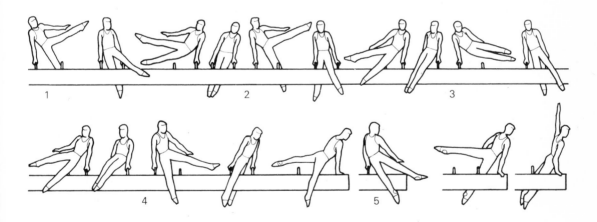

Standard Two
Pommelled Horse
Lesson 3

This exercise is marked out of 10

1	Half left circle of both legs	2.0 points
2	Half left of left leg, half right of right leg	1.0 points
3	Full right circle of right leg	2.0 points
4	Half right circle of left leg, shears right	2.5 points
5	Feint left and remove right leg, front vault left with quarter right turn	2.5 points

Standard Two
Pommelled Horse
Lesson 4

This exercise is marked out of 10

1	Right hand reverse grasp on pommel, half left circle of left leg with half left turn of body	0.5 points
2	Half right circle of right leg	0.5 points
3	Half right circle of left leg front shears right	2.5 points
4	Full right circle of left leg to feint left	3.5 points
5	Half right circle of right leg	0.5 points
6	Half left circle of left leg, full left circle of right leg with three quarters left turn of body dismount	2.5 points

Standard Two   Pommelled Horse   Lesson 3

Standard Two   Pommelled Horse   Lesson 4

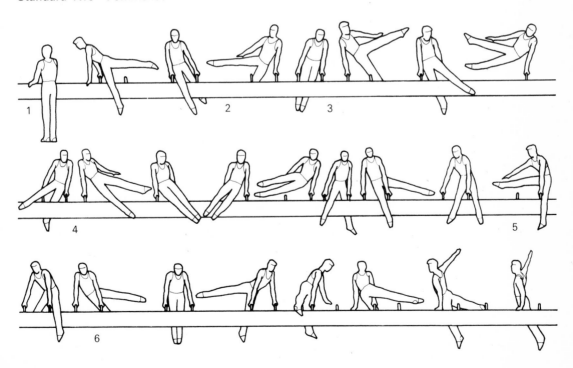

Standard Two
Pommelled Horse
Lesson 5

This exercise is marked out of 10

1	Right hand reverse grasp on pommel, straddle right hand with half left turn	1.0 points
2	Half left circle of left leg	0.5 points
3	Back shears right	2.5 points
4	Half left circle of left leg	0.5 points
5	Half left circle of right leg, front shears left	2.5 points
6	Half left circle of right leg, rear vault dismount	3.0 points

For every event the gymnast must present himself to the master judge before commencing. In the photograph Alexander Detiatin starts his routine on the pommelled horse.

Standard Two
Pommelled Horse
Lesson 6

This exercise is marked out of 10

1	Full left circle of right leg	2.5 points
2	Full left circle of left leg	2.5 points
3	Half left circle of right leg, feint left	0.5 points
4	Half right circle of right leg back shears left	3.0 points
5	Half right circle of right leg, dismount with half right turn of body	1.5 points

Standard Two   Pommelled Horse   Lesson 5

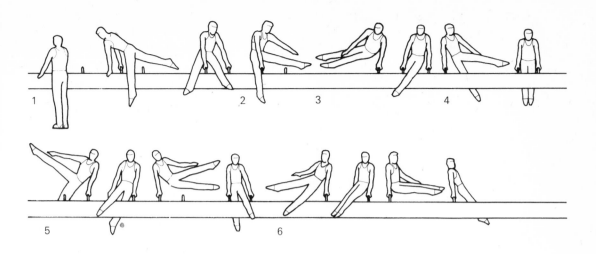

Standard Two   Pommelled Horse   Lesson 6

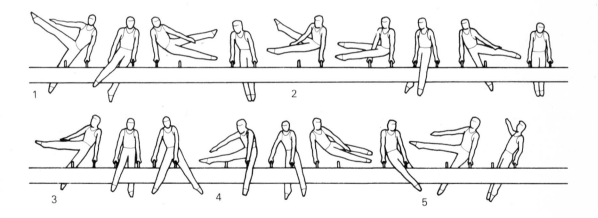

Tom Wilson–a member of the GB team coached by the author of this book. 1975-6 GB Champion, 1976 Olympic Games competitor, 1977 Champions Cup of Great Britain winner. The ring exercise comprises at least eleven movements, predominantly swing, but showing hands and other held strength parts. At Olympic level all the swing parts are shown with straight arms.

Standard Two
Rings
Lesson 1

This exercise is marked out of 10

1	Forward roll to inverted hang	4.0 points
2	Back uprise to bent-arm hang	1.0 points
3	Swing forward to inverted hang	2.0 points
4	Lower to bent inverted hang, extend, dismount	3.0 points

Standard Two
Rings
Lesson 2

This exercise is marked out of 10

1	With straight body, swing to inverted hang	2.0 points
2	Swing down and inlocate to bent inverted hang	3.5 points
3	Back uprise to bent-arm hang	0.5 points
4	Swing back, lower to straight-arm hang	0.5 points
5	Straddle dismount	3.5 points

Standard Two   Rings   Lesson 1

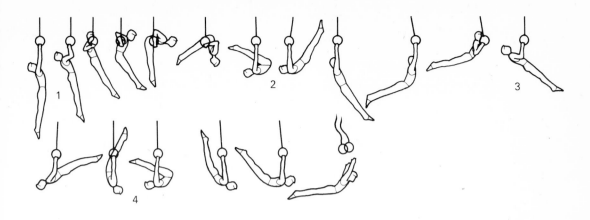

Standard Two   Rings   Lesson 2

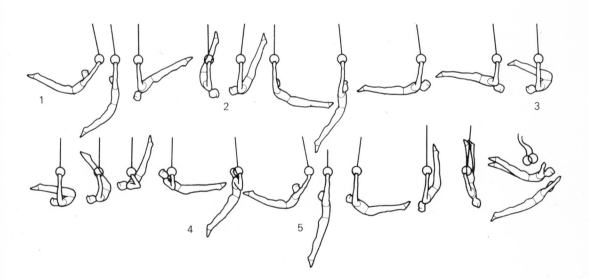

89

Standard Two
Rings
Lesson 3

This exercise is marked out of 10

1	Swing forward uprise	4.0 points
2	Circle to bent inverted hang	1.0 points
3	Beat swing back in bent-arm hang	1.0 points
4	Lower to straight-arm hang swing forward to inverted hang	1.5 points
5	Lower legs to bent inverted hang, extend, dismount forward	2.5 points

Mikhaelyan (USSR) demonstrates a 'back planche' on the rings. This is the first strength part used by aspiring gymnasts but national and international performers must attempt 'crucifix' and other more difficult strength skills.

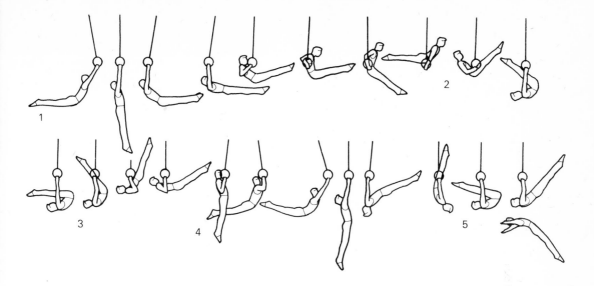

'The straightarm overswing'–this is one of the most important vaults for the gymnast to perfect. From it the complicated 'modern twisting' and 'double rotation vaults' can be learned. Line judge Eugene Kopp makes sure the gymnast's hands are in the correct zone.

Standard Two
Vaulting
Lesson 1

This exercise is marked out of 10

1.20m	10 points
1.15m	8 points
1.10m	6 points •
1.05m	4 points
1.00m	2 points

Running forward high jump.
(Hips facing forward throughout.)

Standard Two
Vaulting
Lesson 2

Squat vault using springboard over horse set at 1.50m and placed sideways.
(Aim for strong thrust, full extension before contacting the floor, arms forwards, upwards in second flight phase.)

Standard Two
Vaulting
Lesson 3

Squat vault using beat board over buck set at 1.20m and placed sideways.
(As in Lesson 2, but aim for more vibrant jump action.)

Standard Two   Vaulting   Lesson 1

1

Standard Two   Vaulting   Lesson 2

2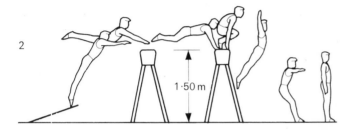

1·50 m

Standard Two   Vaulting   Lesson 3

3

1·20 m

Standard Two
Vaulting
Lesson 4

Straddle vault over buck horse set at 1.20m with rope or lath between board and horse. (Aim to clear rope or lath before opening legs for the straddle – close legs before the landing is made and aim for extensions in the second flight phase.)

Standard Two
Vaulting
Lesson 5

Thief vault using beat board over pommelled horse set at 1.25m. (Aim to bring both legs together and straight before hand contact with pommels is made. Extend hips to obtain flight position while still in contact with hands.)

'Innovation'
Mitsuo Tsukahara (Japan) – inventor of the famous 'Tsukahara' vault which is a cartwheel with a quarter inward turn, from a forward take-off, followed by a free one and a half back somersault from hands. Here he is opening out to perform the Tsukahara with straight body. Scrutinized here by Dr Paul Barnes, one of Britain's top judges (2nd from right).

Standard Two   Vaulting   Lesson 4

4

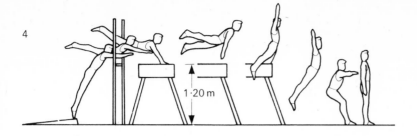

1·20 m

Standard Two   Vaulting   Lesson 5

5

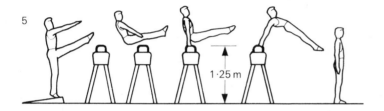

1·25 m

Shigeru Kasamatsu (Japan) demonstrates here a 'half lever', the most popular position from which top gymnasts press to handstand on the parallel bars.

Standard Two
Parallel Bars
Lesson 1

This exercise is marked out of 10

1 Straddle left bar in and right bar out	1.0 points
2 Straddle right bar in	1.0 points
3 Swing back to shoulderstand	1.5 points
4 Roll through cross riding seat to forearm rest	1.5 points
5 Uprise forward, swing back	
6 Straddle forward over right bar	2.0 points
7 Place right foot on left bar and swing left leg forwards, turn to stand on left bar and neck spring to ground	3.0 points

Standard Two
Parallel Bars
Lesson 2

This exercise is marked out of 10

1 Jump to forearms, swing back and uprise	2.0 points
2 Full left circle of right leg over left bar with half left turn of body	2.5 points
3 Swing down forward through bent-arm cross rest	1.0 points
4 Place right leg on right bar, swing left leg to rear and shears turn to rear	2.5 points
5 Swing to rear and flank vault dismount	2.0 points

The 'Stutz' or swinging front change is a half turn on the forward swing to a high front support. This position is performed at most levels of gymnastic competition.

Standard Two   Parallel Bars   Lesson 1

Standard Two   Parallel Bars   Lesson 2

Standard Two
Parallel Bars
Lesson 3

This exercise is marked out of 10

1	Backward roll to shoulderstand	2.5 points
2	Straighten arms and swing down forwards	0.5 points
3	Sink backwards to upper-arm rest and upstart swing to rear	2.5 points
4	Open and close legs (slowly swing down)	0.5 points
5	Full right circle of left leg with half turn of body	2.0 points
6	Roll forwards to outside riding seat on right bar	0.5 points
7	Quarter turn left to front leaning rest through dismount	1.5 points

Standard Two
Parallel Bars
Lesson 4

This exercise is marked out of 10

1	Run forwards and long upstart to upper-arm rest	3.5 points
2	Back uprise with half turn to cross riding seat hands behind	2.5 points
3	Place hands forward in forearm rest	1.5 points
4	Uprise forwards at end of forward swing	
5	Swing backwards and straddle forwards dismount	2.5 points

Standard Two   Parallel Bars   Lesson 3

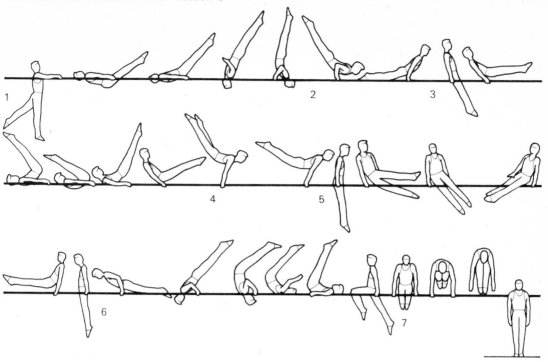

1   2   3

4   5

6   7

Standard Two   Parallel Bars   Lesson 4

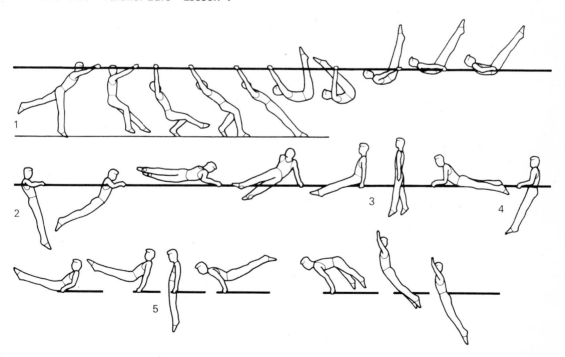

1

2   3   4

5

Standard Two
Parallel Bars
Lesson 5

This exercise is marked out of 10

1 Front standing, alternate grasp, underswing with half turn to upper-arm hang	0.5 points
2 Backward roll in upper-arm rest	3.5 points
3 Upstart from upper-arm rest	2.5 points
4 Swing back place left foot on right bar	2.0 points
5 Full left circle of right leg, swing back to shoulderstand	
6 Cartwheel dismount to left or right	1.5 points

Standard Two
Parallel Bars
Lesson 6

This exercise is marked out of 10

1 From upper-arm hang, uprise forward	3.0 points
2 Swing backwards to shoulderstand	2.0 points
3 Roll forwards and swing backwards, back uprise	3.0 points
4 Swing forwards and rear vault right with half right turn	2.0 points

Standard Two   Parallel Bars   Lesson 5

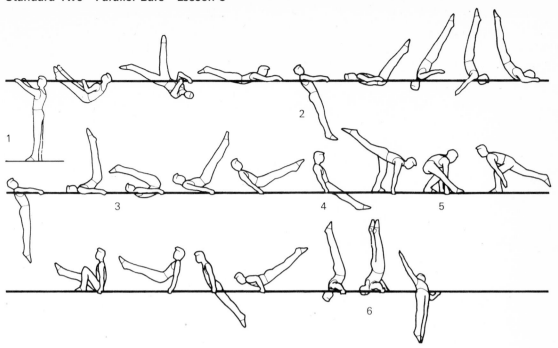

Standard Two   Parallel Bars   Lesson 6

Eberhard Gienger (West Germany), World Champion on the horizontal bar and Olympic medallist in Montreal. Here he shows a perfect forward longswing before stooping in for a forward seat circle into dislocation.

Standard Two
Horizontal Bar
Lesson 1

This exercise is marked out of 10

1 Short underswing to half mill circle forwards to rise above bar, half turn	3.0 points
2 Mill circle backwards to rest position	2.0 points
3 Half mill circle backwards, half mill circle forwards	1.5 points
4 Remove leg to front rest and place feet on bar	1.0 points
5 High jump dismount to front	2.5 points

Standard Two
Horizontal Bar
Lesson 2

This exercise is marked out of 10

1 Upward circle to front rest (quickly)	0.5 points
2 Place right leg over bar with half left turn	1.5 points
3 Mill circle backwards	1.5 points
4 Sink back and place leg between hands, swing forwards and slap hands, regrasp	1.5 points
5 Hook circle backwards to mill rest above bar	1.5 points
6 Remove leg to front rest	
7 Squat dismount	3.5 points

Mitsuo Tsukahara (Japan), double Olympic Champion on the horizontal bar, shows a back uprise pirouette.

Standard Two Horizontal Bar Lesson 1

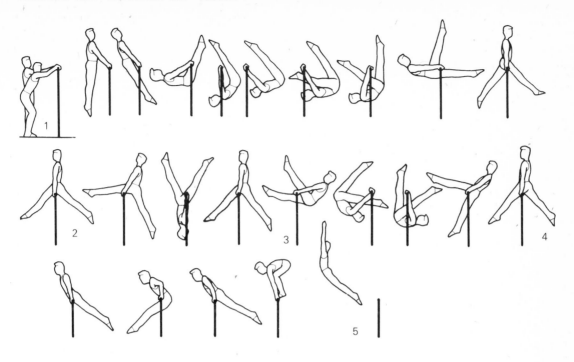

Standard Two Horizontal Bar Lesson 2

Standard Two
Horizontal Bar
Lesson 3

This exercise is marked out of 10

1	Long underswing upstart to front rest	4.0 points
2	Half left turn to mill rest reverse grasp	2.0 points
3	Mill circle forwards to rest position above bar	1.5 points
4	Turn to front rest over grasp	0.5 points
5	High underswing to front (shoot to front) dismount	2.0 points

Standard Two
Horizontal Bar
Lesson 4

This exercise is marked out of 10

1	Upward circle to front rest	1.0 points
2	Lay out forwards, swing to rear	1.0 points
3	Place hands together at rear of swing	0.5 points
4	Straddle legs to rise above bar, grasp outside legs	3.0 points
5	Sink back remove leg and mill circle to rise above	1.5 points
6	Half turn to front rest	0.5 points
7	High underswing to front dismount	2.5 points

Standard Two   Horizontal Bar   Lesson 3

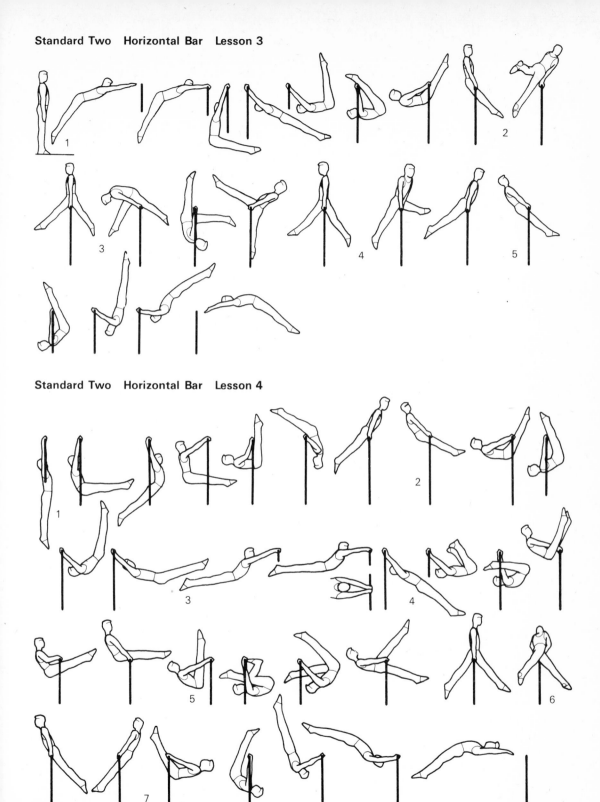

Standard Two   Horizontal Bar   Lesson 4

**Standard Two
Horizontal Bar
Lesson 5**

This exercise is marked out of 10

1	Swing in alternate grasp, swing forwards releasing overgrasp hand, turn to overgrasp	1.0 points
2	Half mill circle forwards to rest	2.0 points
3	Mill circle backwards to rest	1.5 points
4	Sink back, place other leg between hands and circle forwards to back rest	3.5 points
5	Turn, lay out forwards swing backwards	1.0 points
6	Release left then right hand, half turn dismount	1.0 points

**Standard Two
Horizontal Bar
Lesson 6**

This exercise is marked out of 10

1	Lay out and upstart to front rest	3.0 points
2	Short circle backwards to front rest	2.0 points
3	Lay out forwards with half turn swing forwards	2.5 points
4	Change hand, squat legs through and hook swing dismount	2.5 points

106

Standard Two   Horizontal Bar   Lesson 5

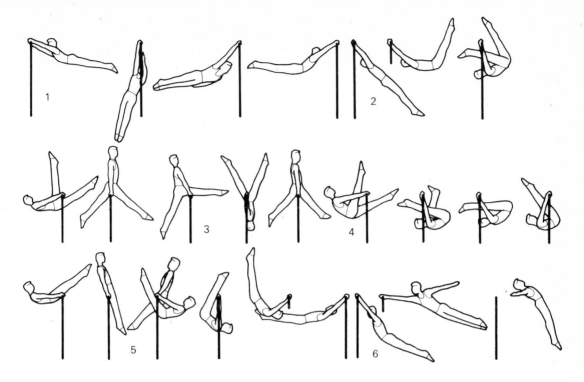

Standard Two   Horizontal Bar   Lesson 6

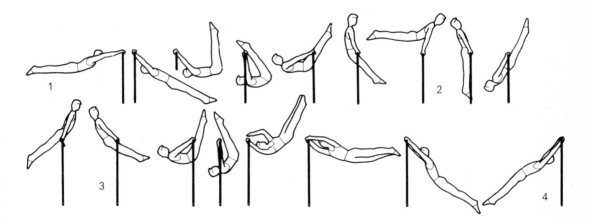

Standard Three
Floor Exercises
Lesson 1

This exercise is marked out of 10

I
1 From attention raise arms
   sideways upwards by
   swinging them forwards and
   swing right leg to rear.
2 Swing right leg forwards
   swinging arms downwards
   to head height to touch toes
   with hands.
3 Swing right leg to rear,
   maintaining arms forward to
   horizontal stand position.
4 Swing right leg to right with
   trunk erect to stand astride
   with arms raised upwards.   1.0 points

II
1 Swing arms and trunk down
   between legs, swing arms
   upwards with quarter left
   turn of trunk.
2 Arms across bend, right leg
   slightly bent.
3 Return arms to upward
   position, turning trunk
   quarter right turn to astride
   position, swing arms and
   trunk downwards between
   legs, swing arms upwards
   with quarter right turn of
   trunk.
4 Lean to rear bending left leg,
   arms extended obliquely.   1.0 points

III
1 2 Push from left leg and
   make three-quarter turn to
   stand in astride position with
   arms forwards.
3 4 Bend forwards placing
   backs of hands on ground
   and roll forwards to long
   sitting   1.5 points

IV
1 Place left leg to the side,
   circle right leg beneath left
   leg to front support.
2 Continuing to swing right
   leg to the rear bend arms to
   Swedish fall.
3 Lower leg and straighten
   arms to front support.
4 Squat legs between hands to
   back support.   1.0 points

V
1 Return to long sitting, arms
   sideways, bend forwards
   placing hands on feet, head
   between arms.
2 Rock backwards with legs
   straight bending arms.
3 4 Continue to roll backwards
   placing upper feet on
   ground and straightening
   arms to front support.   2.0 points

VI
1 Squat legs forward
   maintaining bent left leg,
   with right leg extended
   forwards, circle right leg to
   the right and the left foot
   and the left and right hand.

Standard Three Floor Exercises Lesson 1

I 1 2 3 4 II 1 2

3 4 III 1–2 3–4

IV 1 2 3 4

V 1 2 3–4 VI 1

continued

'A back somersault with full twist'.

2 Extend right leg to the right.
3 Stand erect with left leg
  extended sideways to the left
  and arms upward.
4 Close legs, swing right foot
  forwards.   1.5 points

VII
1 Step forwards and swing to
  handstand left leg leading,
  return to –
2 3 Extended crouch position
  with right leg leading.
4 Return to bent-leg stand,
  knees extended sideways,
  arms across. Bend back
  straight.   1.5 points

VIII
1 Stand erect swinging right
  leg to the right, arms
  sideways.
2 Hop swinging left leg to the
  left in line with shoulders,
  bring both legs together
  bending knees, arms
  remaining sideways.
3 Spring high opening legs
  and extending arms
  sideways upwards. Land with
  legs bent, knees open, arms
  sideways upwards.
4 Straighten legs, lowering
  arms to attention.   0.5 points

Standard Three   Floor Exercises   Lesson 1

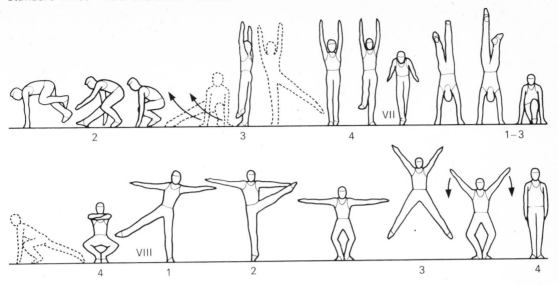

111

Standard Three
Floor Exercises
Lesson 2

This exercise is marked out of 10

I
1 From attention raise left arm
to the left, right arm
forwards and step forwards
with left foot. Swing right leg
to the right raising right arm
sideways upwards.
2 Extended lunge to the right,
raise left arm upwards.
3 Continue circling arms to
the right, straighten right
leg, transfer weight to the
left leg bending left leg with
arms sideways and parallel.
4 Push weight back on to right
leg opening arms and
leaning back.   1.0 points

II
1 Bend left leg, placing right
hand on ground.
2 Turn to the left to back
support.
3 Place right leg to the right,
circling left leg underneath
right leg with quarter turn to
front support.
4 Front support.   1.5 points

III
1 Push back to kneeling, arms
extended forwards.
2 3 Place head on ground
curling to headstand.
4 Open legs to astride
position.   2.0 points

IV
1 Close legs, bend legs.
2 Placing legs on ground, lean
forwards, and place arms to
rear.
3 Swing arms forwards and
upwards extending legs to
land with knees bent and
arms forwards.
4 Spring high with legs
together, arms swinging
downwards to the rear. Land
with legs bent and jump
upwards with arms swinging
upwards, land with legs bent
and arms upwards.   1.0 points

V
1 Extend arms obliquely
sideways, jump with quarter
left turn landing with legs
bent and arms sideways.
2 3 Raise right leg to rear to
forward horizontal stand,
bring both legs together and
bend them moving arms to
rear.   1.0 points

112

continued

Tom Wilson (GB). Competing in 'Champions All' at Wembley, he shows excellent gymnastic poise in this 'side horizontal lever'.

VI

1 2 Dive roll forwards to crouch.

3 Stand erect placing arms sideways, quarter left turn, step forwards with left foot.

4 Swing right foot forwards.   1.5 points

VII

1 2 Cartwheel right with quarter right turn.

3 Extended lunge forward on right leg, arms upwards.

4 Straighten right leg, swinging left leg forward to touch right hand, left leg at the rear.   1.5 points

VIII

1 Swing left leg to the rear placing left arm forwards, raising arms upwards with quarter left turn.

2 3 Swing arms downwards, swinging right leg forwards to touch left hand, right arm backwards and right leg down with quarter right turn placing arms sideways.

4 Close legs and lower arms to attention.   0.5 points

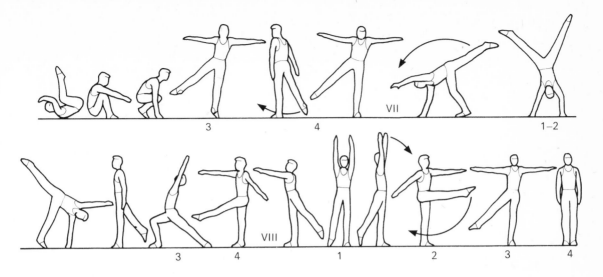

**Standard Three
Floor Exercises
Lesson 3**

This lesson is marked out of 10

I
1 From attention swing arms
  upwards raising head
  upwards.
2 Swing arms downwards and
  backwards bending at knees
  and hips lowering head and
  extend arms sideways with
  legs remaining bent.
3 Stand erect with arms
  upwards, head raised, swing
  left leg to the left.
4 Extend legs to astride
  position, arms upwards.   1.0 points

II
1 Circle arms to the left
  touching left foot and
  continue to circle to the
  right to touch right foot.
2 Extend right leg then left leg,
  extend left arm upwards,
  right arm downwards.
3 Repeat circle of arms in
  opposite direction.
4 Extended lunge on right leg,
  right arm upwards, left arm
  downwards.   1.5 points

III
  Swing trunk towards left leg,
  arms to the rear, extend left
  leg and raise to forward
  horizontal stand, arms
  upwards.   1.0 points

IV
1 Maintain right leg raised,
  quarter right turn, arms
  sideways.
2 Cartwheel to right, raise left
  leg and make quarter left turn.

3 Lowering arms to side and
  closing legs –
4 Attention.   2.0 points

V
1 Bend legs placing arms to
  rear.
2 3 Roll forwards crossing
  legs.
4 Stand erect with half turn.   1.0 points

VI
1 Fall forwards to prone lying
  with arms bent.
2 Spring to left leg bent, right
  leg extended sideways,
  continue to circle right leg
  forwards under right hand.
3 4 Continue to circle right leg
  under left hand and left foot
  with quarter left turn to right
  leg extended sideways, left
  leg bent, hands on ground.   1.5 points

VII
1 Continue to circle right leg,
  placing head on ground and
  raising to headstand with
  legs astride.
2 3 Hold position of
  headstand with legs astride.
4 Return to kneeling, back
  straight.   1.0 points

VIII
1 Push to kneeling with body
  erect, arms extended
  sideways, circle arms to rear,
  bending at hips.
2 Extend hips and knees
  swinging arms forwards and
  upwards to land with arms
  forwards, legs bent.
3 Spring high, throwing legs
  to rear and arms upwards,
  land with arms sideways and
  knees bent.
4 Extend legs and lower arms
  to side to attention.   1.0 points

Standard Three   Floor Exercises   Lesson 3

117

Standard Three
Floor Exercises
Lesson 4

This lesson is marked out of 10

I
1 From attention raise arms
sideways and swing right leg
forwards to horizontal with
the ground and step
forwards on to right leg,
bend right leg scissor kick
forwards.
2 Land on left leg, arms
extended sideways, right leg
raised forwards.
3 Circle arms downwards
inwards placing right leg to
the right.
4 Swing right arm downwards
to join left arm forwards with
quarter left turn, jump, land
on right leg with left leg
extended forwards.   1.0 points

II
1 2 Step forwards with left leg,
step forwards with right leg,
jump upwards and cartwheel
left to stand erect with
quarter left turn, arms
downwards.

3 4 Forward roll with legs
crossed to turn about.   2.0 points

III
1 Fall to prone lying with arms
bent.
2 Elevate right leg and
straighten arms.
3 Return to prone lying legs
together.
4 Half turn right, to sit with
legs raised with hand
support.   1.0 points

IV
1 2 Place arms upwards
maintaining position, roll
forwards to place hands on
feet, trunk folded forwards,
begin to roll backwards.
3 4 Roll backwards over left
shoulder to front support,
thighs on ground arms
straight.   2.0 points

V
1 Push backwards to crouch
with arms extended
upwards.
2 3 Squat legs through hands.
4 Continue to roll backwards
to shoulders to shoulder
support.   1.0 points

I

1   and   2   3

II

4   1–2

III

3–4   1   2   3   4

IV

1   2   3–4   V   1   2–3   4

continued

VI

1 2 Roll forwards, bend left leg maintaining right leg straight with arms at shoulder height.

3 Stand erect, right leg forwards.

4 Right leg to rear, to forward horizontal stand.   1.5 points

VII

1 2 Circle right leg to rear with quarter turn and arms to the right to downwards to the left.

3 Swing right leg forwards, circling arms to rear.

4 Lunge forwards on left leg, arms forwards upwards.   1.0 points

VIII

1 Swing right leg forwards with quarter left turn, right arm upwards, left arm sideways, keep closing legs and changing right and left arm to sideways upwards.

2 Land on right leg, right and left arm circling inwards.

3 Close legs, crossing arms in front, bending legs, spring upwards, arms sideways upwards, and land on both feet arms sideways upwards.

4 Return to attention.   0.5 points

'A side somersault'. Since the late sixties a wide variety of difficult somersaults have been introduced to men's floor exercises. This is one of the most popular.

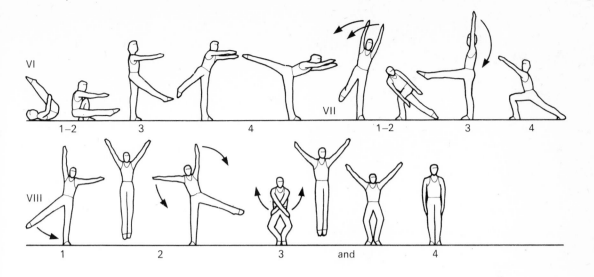

VI

1–2   3   4

VII

1–2   3   4

VIII

1   2   3   and   4

To be a Champion in World, Olympic and European events is a fantastic achievement. To do this Zoltan has developed two new movements – 'The Magyar Walk' (demonstrated here) and 'The Spindle'. Both are complicated circling, travelling and turning movements. A gymnast can only do these by learning perfect basics.

Standard Three
Pommelled Horse
Lesson 1

This exercise is marked out of 10

1	Stand, one hand on pommel and left hand on end, half right circle of left leg and swing to left	1.0 points
2	Back shears right	3.5 points
3	Half left circle of left leg to front rest	0.5 points
4	Half left circle of right leg, half right circle of left leg	0.5 points
5	Full right circle of left leg	3.0 points
6	Rear vault dismount to right	1.5 points

Standard Three
Pommelled Horse
Lesson 2

This exercise is marked out of 10

1	Stand, left hand on pommel, right hand on croup half right circle of right leg to saddle	0.5 points
2	One and a half left circles of left leg	2.0 points
3	Half left circle of right leg and shears left	2.5 points
4	Half left circle of right leg, half circle of both legs	2.5 points
5	Full left circle of right leg, with half left turn of body place left hand on end and flank dismount	2.5 points

Standard Three   Pommelled Horse   Lesson 1

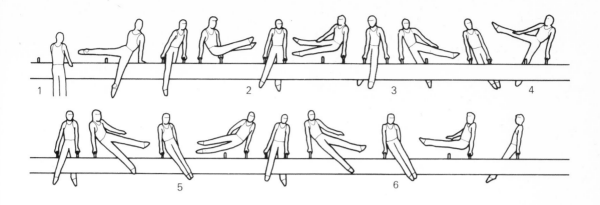

Standard Three   Pommelled Horse   Lesson 2

123

Standard Three
Pommelled Horse
Lesson 3

This exercise is marked out of 10

1	Full left circle of right leg to straddle right hand	1.0 points
2	Half left circle of left leg back shears right	3.0 points
3	Half left circle of left leg, full left circle of right leg	2.0 points
4	Full left circle of right leg	1.5 points
5	Flank vault right	2.5 points

Shigeru Kasamatsu (Japan). The basic practices in balance and flexibility learned in warm-up and floor sessions are combined with strength to produce high single leg movements needed in routines of all levels.

Standard Three
Pommelled Horse
Lesson 4

This exercise is marked out of 10

1	Half left circle of both legs	2.5 points
2	Half left circle of left leg	1.0 points
3	Half right circle of right leg	0.5 points
4	Half right circle of left leg and shears right	1.5 points
5	Full right circle of right leg	1.5 points
6	Rear vault left	3.0 points

Eberhard Gienger (West Germany) shows the 'flanking out' position in double leg circles, the movement which in its variations forms most a pommelled horse routine.

Standard Three   Pommelled Horse   Lesson 3

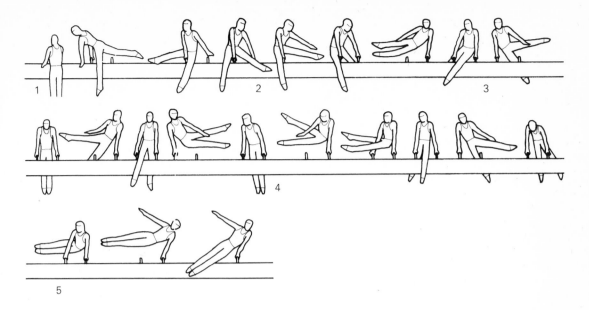

1   2   3

4

5

Standard Three   Pommelled Horse   Lesson 4

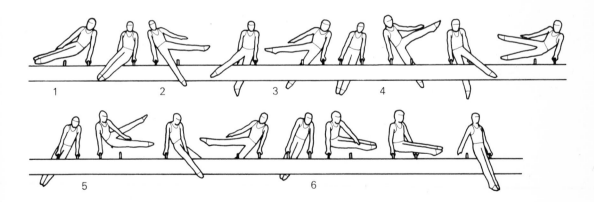

1   2   3   4

5   6

Standard Three
Pommelled Horse
Lesson 5

This exercise is marked out of 10

1	Feint left and throw out back shears left	2.0 points
2	Half right circle of right leg	1.0 points
3	Half right circle of both legs	2.0 points
4	Full right circle of right leg with half right turn of body placing left hand on end	1.0 points
5	Half right circle of left leg, half left circle of right leg to straddle right hand	0.5 points
6	Half left turn of body, regrasping pommel	1.0 points
7	Half left circle of left leg and from feint right flank vault left	2.5 points

Standard Three
Pommelled Horse
Lesson 6

This exercise is marked out of 10

1	Half right circle of left leg, shears right	2.5 points
2	Half right circle of left leg to straddle left pommel	
3	Half right circle of right leg and back shears left	2.0 points
4	Half right circle of right leg, half right circle of left leg, half left circle of right leg	1.5 points
5	Full left circle of right leg to straddle right hand	1.0 points
6	Half right circle of right leg and placing left hand on end rear vault dismount	3.0 points

126

Standard Three   Pommelled Horse   Lesson 5

Standard Three   Pommelled Horse   Lesson 6

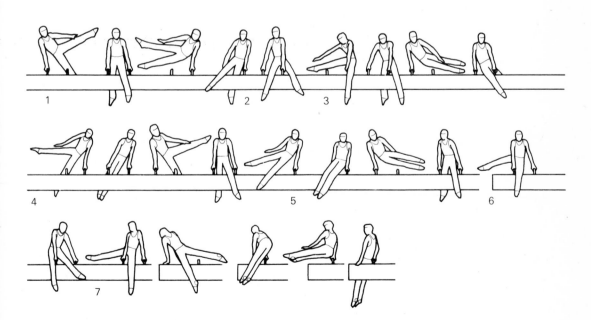

Vladimir Tichonov (USSR) uses strong flexible shoulders to pull from hang, through German hang before longswinging forwards to handstand.

Standard Three
Rings
Lesson 1

This exercise is marked out of 10

1	Raise to cross rest	2.0 points
2	Raise legs to half lever and hold for 3 seconds	1.5 points
3	One and a half forward rolls to inverted hang	2.0 points
4	Inlocation to inverted hang	2.0 points
5	Extend body and release dismount	2.5 points

Standard Three
Rings
Lesson 2

This exercise is marked out of 10

1	Circle up to hook rest on left arm	2.5 points
2	Circle down to inverted hang (bent)	0.5 points
3	Lay out forwards and inlocate	2.0 points
4	Lower with one leg bent to back horizontal lever	2.5 points
5	Lower to back hang, raise to inverted hang	0.5 points
6	Shoot to front dismount	2.0 points

Standard Three   Rings   Lesson 1

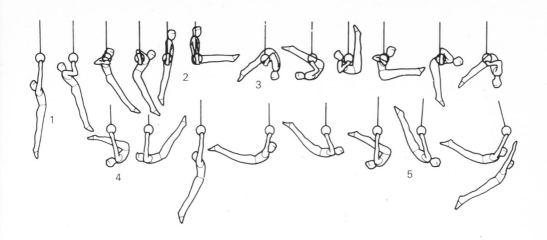

Standard Three   Rings   Lesson 2

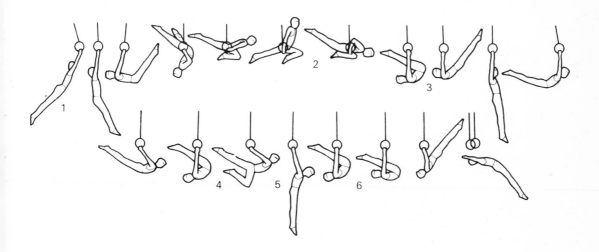

This exercise is marked out of 10

1	Swing forwards and uprise, swing to rear	3.0 points
2	Circle backwards to inverted hang	0.5 points
3	Dislocate to rear	2.5 points
4	Uprise forwards to bent-arm hang	0.5 points
5	Swing to rear and lower to straight-arm hang	0.5 points
6	Swing forwards and straddle dismount	3.0 points

Mitsuo Tsukahara (Japan) performs here, with ease, one of the most difficult strength parts, lowering from handstand, through the 'Maltese' position towards back plant.

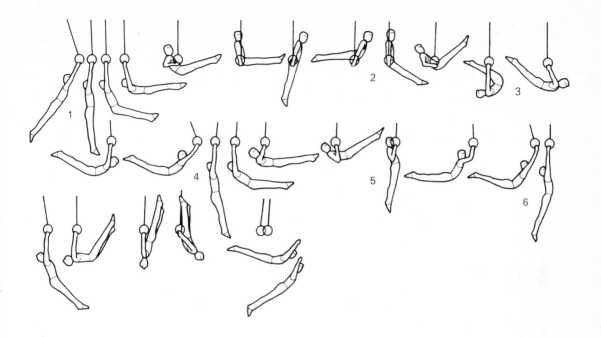

Shigeru Kasamatsu (Japan) performing 'the hecht vault' – 'second flight phase'. In world and Olympic events all gymnasts have to perform compulsory exercises. Beginners start with the type of graduated routines shown in this book.

Standard Three
Vaulting
Lesson 1

This exercise is marked out of 10

1.30m	10 points
1.25m	8 points
1.20m	6 points
1.15m	4 points
1.10m	2 points

Running forward high jump over rope or lath.
(Lean back at take-off, swing arms upwards and forwards obtain legs straight and together before extending the hips after passing over the rope or lath.)

Standard Three
Vaulting
Lesson 2

Back straddle using beat board over long horse set at 1.30m.
(Open the legs and turn when both hands strike the horse. In the beginning stages it is necessary to take one hand at a time from the horse towards the direction in which the turn is occurring. Even though the vault is turned backwards to land the hip extended position is still shown.)

Standard Three
Vaulting
Lesson 3

Forward straddle over long horse, set at 1.20m.
(Open the legs as late as possible after thrust position is made.)

Standard Three   Vaulting   Lesson 1

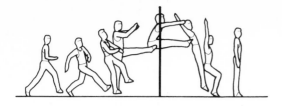

Standard Three   Vaulting   Lesson 2

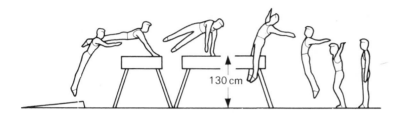

Standard Three   Vaulting   Lesson 3

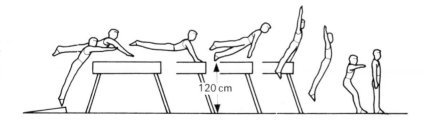

133

Standard Three
Vaulting
Lesson 4

Sheep vault buck set at 1.30m and placed
sideways.
(Draw the knees towards the hands until
the knee angle is approximately 90°, then
elevate the shoulders rapidly, and extend
the hips.)

Standard Three
Vaulting
Lesson 5

Bent-legs squat vault, using spring board,
broad buck set at 1.50m and placed
sideways.
(From the spring board or trampett swing
the legs backwards before the strike
position is obtained. Squat with the legs
bent between the hands. Extend before
landing.)

Standard Three
Vaulting
Lesson 6

Straight-legs squat, beat board, pommelled
horse with handles set at 1.20m. (Elevate
the hips as high as possible. Extend the
hips before landing.)

*Miroslav Cerar (Yugoslavia) demonstrates the
pre-flight*

Standard Three   Vaulting   Lesson 4

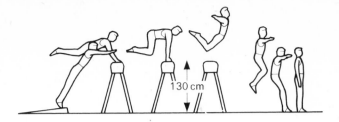

130 cm

Standard Three   Vaulting   Lesson 5

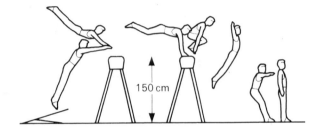

150 cm

Standard Three   Vaulting   Lesson 6

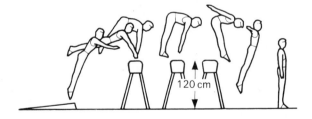

120 cm

'Swing'. Here a Montreal Olympian shows a fully extended swing, preparing for an underswing to upper arms. The parallel bar exercise should show movement above, below and between the bars with transition from one level to another.

Standard Three
Parallel Bars
Lesson 1

This exercise is marked out of 10

1	Jump to upper arm, swing forwards to upstart, swing to rear	1.5 points
2	Lower to bent-arm lever on one arm	2.5 points
3	Raise with straight body to shoulderstand	0.5 points
4	Roll forwards and back uprise to straight-arm rest	1.5 points
5	Swing forwards, swing backwards through bent-arm rest	0.5 points
6	Straddle left bar to front	1.5 points
7	Place right leg over right bar and turn to left in front rest, squat dismount to ground	2.0 points

Standard Three
Parallel Bars
Lesson 2

This exercise is marked out of 10

1	From upper-arm rest, swing to rear and sink to long underswing upstart to upper-arm rest	3.0 points
2	Back uprise and straddle turn to cross riding seat	2.5 points
3	Grasp bars in front and uprise forwards	1.5 points
4	Swing back to shoulderstand	1.5 points
5	Overthrow to stand outside bars	1.5 points

Standard Three   Parallel Bars   Lesson 1

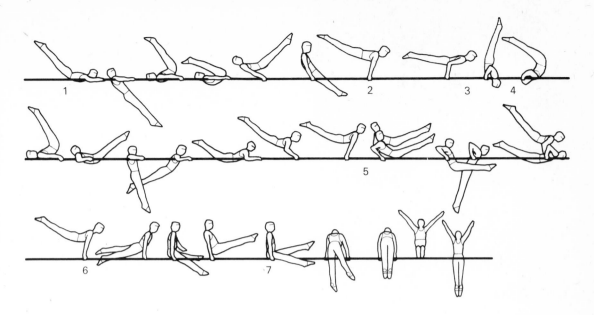

Standard Three   Parallel Bars   Lesson 2

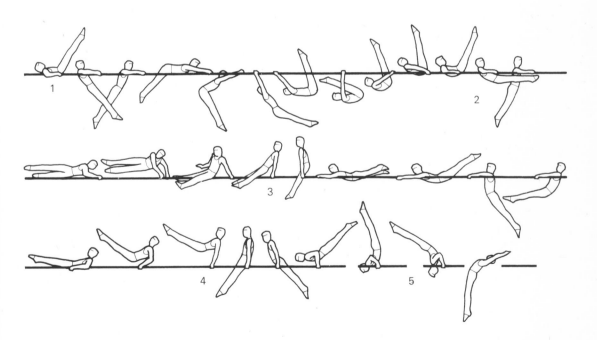

Nikolai Andrianov (USSR) performs a perfect 'flying back roll', a complete somersault from handstand to handstand, on the parallel bars.

Standard Three
Parallel Bars
Lesson 3

This exercise is marked out of 10

1	Jump to over-arm hang and backward roll	2.5 points
2	Swing legs forwards and upstart from upper arms, swing to rear	1.5 points
3	Swing down through bent-arm hang and jump forwards to half lever hold for three seconds	2.0 points
4	Swing to shoulderstand	1.0 points
5	Roll forwards and place left leg on left bar	0.5 points
6	Swing right leg to rear and flank vault to right with half right turn	2.5 points

Standard Three
Parallel Bars
Lesson 4

This exercise is marked out of 10

1	Jump to upper-arm rest and backward roll	2.5 points
2	Uprise forwards and place right leg on bar	1.5 points
3	Swing left leg to rear, half turn to cross riding seat	1.0 points
4	Swing to rear and straddle right bar to half lever	1.5 points
5	Hold half lever for 3 seconds	1.0 points
6	Lift with bent hips and bent arms to shoulderstand	1.0 points
7	Swing forwards and rear vault left with half right turn	1.5 points

Standard Three   Parallel Bars   Lesson 3

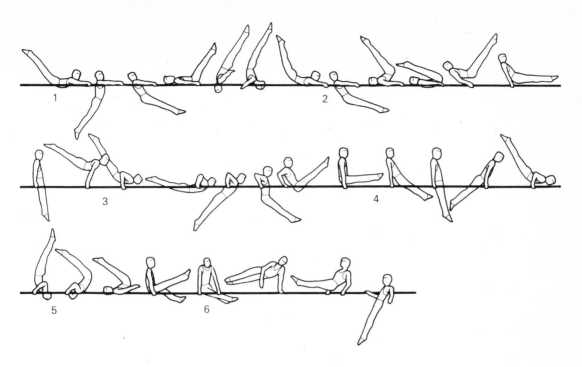

Standard Three   Parallel Bars   Lesson 4

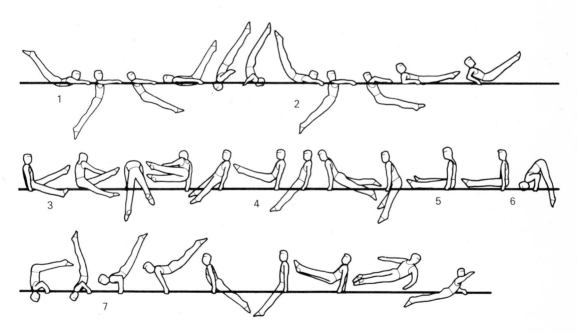

Standard Three
Parallel Bars
Lesson 5

This exercise is marked out of 10

1	Short underswing upstart and swing to rear	2.5 points
2	Swing down forwards through bent-arm rest and jump forwards to cross riding seat	1.5 points
3	Grasp forwards and backward roll	2.0 points
4	Sink back and rest on upper arms	0.5 points
5	Swing down and back uprise	1.5 points
6	Swing forwards and flank vault left dismount	2.0 points

Left. *A 'flying back roll' out of the parallel bars by Nikolai Andrianov (USSR).*

Right. *A delicate shift of weight in preparation for the one-hand stand by that great and affable gymnast, Safronov (USSR).*

140

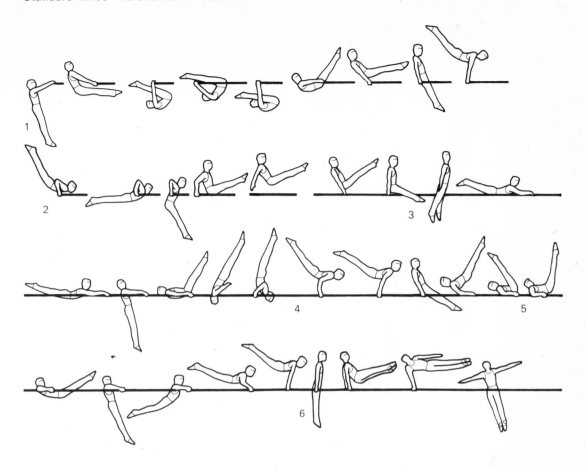

Standard Three
Parallel Bars
Lesson 6

This exercise is marked out of 10

1 Jump to upper-arm hang and uprise forwards	1.5 points
2 Swing to rear and straddle left bar to bent-arm cross rest	1.5 points
3 Swing to rear and sink to upper-arm hang	1.5 points
4 Swing legs forwards and upstart, swing to rear	1.5 points
5 Swing to shoulderstand	1.0 points
6 Swing down forwards and place legs on bars, remove legs	0.5 points
7 Swing rear and front vault right with half right turn	2.5 points

'Stutz turn' to handstand – Nikolai Andrianov (USSR). Super-style gymnast.

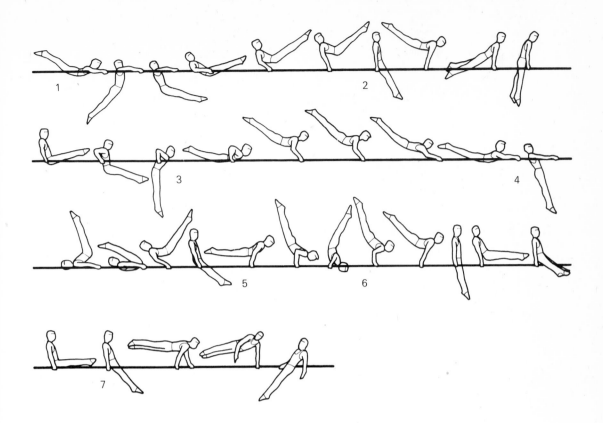

1

2

3

4

5

6

7

Standard Three
Horizontal Bar
Lesson 1

This exercise is marked out of 10

1 Hang in overgrasp, swing
  and squat legs through
  hands to back rest above
  bar-turn to front rest   3.0 points
2 Underswing forwards with
  half turn to left or right   1.5 points
3 Swing forwards in alternate
  grasp and half mill circle to
  rise above bar   1.5 points
4 Change grasp to undergrasp
  and full mill circle forwards   1.0 points
5 Turn to front rest and lower
  legs, swing legs to rear and
  flank vault   3.0 points

*Shigeru Kasamatsu (Japan) in 'top change'
shows the form and extension of a world
champion. Note the eyes, concentrating on the
bar, showing absolute awareness of his body in
relation to the skill being performed.*

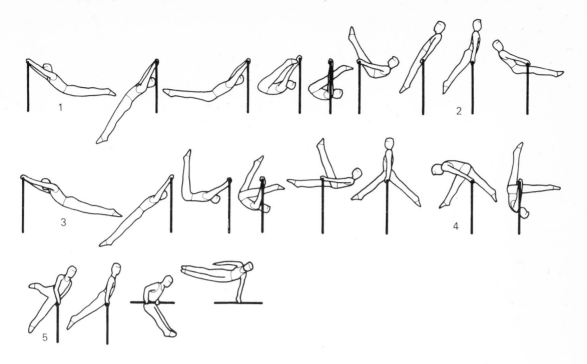

Standard Three
Horizontal Bar
Lesson 2

This exercise is marked out of 10

1	Alternate grasp, swing forwards release overgrasp hand turn and grasp in overgrasp, swing forwards	0.5 points
2	Upstart to front rest	2.5 points
3	Place right leg between hands to mill rest	0.5 points
4	Mill circle backwards	1.0 points
5	Sink backwards remove right leg and place left leg between hands and rise above bar	3.0 points
6	Lay out forwards swing to rear and piked dismount to rear	2.5 points

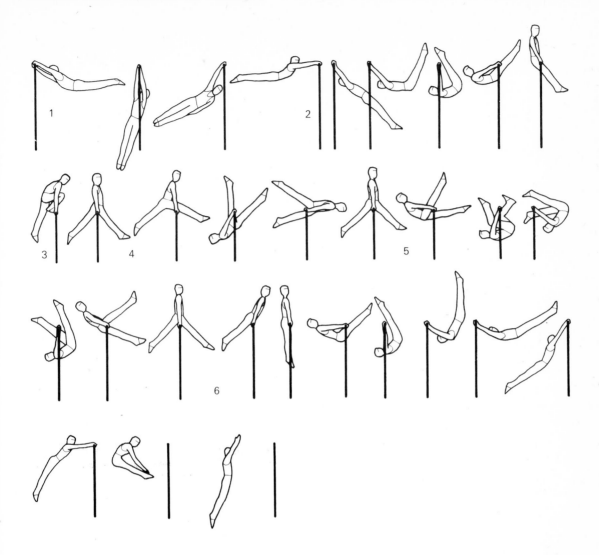

Standard Three
Horizontal Bar
Lesson 3

This exercise is marked out of 10

1 Swing forwards in undergrasp and squat legs between hands to back rest above bar   3.0 points
2 Lay out to rear under bar, swing forwards   3.0 points
3 Bend at hips, swing forwards, place right leg between hands and half hook circle forwards   1.0 points
4 Mill circle forwards to rest above bar   1.0 points
5 Turn to front rest and underswing dismount   2.0 points

Wolfgang Thune (West Germany) shows the 'Voronin hop' on the horizontal bar. Thune has added appeal to the move by making a spectacular sideways arm movement at the height of the flight phase.

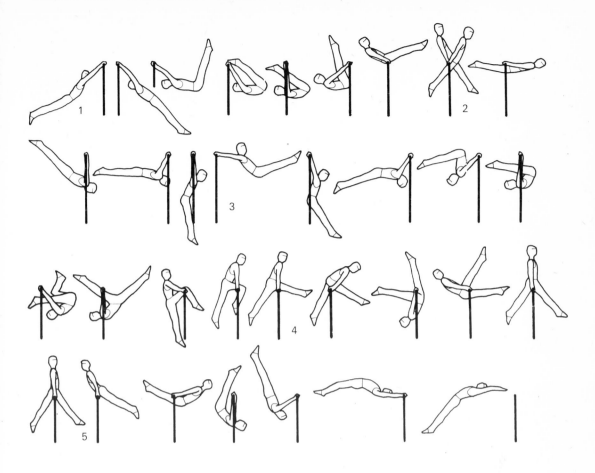

**Standard Three
Horizontal Bar
Lesson 4**

This exercise is marked out of 10

1	Lay out forwards in overgrasp and uprise to rear	3.5 points
2	Short circle backwards	0.5 points
3	Lay out forwards, swing to rear and cross hands swing forwards and turn to overgrasp	0.5 points
4	Swing forwards and half mill circle followed by a half turn	1.5 points
5	Sink to rear and rise immediately above bar	1.0 points
6	Remove leg to front rest, flank vault dismount	3.0 points

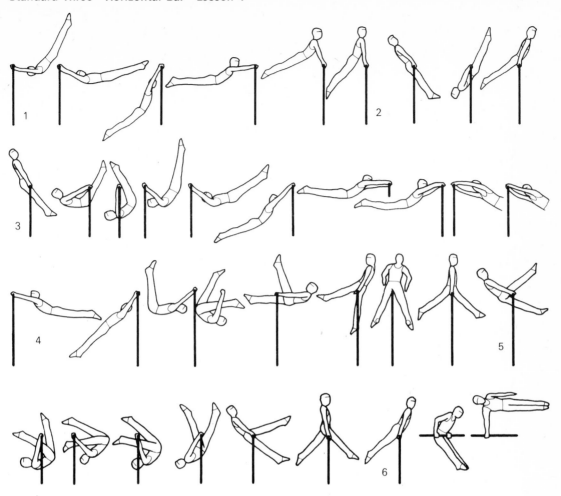

151

Standard Three
Horizontal Bar
Lesson 5

This exercise is marked out of 10

1	Overgrasp, swing forwards and turn to alternate grasp	0.5 points
2	Swing forwards and change hand to overgrasp, upstart	3.0 points
3	Short circle to the rear	1.0 points
4	Underswing to half turn into alternate grasp	1.5 points
5	Swing forwards and place leg between hands, half mill circle forwards, change grasp to overgrasp	1.5 points
6	Sink back and place both legs over bar, hook, dismount	2.5 points

Shigeru Kasamatsu (Japan). A circle straddle movement performed with amplitude. Only by constant repetition and mastery of the basics will you ever produce a skilled performance to this level. One hallmark of a champion is the ability to effortlessly perform simple or advanced skills to a limit beyond the normal execution.

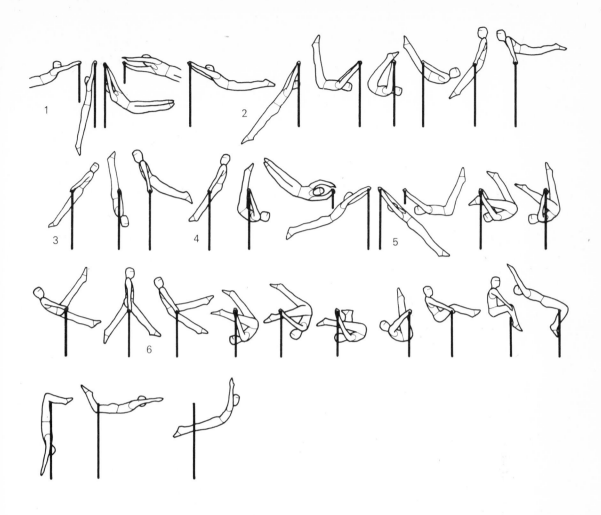

Standard Three
Horizontal Bar
Lesson 6

This exercise is marked out of 10

1	Overgrasp, lay out swing to rear, short underswing upstart	3.5 points
2	Place left leg between hands to mill rest	0.5 points
3	Mill circle backwards	1.0 points
4	Sink back, place right leg between hands and circle forwards to back rest	2.5 points
5	Turn to front rest and squat dismount to ground	2.5 points

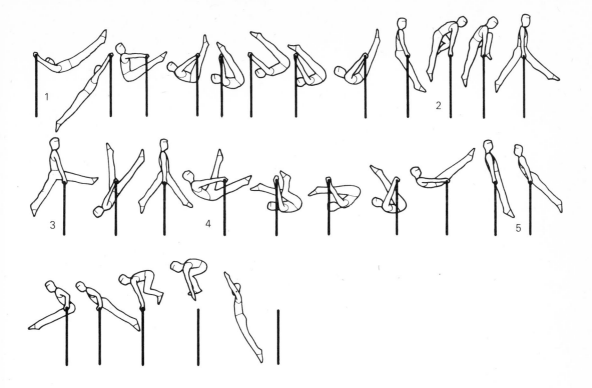

Standard Four
Floor Exercises
Lesson 1

This exercise is marked out of 10

I
1 Rise on toes raising arms
  sideways. Swing arms
  forwards, bend arms and
  elbows to 90°, move elbows
  outwards to bring forearms
  parallel to ground.
2 Extend arms forwards, swing
  arms sideways, bend knees,
  circling arms downwards
  through forwards
  downwards position. Circle
  arms inwards upwards to
  jump, landing on one leg
  arms sideways downwards.
3 Bend left leg, fully extending
  right leg forwards, raising
  arms forwards.
4 Stand erect on left leg,
  moving right leg sideways
  and arms sideways.   0.5 points

II
1 Hop on left leg changing to
  stand on right leg, left leg
  raised and arms sideways.
2 Hop on right leg repeating
  position on left leg.
3 4 Bend right leg, bending
  right arm, lunging and
  extending left arm down left
  leg.   0.5 points

III
1 Three-quarter spin turn on
  left leg to the left, raising
  arms upwards.
2 Back flip.   2.0 points

3 4 Place legs on ground
  stand erect, arms upwards.

IV
1 2 Backward roll over right
  shoulder to support on
  thighs.
3 Push back to deep crouch
  arms forward.
4 Spring to extend right leg
  sideways.   1.0 points

V
1 Circle right leg to left.
2 Continue to circle leg with
  quarter turn.
3 Roll forwards and spring
  backwards, landing.
4 Spring high straddle legs,
  place arms sideways.   0.5 points

VI
1 Lean left, lunge right, left
  arm across body in front.   0.5 points
2 Spin turn on left foot to left.
3 4 Kick to handstand.

VII
1 2 Hold handstand, roll down
  chest.   1.0 points
3 Front support.
4 Push backwards to deep
  crouch.

VIII
1 Roll to the right.   1.0 points
2 Continue rolling.
3 4 Extend legs to invert
  support on shoulders.

IX
1 2 Roll down, bend right leg
  stand with –

continued

Shigeru Kasamatsu (Japan). In this 'Y' Scale Kasamatsu will lose no points for a perfect balance, showing hip girdle flexibility.

3 4 Quarter turn to left, carry on turning a further quarter turn swinging left leg to rear, step forwards with right leg, extend arms upwards.   0.5 points

X
1 2 Step forwards twice hop on right leg, swinging left leg forwards.
3 4 Scissor kick to land on left leg, jump forwards to balance on right leg, forward horizontal stand.   1.0 points

XI
1 Circle arms outwards, bring legs together, jumping and landing on left leg, right legs sideways, arms sideways, circle arms upwards.
2 Crossing arms, straddle stand.
Lower trunk forwards to straddle, stand arms sideways trunk horizontal.   0.5 points

XII
1 Lunge left, right arm forwards left arm backwards, swing.
2 Swing right arm backwards extending left leg, arms sideways. Bring legs together, circling arms inwards, bending legs spring high legs astride, arms upwards sideways.
3 Land bending legs, arms sideways upwards. Circle arms inwards extending legs to arm stand with arms sideways upwards. Maintain position and lower arms to –
4 Attention.   1.0 points

Standard Four   Floor Exercises   Lesson 1

159

Standard Four
Floor Exercises
Lesson 2

This exercise is marked out of 10

I
1 Rise on toes and raise arms
   forwards, bend legs and
   lower arms, spring with arms
   swinging backwards, land
   with arms forwards.
2 Spring high with arms
   upwards and knees bent
   backwards, land with arms
   crossed and knees bent.
3 Spring high with legs astride
   and arms sideways upwards,
   land sweeping arms
   downwards backwards.
4 Swing arms forwards.   1.0 points

II
1 2 Flic-flac to stand with
   arms upwards.
3 Lower arms sideways, step
   forwards.
4 Scissor kick.   2.0 points

III
1 2 Step forwards with right
   and left legs hop step.
3 Hand spring to legs bend
   arms sideways, place hands
   on ground.
4 Elevate to handstand.   2.0 points

IV
1 2 Hold handstand, bend legs
   and kick backwards.

3 Land on feet, spring with
   half turn.
4 Land sweeping arms
   backwards.   1.0 points

V
1 2 Swing arms forwards.
3 4 Forward roll with straight
   legs to half lever hold.   1.0 points

VI
1 Bend left leg and spring with
   half turn.
2 Front support spring legs
   forwards passing straight
   right leg between hands.
3 Circle right leg to the right
   continue circling right leg,
   join both legs together circle
   both legs to –
4 Back support.   1.0 points

VII
1 Lower to long sitting, sweep
   arms forwards over head to
   feet, roll backwards on to
   shoulders.
2 3 Roll backwards through
   handstand, lower to –
4 Forward horizontal stand.   1.0 points

VIII
1 2 Turn to side horizontal
   stand on left leg, spring to
   land on right leg, left leg
   raised arms sideways.
3 Circle inwards above
   forearms.
4 Lower leg and arms. Recover
   to attention.   1.0 points

Standard Four
Floor Exercises
Lesson 3

This exercise is marked out of 10

I
1 Rise on toes with arms
   sideways, two steps
   forwards.
2 3 Hand spring to land on
   bent legs, arms forwards.
4 Stand turning quarter turn to
   right.   2.0 points

II
1 2 Quarter turn to left
   stepping forward with left
   leg.
3 Circle arms inwards turning
   half turn to left.
4 Forward horizontal stand.   1.0 points

III
1 Swing right leg forwards with
   quarter left turn of body
   raising right arm upwards
   left arm sideways.
2 3 Cartwheel.
4 Balance position on right
   leg.   1.0 points

IV
1 2 Side horizontal stand on
   right leg, right arm upwards
   left arm by the side.

3 4 Recover to attention with
   quarter right turn, raise arms
   upwards sideways bend
   forwards.   1.0 points

V
1 2 Backward roll to front
   support, squat one leg
   between hands carry on
   circling both legs to the
   right.
3 4 Circle both legs forwards
   to –   1.0 points

VI
1 Back support, raise left leg
   and turn three-quarter turn
   to the right to straddle,
   stand.
2 3 4 Raise arms sideways,
   trunk inclined forwards.   1.0 points

VII
1 2 3 4 Bent arm, bent leg,
   press to handstand.   2.0 points

VIII
1 Bend legs and kick down
   to –
2 Jump high with arms
   sideways, land with bent
   legs arms circling
   downwards inwards.
3 Spring with full turn to land
   with bent legs arms
   sideways.
4 Recover to attention.   1.0 points

162

**Standard Four
Floor Exercises
Lesson 4**

This exercise is marked out of 10

I
1 From attention circle arms
  upwards to the right, raise
  leg to the right, circle right
  arm downwards to right
  side.
2 Continue circling right arm
  to upwards and lower left
  arm to sideways, bending
  right leg.
3 Transfer to left
  corresponding position right
  arm behind back.
4 Extend left leg and arms
  sideways.   1.0 points

II
1 2 Cartwheel to handstand,
  roll forwards to crouch.
3 Stand.
4 Lower to side horizontal
  stand.   2.0 points

III
1 Recover to attention.
2 Half turn to the right, fall to
  prone.
3 Circle left leg underneath
  hands turning to back
  support.
4 Lower to long sitting.   1.0 points

IV
1 2 Roll backwards over right
  shoulder to front support.
3 Turn to back support.
4 Sweep right leg and left leg
  and turn to front support.   1.0 points

V
1 Jump to squat, jump high
  and –
2 3 Cartwheel to the right.
4 Lunge right arms raised
  upwards, circle arms
  downwards.   1.0 points

VI
1 Push from right leg circling
  both arms to stand on left
  leg.
2 Sweep left leg forwards and –
3 4 Kick to handstand.   2.0 points

VII
1 2 Hold handstand, quarter
  turn left.
3 4 Roll down crossing legs
  and turning to crouch.   1.0 points

VIII
1 2 Stand, step forwards two
  paces and –
3 Arab spring, jump with legs
  astride to land legs bent,
  arms sideways downwards.
4 Recover to attention.   1.0 points

164

Alexandre Detiatin (USSR), shows the modern trend in difficult circling movements on one handle. Note the strong grip, spaced as widely as possible, and the straight arms. The wrists are 'cocked'. The small joints must be supple too.

Standard Four
Pommelled Horse
Lesson 1

This exercise is marked out of 10

1	Double rear vault to cross rest in saddle left leg forwards half left circle of left leg	3.0 points
2	Full left circle of right leg	1.0 points
3	Half left circle of right leg, front shears left and right	2.5 points
4	Half right circle of left leg, full right circle of both legs	2.5 points
5	Rear vault right dismount	1.0 points

Standard Four
Pommelled Horse
Lesson 2

This exercise is marked out of 10

1	Full right circle of left leg to straddle left hand	2.0 points
2	Half right circle of right leg back shears left	1.5 points
3	Half right circle of right leg, full right circle of right leg	1.0 points
4	Half right circle of left leg and front shears right, front shears left	2.5 points
5	Full left circle of right leg	1.5 points
6	Double rear vault left dismount	1.5 points

Wolfgang Thune (West Germany) shows excellent flank extension here in a 'rear out'.

166

Standard Four   Pommelled Horse   Lesson 1

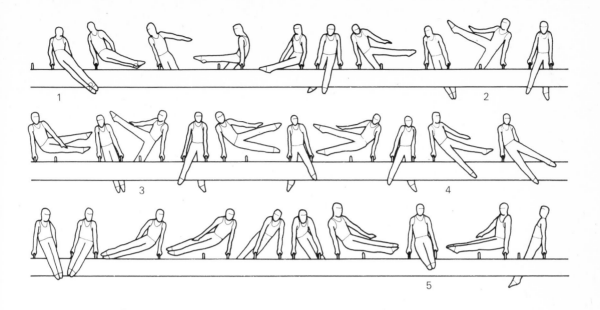

Standard Four   Pommelled Horse   Lesson 2

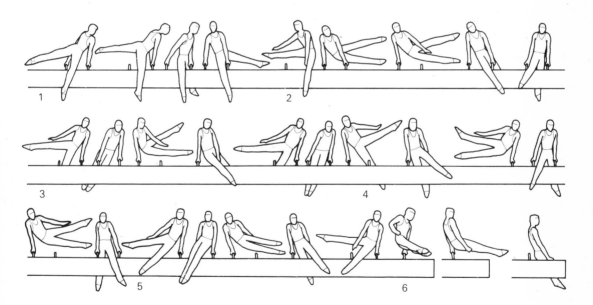

Standard Four
Pommelled Horse
Lesson 3

This exercise is marked out of 10

1	Half left circle of left leg back shears left	2.5 points
2	Half right circle of right leg, full right circle of left leg	1.0 points
3	Half right circle of both legs	1.0 points
4	Full right circle of right leg	2.0 points
5	Half right circle of left leg	2.0 points
6	Half right circle of left leg with half right turn of body, full right circle of right leg dismount	1.5 points

Standard Four
Pommelled Horse
Lesson 4

This exercise is marked out of 10

1	Left hand on end, right hand on handle double rear vault to cross rest in saddle right leg forwards half right circle of right leg	3.0 points
2	Half right circle of left leg, shears right, shears left	2.5 points
3	Single feint right and half left circle of left leg, back shears right	1.5 points
4	One and a half left circles of left leg	1.0 points
5	Double rear vault left dismount	2.0 points

Standard Four   Pommelled Horse   Lesson 3

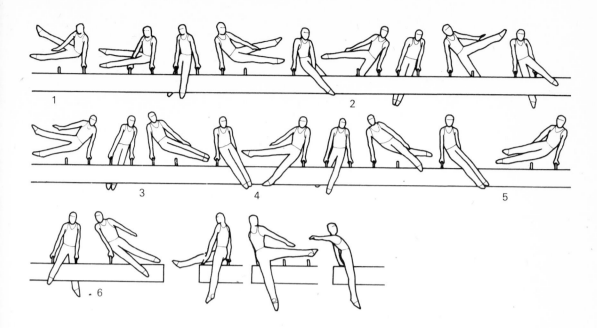

1   2   3   4   5   - 6

Standard Four   Pommelled Horse   Lesson 4

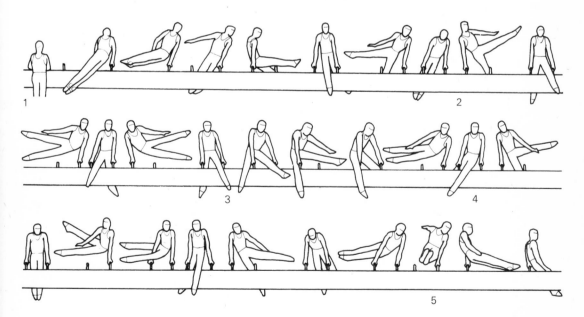

1   2   3   4   5

Standard Four
Pommelled Horse
Lesson 5

This exercise is marked out of 10

1	Full left circle of both legs	2.5 points
2	Half left circle of right leg, front shears left	1.0 points
3	Full left circle of left leg	1.5 points
4	Shears right	1.5 points
5	Half right circle of left leg, half right circle of both legs	1.0 points
6	Full right circle of left leg	1.0 points
7	Extended front vault dismount	1.5 points

Standard Four
Pommelled Horse
Lesson 6

This exercise is marked out of 10

1	Single feint left, full left circle of both legs	2.0 points
2	Half left circle of right leg, shears left, shears right	2.5 points
3	Half right circle of left leg, full right circle of both legs	2.0 points
4	Half right circle of right leg, back shears left	1.5 points
5	Half right circle of right leg transferring right hand to left pommel, rear vault dismount	2.0 points

Standard Four   Pommelled Horse   Lesson 5

Standard Four   Pommelled Horse   Lesson 6

171

Standard Four
Rings
Lesson 1

This exercise is marked out of 10

1	Swing forwards and dislocate	1.5 points
2	Circle to front rest	2.5 points
3	Raise legs to half lever and hold for 3 seconds	0.5 points
4	Lower forwards with straight body to inverted hang	1.0 points
5	Swing down forwards and inlocate to bent inverted hang	1.5 points
6	Swing down forwards and with half turn of body straddle backwards dismount	3.0 points

Nikolai Andrianov (USSR), champion of the Montreal Olympics, performs a 'backward longswing' on the rings.

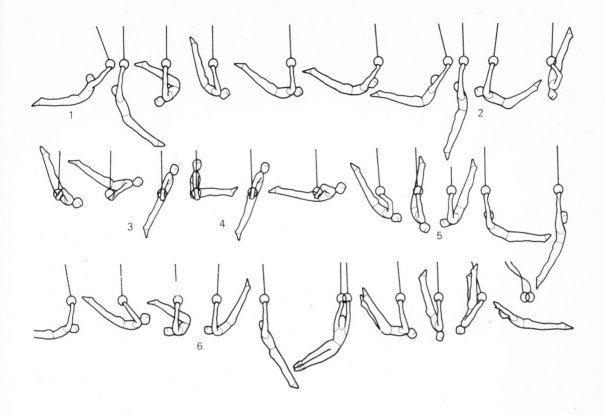

Standard Four
Rings
Lesson 2

This exercise is marked out of 10

1 Swing forwards and uprise
  to cross rest   2.0 points
2 Circle forwards with straight
  body to inverted hang   0.5 points
3 Swing down forwards and
  inlocate to inverted hang   2.0 points
4 Upstart to cross rest, swing
  to rear   2.0 points
5 Sink backwards through
  inverted hang and dislocate   1.5 points
6 Straddle backwards and
  dismount   2.0 points

*Miroslav Cerar (Yugoslavia), the greatest
Yugoslav gymnast of all time, shows a 'front
horizontal lever' on the rings.*

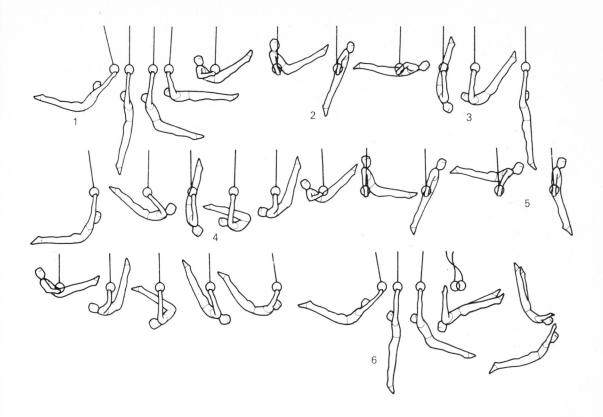

Standard Four
Rings
Lesson 3

This exercise is marked out of 10

1 Swing to inverted hang, lower to back horizontal lever	2.0 points
2 Lower to back hang, raise to inverted hang	1.5 points
3 Swing down and back uprise to cross rest	2.5 points
4 Sink to bent inverted hang, dislocate	1.5 points
5 Swing forwards and straddle backwards dismount	2.5 points

Danut Grecu (Romania). The World and European Champion on rings shows part of his ring optional start. He hangs beneath the rings and circles slowly backward to 'the crucifix'. The start is called 'the Azaryan' after a former Russian Olympic medallist.

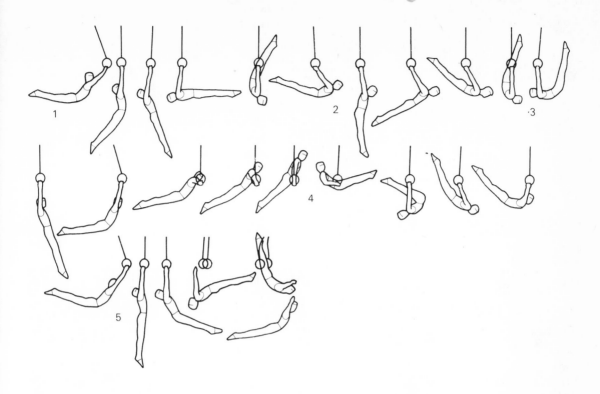

1

2

·3

4

5

Standard Four
Rings
Lesson 4

This exercise is marked out of 10

1	Circle up to cross rest, sink back to inverted hang	2.0 points
2	Dislocate to inverted hang	2.0 points
3	Upstart to cross rest	2.0 points
4	Circle forwards to inverted hang	0.5 points
5	Inlocate to bent inverted hang	2.0 points
6	Extend forwards dismount with half turn	1.5 points

Victor Klimenko (USSR), former USSR Champion, demonstrates a 'dislocate'. This shows the high level of specific muscular conditioning needed to perform modern powerful gymnastic movements on the rings.

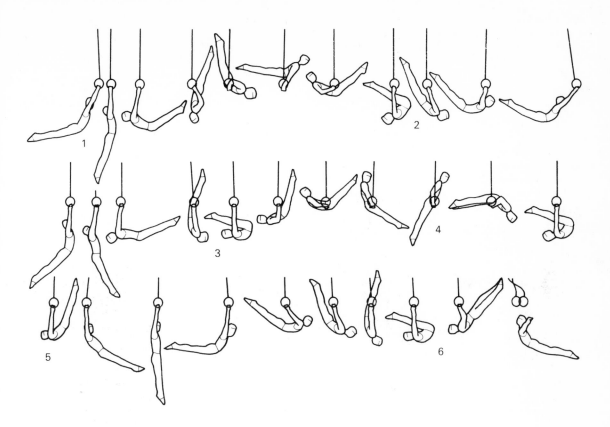

Barry Winch (GB) shows a full twisting longarm!

Standard Four
Vaulting
Lesson 1

This exercise is marked out of 10

1.40m	10 points
1.35m	8 points
1.30m	6 points
1.25m	4 points
1.20m	2 points

Running forward high jump.
(Use the beat board to obtain better elevation. Extend the hips before landing.)

Standard Four
Vaulting
Lesson 2

Straight-legs-squat vault over buck set at 1.30m and placed sideways.
(Use the beat board to obtain better elevation. Extend the hips before landing.)

Standard Four
Vaulting
Lesson 3

Bent-legs-squat vault over horse set at 1.20m.
(Swing the legs high to the rear obtaining an angle of at least 35°. Squat the legs between the hands. Extend hips before landing.)

Standard Four   Vaulting   Lesson 1

Standard Four   Vaulting   Lesson 2

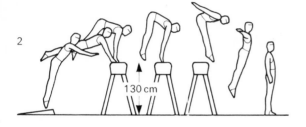

130 cm

Standard Four   Vaulting   Lesson 3

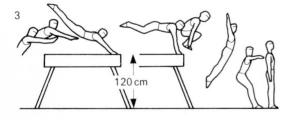

120 cm

**Standard Four
Vaulting
Lesson 4**

Straddle vault over horse set at 1.20m.
(Swing the legs high to the rear, and
straddle dismount, with strong thrust, from
the end of the horse.)

Note: These two exercises on the vaulting
table are merely put in as examples,
because this apparatus is popular for
demonstrations. The other vaults shown in
this book can be attempted with much
success on the vaulting table.

Extreme caution and the full use of crash
mats is advised when vaulting-table
exercises are being tried out. The vaulting
table should never be used in
demonstration without crash mats.

**Standard Four
Vaulting
Lesson 5**

Cartwheel over vaulting table set at 1.60m.
(Jump up from springboard or trampett
with shoulders square. During the first
flight phase elevate the left hand to obtain
the quarter turn to handstand. In the
dismount phase do not angle the shoulders
or hips. Swing extended body to land.)

**Standard Four
Vaulting
Lesson 6**

Straddle vault over vaulting table set at
1.45m – slightly lower than in Lesson 5.
(Swing the legs high backwards to the
strike position. Straddle dismount,
extending hips to land.)

Standard Four   Vaulting   Lesson 4

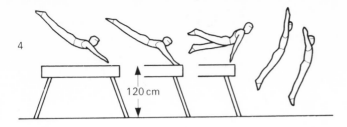

4

120 cm

Standard Four   Vaulting   Lesson 5

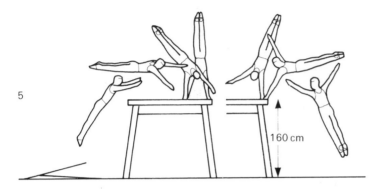

5

160 cm

Standard Four   Vaulting   Lesson 6

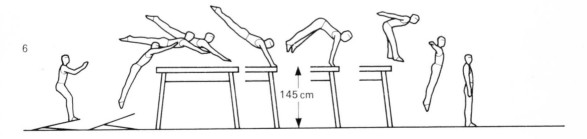

6

145 cm

Shigeru Kasamatsu (Japan) shows the support shoulder stand position used after an underswing. This position is used at all levels of competitive gymnastics.

Standard Four
Parallel Bars
Lesson 1

This exercise is marked out of 10

1 Short underswing upstart to upper-arm rest	0.7 points
2 Back uprise to cross rest	0.7 points
3 Swinging front change to upper-arm rest	1.5 points
4 Swinging the legs forwards upstart from upper arms	0.7 points
5 Straddle forwards over left bar	0.7 points
6 Swing to handstand and hold for three seconds	2.5 points
7 Half turn onto left bar	1.2 points
8 Straight-leg squat, dismount	2.0 points

Standard Four
Parallel Bars
Lesson 2

This exercise is marked out of 10

1 Short underswing upstart to straight-arm rest	1.5 points
2 Swing to rear and circle right leg over right bar with half turn of body to cross rest legs raised forwards	1.5 points
3 With bent arms and body lift to handstand and hold for 3 seconds	2.5 points
4 Sink to upper arms and backward roll	1.5 points
5 Uprise forwards	1.0 points
6 Swing to rear and double flank vault left dismount	2.0 points

Standard Four   Parallel Bars   Lesson 1

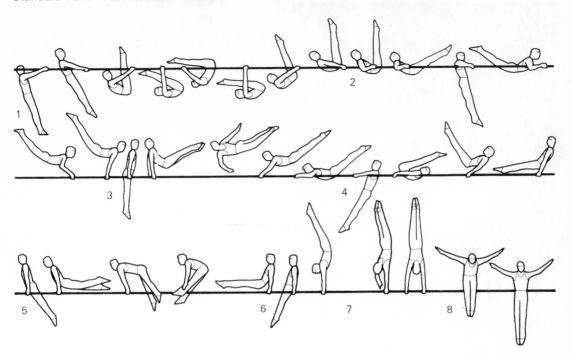

Standard Four   Parallel Bars   Lesson 2

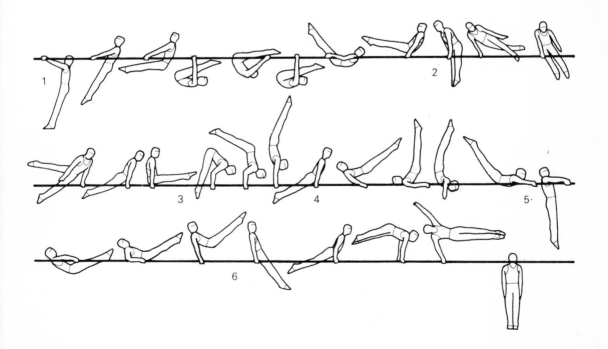

Sawao Kato (Japan) performs a 'back uprise half turn'. His Olympic successes are: 1968 Mexico City – all round Gold, team Gold, floor Gold, rings Bronze; 1972 Munich – all round Gold, team Gold; 1976 Montreal – team Gold, all round Silver, parallel bars – Gold.

Standard Four
Parallel Bars
Lesson 3

This exercise is marked out of 10

1 At the end of the bars undergrasp circle to front rest legs raised forwards	3.0 points
2 Swing legs to rear and circle right leg over left bar, with half turn of body raise to half horizontal lever	1.5 points
3 Lift to shoulderstand, roll forwards to upper-arm rest	2.5 points
4 Swing to rear and sink through bars to long underswing upstart	1.5 points
5 Swing to the rear and straddle right bar forwards, followed immediately by a rear vault dismount left	1.5 points

Standard Four
Parallel Bars
Lesson 4

This exercise is marked out of 10

1 From upper arms swing forwards and uprise	1.0 points
2 Swing to handstand and hold for three seconds	2.5 points
3 Swing down and sink to upper-arm rest	0.5 points
4 Back uprise and straddle forwards over left bar to bent-arm cross rest	2.5 points
5 Swing back to horizontal front lever on right arm	1.0 points
6 Swing forwards and placing right hand on left bar circle legs to front leaning on rest on rear bar	1.0 points
7 Straddle forwards dismount	1.5 points

Standard Four   Parallel Bars   Lesson 3

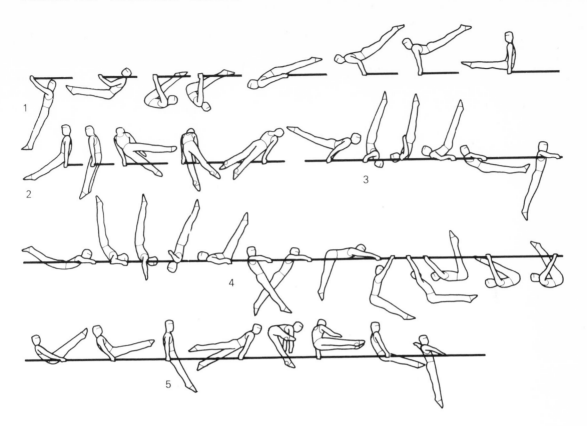

Standard Four   Parallel Bars   Lesson 4

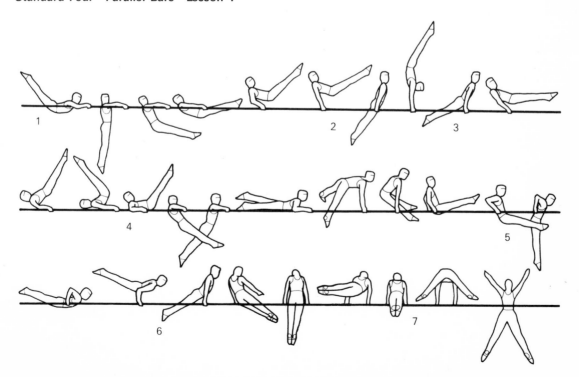

Standard Four
Parallel Bars
Lesson 5

This exercise is marked out of 10

1	Swing forward to upper-arm rest, forward roll to upper-arm rest	2.5 points
2	Swing back and half turn to upper arms	1.0 points
3	Swing to rear and sink through bars, to long underswing upstart	1.5 points
4	Swing to the rear and straddle left or right bar to cross rest, with bent arms	1.5 points
5	Swing to handstand and hold for three seconds	2.5 points
6	Cartwheel left dismount	1.0 points

Standard Four
Parallel Bars
Lesson 6

This exercise is marked out of 10

1	Uprise backwards to horizontal lever on right arm	2.5 points
2	Swing forwards, circle right leg over left bar with half left turn of body	0.5 points
3	Swing backwards to handstand and hold for three seconds	2.5 points
4	From handstand lower to upper arms	0.5 points
5	Backward roll	1.0 points
6	Swing forwards and uprise forwards	1.0 points
7	Swing backwards and double rear vault dismount	2.0 points

188

Standard Four   Parallel Bars   Lesson 5

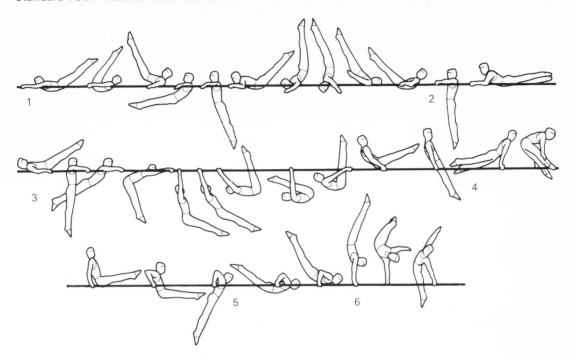

1   2   3   4   5   6

Standard Four   Parallel Bars   Lesson 6

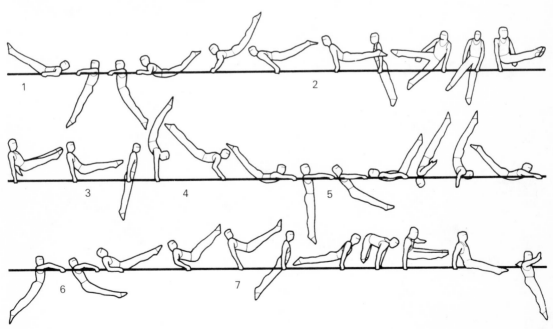

1   2   3   4   5   6   7

Standard Four
Horizontal Bar
Lesson 1

This exercise is marked out of 10

1 In undergrasp, swing forwards and upstart to handstand	2.0 points
2 Swing down forwards in three-quarter long swing	1.5 points
3 Change hands to overgrasp at height of swing	1.0 points
4 Swing forwards and circle to front rest	2.0 points
5 Lay out forwards and turn to alternate grasp	1.0 points
6 Upstart to front rest	1.0 points
7 Front vault dismount	1.5 points

'The Stalder straddle'. In top-class work extreme range of movement and a strong grip are essential.

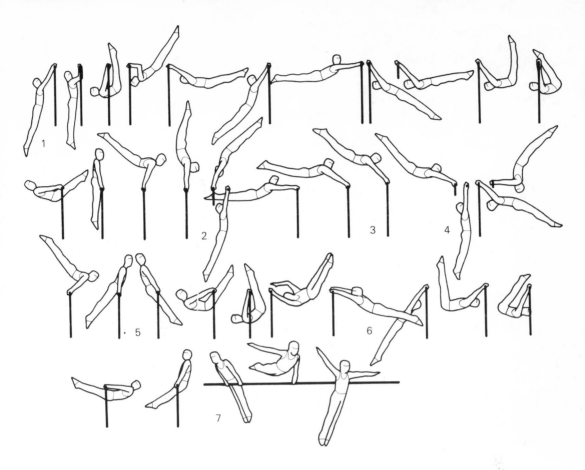

Standard Four
Horizontal Bar
Lesson 2

This exercise is marked out of 10

1 Undergrasp, swing forwards and half free seat circle forwards with half turn to front rest	2.0 points
2 Underswing forwards and back uprise to front rest	1.5 points
3 Clear circle to rear and swing down forwards	2.5 points
4 Circle forwards to front rest	2.0 points
5 Short underswing upstart, place feet on bar between hands	1.0 points
6 Underswing forwards and remove feet from bar, dismount	1.0 points

'A flying straddle' by a Japanese team member. The gymnast seems to 'fly' above the apparatus. He is in fact more than twelve feet above the landing mat.

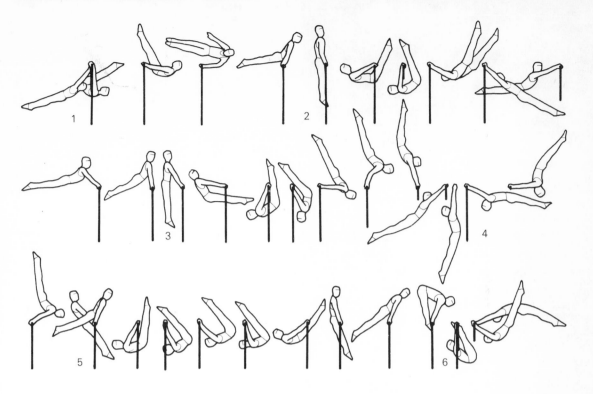

Standard Four
Horizontal Bar
Lesson 3

This exercise is marked out of 10

1	Swing forwards in overgrasp, squat legs between hands and extend body to rear, swing forwards in back hang	1.0 points
2	Swing forwards and upstart to back rest	2.5 points
3	Back seat circle to back rest	1.5 points
4	Sink backwards and remove legs, short underswing upstart	1.0 points
5	Clear circle to front rest	1.5 points
6	Short underswing forwards, swing to rear and uprise to cross rest, knees bent and upper foot placed against the bar	1.5 points
7	Swing to the rear and dismount forwards	1.0 points

Paata Shamugia (USSR). The complicated turning movements from longswings become second nature to the champions. Perfect your simple turns by learning the standards to the highest level and the path to progress will open to you.

194

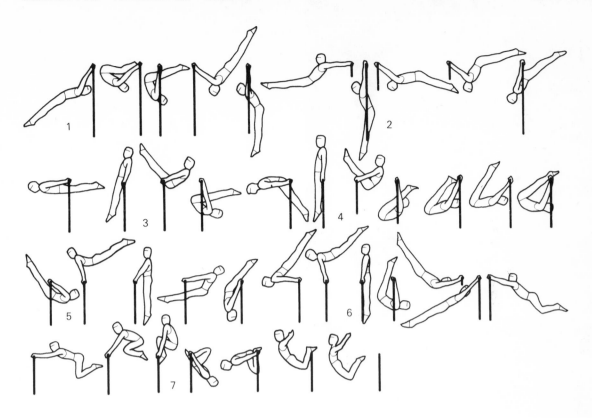

Standard Four
Horizontal Bar
Lesson 4

This exercise is marked out of 10

1 Without swing, upstart to front rest	1.5 points
2 Forward roll to front rest, place feet on bar between hands	1.5 points
3 Underswing with half turn, removing feet	1.5 points
4 Circle forwards to front rest, in overgrasp	2.5 points
5 Short underswing upstart to front rest	1.0 point
6 Squat dismount forwards	2.0 points

Hiroshi Kajnama (Japan) performing 'inverted giants'. After years of basic training, many competitions and demonstrations, a gymnast may reach world class level. In Japan there are hundreds of world class performers all working toward Olympic participation. With such fierce competition only the best technicians and most determined achieve the top results.

196

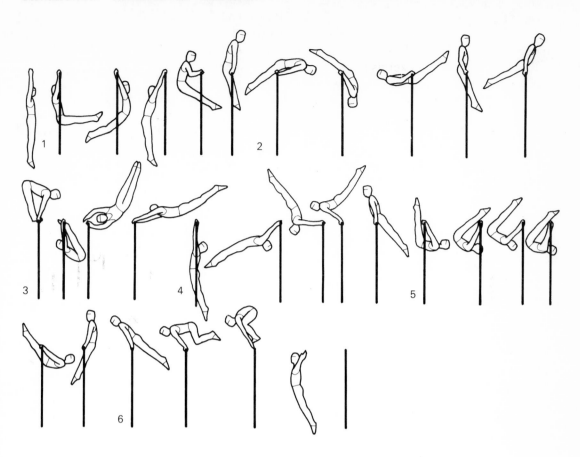

Standard Four
Horizontal Bar
Lesson 5

This exercise is marked out of 10

1 Swing forwards and squat legs between hands, back upstart to back rest	2.0 points
2 Sink to rear and removing legs short upstart to front rest	1.0 point
3 Forward roll and lay out to rear	1.5 points
4 Cross right hand over left and swing down forwards	1.0 point
5 Back uprise changing hands to overgrasp	3.0 points
6 Underswing dismount with half turn	1.5 points

Standard Four
Horizontal Bar
Lesson 6

This exercise is marked out of 10

1 Swing forwards in overgrasp and straddle bar to back rest in undergrasp	2.0 points
2 Extend to rear, swing forwards and bend at hips	0.5 point
3 Half seat circle forwards above bar	2.5 points
4 Free seat circle forwards with half turn to front rest	2.0 points
5 Short underswing forwards upstart to front rest	1.0 point
6 Place both feet on bar outside hands and hand and foot circle dismount	2.0 points

Standard Four   Horizontal Bar   Lesson 5

Standard Four   Horizontal Bar   Lesson 6

Evaluation of performance

Evaluation of performance is best left to the experienced coach – better still to the judge. At this point it is best to contact the British Amateur Gymnastics Association (BAGA) and obtain the services of a judge. There is probably one in your area.

On the subject of judging, much has been said and written but, for the purpose of the lessons, the ability to recognize quality in a performance is of paramount importance. Send to the BAGA for the *International Code of Points for Judges.* This will improve your knowledge of gymnastics and may lead you to take a judging qualification at one of the courses held by the BAGA. Your club coach or a gymnast of international or national standard is the next best guide. The following extracts from the *International Code* are reproduced by kind permission of the Fédération Internationale Gymnastique.

Evaluation of execution

Deductions will be made for poor form and incorrect technical execution. All set exercises are marked out of 10 but the total number of marks allotted to voluntary exercises depends on content.

1   Execution errors in form apply to poor foot, leg, head, arm, hands and body holding, stops, touching etc.

2   In the group of technically incorrect execution belong among others the following errors: if the shoulders are too far forward upon regrasping the parallel bars in a swinging front turn or if there is too much arch in the back; when the regrasp of the back salto on the parallel bars is too late, or executed with the shoulders too far forward; unimpressive uprises, lack of amplitude and executed too low, too little freedom in double leg circles or scissors in which only the legs but not the hips are raised high on the side horse; handstands not held vertically (shoulders too far forward); handstand pirouettes on parallel bars and on the floor in which the body is not in a vertical position; supporting, hanging and standing scales in which the body is not held in a level position; crosses with bent arms or not held with arms level, etc.

General execution errors and corresponding deductions

1   *Poor* position of feet, legs, arms, hands, head and body; or open legs at instances where this is not required by the movement, every time   *up to 0.3 point*
2   *Touching* the body of the horse, the pommels, the rails, the standards for the parallel bars; the floor or the base support of the parallel bars; the horizontal bar, the uprights of the horizontal bar; or the ropes of the rings: touching these with the feet, legs or with the seat or other parts of the body if the touching of these is not required by the execution of the movements, every time   *0.1 to 0.3 point*
3   *Stops (or hesitations) of the exercise* will always be punished according to the extent of the error; however, taking into consideration the difficulty rating of the part or the connecting exercises which are the causing factor to the stop, every time deduct   *0.1 to 0.3 point*

4   *In the case of a definite sit down* on the apparatus, deduct every time in relation to the duration   *0.3 to 0.5 point*
5   *Falling on the apparatus* forward, sideward, or backward is identical to a definite sit down and should be treated the same way, and of course in addition to the stipulated *0.3 to 0.5 point* deductions, further deductions for poor form.

Deductions for technical insufficiency of the execution

1   *Walking in handstand* : 0.1 per step, at the most deduct   *up to 0.5 point*
2   *Interrupted motion in upward movements*

'The Rising Sun'. After a tremendous battle, the Olympic title at Montreal was won by Japan by 0.20 of a mark. This is the merest margin considering that the result is over sixty routines and almost 1200 points in the team scores. Russia were second, East Germany third.

3   *Two or more starts* to a hold part or to a strength part, or to any other upward movement   *0.1 to 0.3 point*
4   *Strength parts* that are executed with swing, or swing parts that are executed with strength, shall be penalized with   *0.1 to 0.3 point*
5   *The time duration for hold parts is 2 seconds*
6   *Non-observation of these time durations* will bring the following deductions:

201

(a) held for 1 second only   *0.2 point*

(b) not holding at all, is not to be credited as a hold part and event penalty in combination, if there is a lack of proportion between the different parts such as not enough hold parts and devaluation as a difficulty part will result also.

(c) A too long duration of more than 3 seconds results in deductions of   *0.1 to 0.3 point*

7   On the *rings*

(a) Handstands with bent arms *or* touching the ropes with the arms   *0.2 to 0.3 point*

(b) Handstands with bent arms *and* touching the ropes with the arms   *0.3 to 0.5 point*

(c) Cross or inverted cross, or free support scale with bent or not completely horizontal body, or not completely horizontal arms during cross-hang   *up to 0.5 point*

(d) Swinging of ropes   *0.1 to 0.3 points*

(e) Fall from handstand into hang (if fall was not planned)   *0.2 to 0.5 point*

8   *Floor exercises*

(a) All the *stand faults* during and after an exercise must according to para. 13 be penalized each time   *up to 0.5 point*

(b) If there is harmony, rhythm, suppleness and amplitude missing during the execution of a part or combination, the deduction is each time   *up to 0.2 point*

(c) If the faults are prevalent throughout the exercise   *up to 1.0 point*

(d) When gymnastic movements and connections are not executed according to correct technique and form, and without personal expression and presentation, as much as wrong posture before and after the exercise the total deduction can be   *up to 0.5 point*

(e) If, in the *standing scales*, the horizontal line does not pass through the knees and the upper-shoulder or shoulders, or if the arm or arms are not in line with the line of the body or higher, the deduction is   *up to 0.2 point*

(f) Concerning the *amount of running steps* before jumps, handsprings and saltos, we refer to Article 33, para. 19*a*).

9   *Side Horse*

(a) *Lack of amplitude* during double leg circles, this means if the hip movement is limited and if the circle is done only by the leg movement, the global deduction for an exercise is   *up to 0.5 point*

(b) *Forward scissors without hip movement*, which means that the horizontal line does not pass through the upper hip and the shoulder of the supporting arm; or backward scissors, where the upper hip is not at least halfway between supporting shoulder and horse-body result in deduction each time of   *up to 0.2 point*

(c) For an *additional support* of one hand during a turnswing, deduct   *0.3 point*

10   *Generalities.* Horizontal support scales, horizontal hang scales, 'L' supports and straddle 'L' supports which are not held horizontally, handstands wrong technically, support non-vertical or shoulders advanced forward, late support after Stützkehre or saltos backward on the parallel bars or too quick passage from one part to the other, etc. – deduction each time   *up to 0.3 point*

11   On the rings and the horizontal bar, a gymnast has the *right to be lifted* to grip the apparatus by the team leader, team member or a gymnast from his group, but the evaluation starts whenever the feet of the gymnast are no longer in contact with the floor or mat, otherwise deduction for execution   *up to 0.2 point*

12   *On the rings, a small preliminary swing is not allowed* (like for the horizontal bar), in case of swinging there will be a deduction of   *0.3 point*

13 *Posture and stand after an exercise.* If the exercise on the apparatus is not completed with a good stand and in a correct posture, or if during or after a floor exercise similar faults are made, the deductions are:

(*a*) Little step or skip, or incorrect posture after an exercise *up to 0.2 point*

(*b*) Several steps or hops in the same instance as 13*a* or touching the floor with one or two hands without support or bad posture after exercise *up to 0.3 point*

(*c*) Support of one or two hands on the floor, kneeling or sitting or any other fall *up to 0.5 point*

Interruption of an exercise

Through falling, loosing the grip, or without loosing grip with weight on the floor.

1   When falling from the apparatus or standing on the floor without releasing the grip, and interrupting the exercise, the exercise may not be repeated, but continued immediately or at the latest within 30 seconds; a specific deduction will be made.

2   During the 30 seconds, the gymnast is free to move about as he pleases. If the exercise is not continued at the end of these 30 seconds, it shall be considered completed, and the value of the exercise in this case will be limited to the work done up to the interruption.

3   The superior judge checks this time and informs the gymnast at the completion of 10, 20 and 30 seconds. He then calls 'time' at the end of the 30 seconds.

4   When continuing the exercise, the gymnast must not repeat the last completed part of the exercise, but must start with the part that follows. Movements that are needed here in order to arrive at the proper starting position shall not be considered in the evaluation of the exercise, unless the

World and Olympic Champions on the winners' stand, at the World Championships: (left to right, front) Kajiyama, Kato, Kasamatsu; (left to right, back) Kenmotsu, Honma, Tsukahara.

gymnast uses more than one intermediate swing to arrive in the support position.

5   The deduction in any case will be 0.5 point

(*a*) In case of deductions for form according to Article 38, para. 4, the usual deductions will be given.

(*b*) Tearing of clothing or bandages (taping), health problems or tearing of hand-guards can in no way be taken into consideration when an exercise is interrupted.

Safety rules in the gym

Small injuries impede progress. Large injuries impede club and national progress. Make sure that you observe the following rules:

1 Never train unless a qualified teacher or coach is present.

2 Mats must be smooth; any worn ones should be replaced.

3 Crash mats at least 30 cm (one foot) thick must be used for all somersaults and dismounts from the apparatus with normal agility mats underneath to prevent 'bottoming' and slipping.

4 Never train without warming-up first.

5 Maintain good health habits even in off season.

6 Do not train if unwell.

7 Remove all sharp projections or cover them.

8 Never leave track suits or other clothing on the floor.

9 Remove rings, watches and necklaces.

10 Do not train on the floor in socks, wear gym shoes.

11 Allow at least two hours to pass after eating, then begin training.

12 An accident record book should always be kept; it should always be in the gym office.

13 A telephone should always be available.

14 The telephone number and address of the nearest doctor should be fixed to the wall or telephone in case of emergency.

15 A Red Cross first-aid box, with all essential items, should be available at all times.

16 Never attempt new exercises without an adequate study and practice of the skills involved.

17 'Stand ins' or spotters must be available and actively involved until an exercise has been mastered to a consistent level.

18 Do not rush through the lessons. Your gymnastic ability depends on the amount you understand – study the lessons at home, concentrate in the gym.

19 Stop before you get any blisters. They hamper the performance of any exercise.

20 Use hand straps to give protection and to increase the amount of time you can spend in contact with the apparatus.

21 If an accident does occur, do not attempt to treat the injured person unless you are qualified to do so. In the event of serious accident do not move the injured person but contact a doctor immediately.

'Montreal victory wave'. The 1976 Olympic team Champions retain their title held from Rome, Tokyo, Mexico City and Munich.

DATE DUE

GAYLORD			PRINTED IN U.S.A.

Lavender
the grower's guide

CONTENTS

THIS BOOK IS
DEDICATED
TO MY SON, JASON,
AND TO ALL
LAVENDER LOVERS,
ENTHUSIASTS,
RESEARCHERS,
COLLECTORS AND
GROWERS AROUND
THE WORLD.

MAY THE PERFUME
AND VISION OF
LAVENDER BRING
EVERLASTING LIGHT
INTO YOUR LIVES.

FOREWORD

Virginia McNaughton has produced an excellent account of the genus *Lavandula*, long awaited by gardeners and collectors. She has used her expertise as a botanist and her extensive experience of growing and observing lavender in the South Island of New Zealand to present an overview of the genus together with comprehensive information about the species and cultivars. The author has drawn on the available literature on the classification of *Lavandula* but has not set out to write a botanical monograph. She has instead written a most lucid and helpful book which will be read with great interest by all lavender enthusiasts.

L. x intermedia 'Old English'

Lavender has long been a cottage garden favourite and of course used widely by garden designers in more formal settings to create elegant sweeps of colour and texture. Lately there has been an explosion of interest in the more unusual species lavenders and in the new hybrids and cultivars now flooding the market. This is reflected in the enormous range of lavenders to be seen on the specialist stands in flower and horticultural shows. I am frequently asked why there is not an authoritative book on lavender to support this wave of enthusiasm and am delighted to introduce its arrival.

The climate in parts of New Zealand and Australia appears to favour the cultivation of lavender. Lavender farming has become an increasingly popular activity in both countries and many new hybrids, especially within Section *Stoechas*, have originated there in the last five years or so. These are now listed and described for the first time within one publication. The reader will also appreciate the lists of cultivars in other sections, notably those within Section *Lavandula*, which contains the most widely grown lavenders — the *L. angustifolia* and *L. x intermedia* cultivars. Many of these lavenders originate in the United Kingdom, mainland Europe or the United States of America, while some have been selected in New Zealand and Australia. The descriptions of these cultivars together with beautifully detailed illustrations will be particularly helpful to gardeners with no specialist knowledge of lavender, but there is much for experienced growers to learn also. Equally welcome are the chapters on cultivation and propagation, given pride of place at the start of the book.

The amount of detail in the descriptions of the lavenders, which use both qualitative and quantitative measures, will be of considerable interest to botanists and taxonomists. Nomenclature issues, longstanding problems in the lavender literature, are addressed and we must thank the author for unravelling the double naming that has occurred across the cultivars. Nursery owners interested in checking their labelling should find the chapters on the botany and classification of lavenders essential reading and a reliable reference for some time to come.

Virginia McNaughton is to be congratulated on writing a book that will be welcomed alike by gardeners and the nursery trade, collectors and botanists.

Joan Head
Editor, **The Lavender Bag**
Nottingham, England

L. 'Pippa White' and
L. 'Tickled Pink' amongst
standard roses

INTRODUCTION

Yoda – a lavender loving cat

I have occasionally been asked whether increased interest in lavender this decade will continue or whether it is just another phase or gardening trend that will eventually wane. My personal belief is that lavender is just as popular as it has been for centuries, and with increased promotion it will remain well established — very much 'a herb of our time and for the future'. This increased publicity and awareness have been facilitated by recent advances in communication systems like the Internet, ensuring that information is disseminated globally, reaching both populated and remote areas. There is a realisation that lavender can be grown in many conditions and altitudes and is a very adaptable plant. With this expanded awareness, more people are growing lavender commercially for oil and other commodities. Coinciding with a marked increase in the number of lavender farms, many new cultivars have been introduced to the market. However, there has been a corresponding confusion among the public about lavender varieties and their uses.

The aim of this book, therefore, is to describe some of the lavender cultivars available on the world market and hopefully to clarify some of the errors that have been perpetuated for years in the lavender nursery industry. It will not answer all problems, because ultimately good naming is dependent on reliable, accurate sourcing of original stock. However, the public is becoming increasingly discerning about its needs and hopefully there will be a cultivar somewhere in these pages to meet most requirements. The range and diversity within the *Lavandula* genus are extensive with varieties to match most garden settings and colour schemes.

It is perhaps not surprising that interest in lavender seems to be increasing in the 1990s, particularly with the turn of the century imminent. Spiritually, lavender is considered a plant that will raise perceptiveness and take an individual to higher states of consciousness during meditation. Since fabled Lemurian times, special devas or plant guardians were appointed to look after the plants until such time as mankind was able to absorb greater knowledge. Its therapeutic use in aromatherapy and its wide range of healing applications as well as its other fragrant and ornamental uses make lavender one of the most versatile herbs. It is truly a magical plant and those who have ever been enticed and enchanted by its sweet, heady perfume become enamoured for life.

The view of a field of lavender in bloom is both beautiful and calming, and forever captivating.

Although this book is primarily intended as a botanical reference to the wonderful world of lavender and does not include a detailed history or recipes, it will reveal the diversity of one of the world's most revered plants. Enjoy your time in this exciting world and may your curiosity and passion grow with each new lavender in your garden.

How to use this book

Before delving into any of the detailed descriptions in this book, readers are urged to first consult the chapter on 'The Botany of Lavender', together with the chapter on 'History, Classification and Lavender Species', for an overview of the *Lavandula* genus. You may also find it necessary to regularly refer back to 'The Botany of Lavender' to verify particular characteristics when consulting individual cultivar descriptions.

Both qualitative and quantitative measurements have been used in this book to try to overcome differing growing conditions. The qualitative measurements may be of more use to those growing in other countries as quantitative measurements tend to be subjective.

Many of the terms used in the descriptions may be technical but readers will find a useful glossary and descriptive photographs to assist them. General terms such as 'autumn' or 'summer' have been used to avoid possible confusion over calendar months for gardening enthusiasts in the northern hemisphere.

Writing mainly for New Zealand conditions, I am aware that there will be differences in climate, pests and diseases, etc for other growers, but I hope at least the basics are presented in sufficient detail for those who have not grown lavender before.

It can be difficult to photograph lavender and although the best attempt has been made to colour-match specific cultivars with the images in this book, readers may find slight variations between their lavender and the photographs reproduced here.

Virginia McNaughton
Christchurch, New Zealand

ACKNOWLEDGEMENTS

My heartfelt thanks to:

Hal Tapley and Deborah Ward, who spent literally hours waiting for weather conditions to settle so that they could take the photographs. Their patience was truly remarkable and, without them, this book would never have been created.

Henry Head of Norfolk Lavender, Rosemary Holmes and Edythe Anderson of Yuulong Lavender Estate, Mr Tomita and the Publicity Office of Farm Tomita, Noriko Iwao, and Andrew Van Hevelingen of Van Hevelingen Herbs, for their most valuable contributions to this book. Their time and willingness to share information have been most appreciated.

Joan Head, who offered her valued support, sage comments and precious time to read the draft before it was even edited! You can blame me for *The Lavender Bag* not being out on time.

Peter Carter, my right-hand man, and Susyn Andrews, Chris Barnaby, Mark Braithwaite, Rob Burrows, John Fletcher, Geoff Genge, Elsie Hall, Lorraine and Kerry Hoggard, Wayne Horrobin, Margaret Hughes, Grace and Eion Johnson, Peter Smale and Dr Roger Spencer, who readily offered information when asked.

Avice Hill, a pioneer in her field and without whom this book would never have eventuated.

The Plant Variety Rights Office, New Zealand, for the kind use of their light box.

Carol White of Lavandula, Chris Fairweather, Bridestowe Estate Lavender Farm and Plant Growers Australia who offered photographs.

Dr Noel Porter for giving his valued opinion on oil analysis.

Bill Sykes for his initial research into lavender species and cultivars in New Zealand and his important notes on the genus.

Dr Tim Upson for his current research into the classification/reclassification of the genus.

Professor Arthur O. Tucker, who was unable to contribute an article for the book due to other commitments. He has, however, superbly filled the role of one of the main contributors to Genus *Lavandula* in recent times. Without his and Karel Hensen's research into lavenders and lavandins, many lavender books would either never have been written or be poorer in the information they contained.

Warwick Forge, without whom none of this would have been possible, and Julie Stokes and Stacey Zass for trying to work out the complexities.

My husband, Dennis Matthews, and parents, Gillian and Bevan Button, who were long-suffering but very supportive.

Jason, who really has been marvellous throughout the whole process.

GENERAL
CULTIVATION

The two basic requirements for successful lavender growing are full sun and good drainage. Lavender is a very hardy plant and will tolerate neglect, but for optimum results it will flourish best if these two requirements are met, in return providing you with a picturesque display over the summer months.

SOIL REQUIREMENTS

The best soil for growing lavender is a gritty or sandy loam with a pH factor between 6.0 and 8.0. In France, lavender grows naturally in well-drained calcareous (limestone-derived) and stony ground. Not everyone is fortunate enough to have this type of soil, but a considerable range of light, well-drained soils are generally quite suitable for lavender growing.

In wetter or more clay-based soils lavender can be grown successfully on mounds. Lime will need to be added to clay soils to increase their pH level and friability. Rather than attempting to turn wet, poorly drained soil into an area for lavender growing, it is probably better to find a more suitable site. After torrential rain or an unusually heavy shower, lavender will tolerate 'wet feet' or poor drainage for a short time providing the ground is free-draining, ultimately leading to fast water removal.

Lavandula stoechas cultivars will usually cope with a more acid soil than *L. angustifolia* cultivars. However, the majority of lavenders are very adaptable and a high pH factor in soil is probably more critical for commercial production.

CLIMATE

Lavandula angustifolia and *L.* x *intermedia* cultivars are reasonably tolerant of cold temperatures, winds, rain and snow providing they have good drainage. *Lavandula stoechas* cultivars will withstand similar conditions with frosts to minus 5°C or less, and even snowfalls, providing snow does not lie on the plants for more than a few days. They are less tolerant of harsh conditions than *L. angustifolia* and *L.* x *intermedia* cultivars but will withstand wet or damp weather and lower temperatures in winter providing the ground is well drained.

Late frosts in spring will blacken young spikes on all lavender. Dead spikes are best removed by lightly pruning to allow new spikes to form and promote flowering slightly later in the season. Frost can also cause damage to other parts of the plant, resulting in the browning of stems and leaves, e.g. *L. dentata*. If not too severely affected, the plant will recover to produce new growth in these areas, although it may not return to its normal robust state until summer. *Lavandula dentata* var. *dentata* is less tolerant of frosts than *L. dentata* var. *candicans* but neither will survive harsh frosts. They are best grown against a sunny wall in climates that experience mild to medium frosts.

Frost-tender plants, such as those in the *Pterostoechas* group, need to be either repropagated over the winter or grown in pots so that they can be moved into a sheltered position such as a conservatory, a glasshouse or under a verandah when autumn arrives.

WATERING

It is generally thought that lavender is a drought-tolerant plant. This may be the case where plants are mature and grown in dry conditions with little wind. Where winds are prevalent, strong and of a drying nature, lavenders can desiccate quickly and die. Young lavender, in particular, needs to be watched for any sign of desiccation. Good irrigation or adequate rainfall is important in spring to establish new plantings, and increase stem length and the number of spikes. It will also help to minimise stress for the long hot summer ahead. Older plants are much more likely to withstand dry conditions.

When transplanting stock, planting new plants or encouraging young plants, watering is vital to prevent undue loss. Where soil moisture-holding capacity is high or rainfall is sufficiently high, watering is best kept to a minimum or not given at all.

The highly fragrant notes produced by the linalool/linalyl acetate content in oil can be greatly reduced in plants suffering from water stress.

The method of watering must be considered carefully before planting a large area of lavender. Overhead sprinklers are suitable for plants when they are starting growth for the season but once the stems have elongated and spikes are almost fully developed, sprinklers may cause the bush to split open in the centre. There is also the risk of bacterial and fungal diseases, particularly in more humid conditions. For that reason, trickle irrigation is a better choice.

In a garden situation, however, much of the irrigation will be by overhead sprinklers and this may cause problems in large unpruned bushes.

Plants that have been grown in harsh, dry conditions will survive but may appear stunted with short flower stems (peduncles) and much-reduced spikes (inflorescences). Watering will be necessary if some plants have been lost due to very dry conditions or if a commercial crop is grown. Trials in New Zealand have shown marked differences in oil quality between plants that have been unduly stressed compared with those that have not. The plants receiving sufficient rainfall during spike development maintained the higher notes (linalool/linalyl acetate) in their oil samples whereas those suffering from drought and high temperatures produced oil samples with the higher notes obviously missing. Extreme heat, wind and dryness can cause the volatile sweeter notes to evaporate prior to distillation. There is some question whether ultraviolet light (radiation) plays a role in the loss of some of the components in lavender oil but this has not been fully investigated.

Overwatering or high rainfall (particularly in potted plants) can stress plants in the other direction causing lush growth, resulting in plants that are incapable of holding a compact form and causing foliage to split open and stems to sprawl. Too much water can result in flooding and leave the plants susceptible to root rot and other fungal and bacterial diseases. Equally, high rainfall combined with humidity can result in bacterial and fungal diseases.

As each area's climate differs, it is really a matter of observation of the local environment to determine how much water lavender will require in a particular location. Once a happy growing medium is established, plants will thrive and perform at their best.

PRUNING

To overcome the problem that overhead sprinklers can impose, a careful pruning regime needs to be implemented.

Keeping plants in shape is one of the best ways of maintaining a young, healthy and vigorous bush. Pruning should begin when the plant is still in the pot and continue at least once a year for the whole life of the lavender bush. Cut back at least one-third of the bush; in *L. stoechas* cultivars, this can be one-half. *Lavandula stoechas* cultivars are best cut in early to mid-autumn, well before the chance of a frost. Pruning in spring will prevent a spring flowering, promoting a late spring/early summer flowering instead. Plants pruned in spring will need to be cut again in autumn, as they will be top-heavy from all the flowering. If cut in early to mid-autumn, they will flower (in colder areas) in spring and then again in late summer/autumn. In warmer areas that do not experience such winter cold, pruning may take place when convenient or when the plant has finished flowering.

If *L. stoechas* cultivars are pruned heavily in summer immediately after the plants have produced their first flush of flowers, there is a tendency for the plants to put on a new flush of growth and new flower stems, which can easily be damaged by snowfall in winter. A light pruning is therefore recommended at this time followed by a heavier cut in mid-autumn to keep the plants more compact for the colder months ahead.

Where severe winter conditions occur and *L. stoechas* cultivars need to be overwintered inside, pruning may be necessary after the first flowering.

Lavenders such as *L. dentata* var. *dentata* and *L. dentata* var. *candicans* generally require little pruning unless they have been grown as a hedge or have become too large for their situation. The best time to prune in these circumstances is summer.

Lavenders from the *Pterostoechas* group may require occasional light pruning. Some have a tendency to sprawl but do not always take kindly to hard pruning. They are particularly frost-tender.

All *L. angustifolia* and *L.* x *intermedia* cultivars require pruning after flowering or in autumn. Lavender hedges need pruning twice a year. The first trim is best in spring when only the sides should be cut to allow for top flowering. If a free-flowing hedge effect is desired, then this pruning could be missed altogether. The second pruning should be in autumn, well before any frosts are due. Both the sides and top should be cut back hard so as to maintain the shape of the hedge.

Lavandula stoechas, *L. angustifolia* and *L.* x *intermedia* cultivars may be pruned back by one-third to one-half. If necessary they can be cut back to three sets of leaves or three leaf nodes from the base. If cut any lower, the stems will die. Although it sounds like drastic surgery, this helps to keep bushes young and healthy. Lavenders that have not been kept well pruned have a tendency to become woody in the centre of the bush. If they are old bushes, it may be too late to do anything. For instance, if they have reached three years of age and have never been pruned, then pruning at this stage may not achieve anything and it may be better to replace the bush.

TOP
L. angustifolia 'Twickel Purple'
before pruning

CENTRE
L. angustifolia 'Twickel Purple'
immediately after pruning

BELOW
L. angustifolia 'Twickel Purple'
with new growth in spring

If, however, there is young growth just above the woody part, the plant can be pruned back to within three nodes of this. Do not cut too far back into the old wood, or the lavender will die. This technique may force new growth further down the stem and eventually allow the bush to be reshaped. However the success of this treatment will depend on the type of lavender, as some cultivars are more prone to woodiness than others.

The secret to pruning is to start when the plants are young and still in pots, by pinching out the new growth to encourage lateral branch formation and cutting off flower buds in the first year (if growing for commercial reasons) to ensure a larger bush and abundant spikes for the following season.

LAVENDER LONGEVITY

Lavandula angustifolia and *L.* x *intermedia* cultivars will live for many years if well maintained and well pruned. This longevity is of course also dependent on soil type and other climatic conditions. Plants grown in lighter soils will live longer than those in heavy clay-based soils.

In commercial production, lavender may need to be replaced every eight to ten years to maintain optimum flower spike–producing capacity. In a home garden situation, however, they will look beautiful for many more years than this.

Lavandula stoechas cultivars have a lifespan of three to ten years depending on how they have been cared for. Often they are allowed to grow large and woody, becoming prone to splitting open, and need to be removed. Again, hard pruning once a year will prevent this and will prolong the life of the plant.

HUMIDITY

Many lavenders will tolerate humidity and maintain a reasonably compact shape but some, like *L. angustifolia* and *L.* x *intermedia* cultivars, are more prone to pests and diseases in such conditions, particularly with prolonged damp periods. Spacing plants well apart to allow for adequate air movement around and between plants can overcome this problem. Drainage must also be very good in such conditions.

LATITUDE/ALTITUDE

Lavandula angustifolia and *L.* x *intermedia* (known as lavandins) grow in Provence in France at a latitude of 44° to 45° North. This is an area well known for its lavender fields and tourist 'lavender trail'. Winter temperatures are 2°C to 4°C and summer temperatures 20°C, dry and sunny, with adequate rainfall in spring. *L. angustifolia* grows naturally at approximately 600m to over 1000m above sea level while *L. latifolia* and *L.* x *intermedia* occur at lower altitudes.

Elsewhere in the world, these plants still thrive when grown at much lower altitudes and different latitudes, with *L. angustifolia* cultivars tending to withstand harsher conditions than either *L.* x *intermedia* or *L. latifolia*.

FERTILISER

Lavenders and lavandins are lime-loving, growing on limestone-based soils in their natural habitat. Therefore they grow and yield best where there is adequate calcium in the soil. Lime may be added in autumn or be incorporated before planting.

If in doubt, have the soil tested before applying any fertiliser. Blood and bone is beneficial as a nitrogen source (50 kg/ha per application) in spring and again after flowering. Apply prior to rain or watering.

Avoid using excessive amounts of fertiliser (including nitrogen-based fertilisers) and never use strong manures such as pig or chicken manure.

In commercial production, young lavender may require a higher nitrogen application (100 kg/ha), half applied in spring and half after flowering, until mature (three years). Nitrogen application will increase stem length for cut-flower production. Lower rates appear to be needed for older, mature plants for general maintenance or oil production, but for cut-flower production nitrogen application will be required at a higher rate.

For the home garden, application of a well-balanced compost and some lime will benefit the plants. If this is not possible, lavender will grow happily without any externally added fertiliser for a while but older plants may tend to show signs of nutritional stress if the soil is poor.

Lavandula stoechas cultivars will tolerate more acid soils than *L. angustifolia* cultivars, but will also benefit from an occasional application of compost or blood and bone.

LAVENDERS IN CONTAINERS

Some of the smaller-growing lavenders such as *L. angustifolia* 'Nana Alba', *L. angustifolia* 'Irene Doyle', *L. angustifolia* 'Blue Cushion' and *L. angustifolia* 'Lavenite Petite' are suitable for pot culture as they keep a reasonably compact, small form naturally. Other slightly larger lavenders such as *L. angustifolia* 'Munstead' and *L. angustifolia* 'Hidcote' can be container-grown but really need to be transplanted to the garden after two years unless placed in a very large container.

Some *L.* x *intermedia* cultivars such as 'Grosso' and 'Hidcote Giant' can be grown in very large containers for the first two years but the containers will need to be given sufficient space on the patio or in the garden for the spikes and peduncles to spread out.

Many forms of *L. stoechas* cultivars and *L. dentata* var. *candicans* are grown as topiaried plants in containers but do need routine care to guarantee their longevity in such conditions. Being gross feeders they tend to turn yellow and show other symptoms of nutritional stress, so will require adequate feeding to maintain green foliage.

All potted lavenders require a well-drained potting mixture as well as good drainage at the base of the container. They need annual repotting with a suitable potting mix containing sufficient controlled-release fertiliser to keep them healthy. Adequate watering of the plants will need to be maintained through the long summer months to ensure they do not dry out, since dehydrated lavender is difficult to revive. Winter watering needs to be kept to a minimum and overwatering at any time must be avoided. If these few basic rules are adhered to, then success is guaranteed.

TRANSPLANTING

Lavenders and lavandins generally transplant well but will usually not flower much during the first summer following transplanting. The best times to transplant are late autumn/early winter and very early spring.

Water plants well before moving them to a new position. Cut back and trim damaged roots and remove any flowering material if still present. Once a plant has been shifted, it is best to cut off spikes in the first summer following transplanting. Flower production will be restored by the second summer in the new position.

Lavandula stoechas cultivars are better moved in early spring for successful transplanting.

PLANTING IN THE GARDEN

The distance between lavenders is largely a matter of preference. If planting for ornamental purposes, lavender may be used en masse planted either well apart as separate entities or close together to form a canopy effect. Other lavenders may be planted singly or as hedges.

When planting *L. angustifolia* cultivars as individual plants, they need to be at least 70cm apart for medium-sized bushes and 30–40cm apart for hedges. Smaller-growing plants will need individual spacing of 50cm, and 25cm apart for hedges. Lavandins and *L. stoechas* cultivars require individual spacing of 1m, and 50–70cm apart for hedges.

WEED CONTROL

Like pruning, weed control is also important. Careful preparation of the ground prior to planting is a priority. A decision must be made as to whether weed control will be maintained organically, through hand-weeding, mechanical cultivation and mulching, or by other means such as spraying with selective herbicides.

Weedmat or thin polythene may be used with good effect but is more economical for small areas. Mulching is not recommended for humid or high rainfall areas. But in drier, windier conditions, newspaper or cardboard with peastraw placed on top (and the odd stone if necessary to prevent mulch blowing away) appears to be quite effective between plants, providing the mulch is kept well clear of the base of the bush and does not touch the foliage. The latter method is more suited to smaller gardens.

White sand, seashells or limestone may also be used as mulch but they tend to attract their own specific weeds, so a certain amount of hand-weeding may still be needed with this method. The one advantage of these mulches is that the light is thrown back into the centre of the bushes, thus reducing the impact of fungal diseases.

With the diverse range of colours now available in lavenders, a cultivar can be found to complement the colour scheme of most gardens.

An alternative to organic methods of weed control is herbicides, which may be used to clear the ground prior to planting. Some herbicides have been found to be effective around plants, particularly for weeds such as clover, grasses and dandelion. Investigate local regulations concerning the use of such herbicides on a crop like lavender. If unsure as to how a spray will affect lavender, try spraying around a couple of bushes first or consult your local spray expert. Keep in mind that some sprays have considerable residual effects in the soil.

HARVESTING AND DRYING

Optimum timing for the cutting of lavender is determined by the end use for the spikes. Cutting is best undertaken in the morning once the dew has evaporated and before the heat of the day. However, for larger quantities, cutting needs to continue throughout the day.

If harvesting for dried flowers where the spike is to remain intact, cut when the first two flowers on the spike have opened. This requires carefully observing the bush so that all the spikes can be cut when the majority are ready. If picked at first flower break, the flowers, once dried, will stay on the spike. If cut when too many flowers have opened, the flowers, when dried, will drop off and will be suitable only as stripped lavender for use in lavender bags or pot pourri.

Harvesting at 'Lavandula' near Daylesford, Victoria, Australia

For the fresh flower market, spikes are best cut while in bud or when one-quarter to one-third of the flowers on the spike are open. The best method at present for preserving cut lavender flowers is to change the water daily. More research is needed in this area.

The optimum time to cut for oil depends on the cultivar, but generally when half the flowers on the spike have withered.

For drying, lavender stems are bunched together with a rubber band or tie that allows for shrinkage of the stems as they dry. Rubber bands on the stems can be attached to hooks hanging from the ceiling. Lavender needs to be dried in a dark, dust-free place with good ventilation to allow for quick and complete drying.

Once dried, bunches may be left hanging or placed in suitable containers such as dry cardboard boxes and stored in a cool, dry, low-light area.

PLANT BREEDER'S RIGHTS, PLANT VARIETY RIGHTS AND PLANT PATENTS

As with many other plants, many lavenders are now protected by a Plant Breeder's Right, Plant Variety Right or Plant Patent. These provisions disallow the propagation of plants for commercial use by anyone other than licensed growers. Such rights or patents are usually registered to protect plants that have been bred or raised by a nursery or individual and have been proven to be significantly different in one or more characteristic from other cultivars on the market. Only new plants bred in cultivation can be protected in this way.

The rule of non-propagation and selling imposed by such rights or patents needs to be respected as the owner, whether it be nursery or individual, has usually spent many years, money and time in assessing the plant and then having it formally tested. Heavy penalties may be imposed on anyone selling plants illegally.

It is not intended to catalogue plants protected by such rights or patents in this book, as legislative provision differs in each country and some of the newly released cultivars are only now being tested. If unsure of requirements in your locality, check with the national authority responsible for such rights or patents, especially before selling an unfamiliar lavender plant.

PROPAGATION

Lavender must always be propagated from soft or semi-hardwood cuttings to maintain the true characteristics of a particular cultivar. Lavender grown from seed is likely to be considerably variable, with most seedlings being discarded as inferior due to cross-pollinating by bees, thus hybridising the seed and rendering resultant seedlings unsuitable for sale.

Some lavender cultivars are easy to root and others are not. Softwood cuttings may be taken in spring, and softwood and semi-hardwood cuttings 5–10cm long in autumn. Remove any flowering material, dip cut ends in rooting hormone and place in a gritty, free-draining mixture on a hot bed, with or without mist. New roots will form in three to six weeks. Cuttings may also be placed in a cold frame where they will take approximately 12 weeks in winter or slightly less time in spring. The timing of root formation will depend on the type of cultivar and the climate. These are general guidelines only.

An alternative propagation method is to take longer 15cm cuttings in late winter and place in well-drained, gritty soil and wait until they root. This is a technique sometimes used with old-fashioned roses. Once rooted, the cuttings can be potted or planted out.

The medium around cuttings must remain damp but not saturated.

Occasionally large plants of *L. angustifolia* cultivars can be divided, especially if they have been pruned low and enough of the lower stems has been covered with soil to allow them to root in the ground.

Tissue culture is used nowadays for propagating a large number of plants quickly, particularly useful for commercial growers or bulk-selling opportunities. Tissue is taken from leaf buds and grown under sterile conditions. In time, a callus is produced, from which small plantlets develop, hopefully with stems and roots. These plantlets eventually are transferred to a potting mixture and will gradually become hardened.

Traditionally grown cuttings, once rooted and transferred to their new pots, need to be hardened slowly. Sudden temperature changes can shock young plants. They need to be watched carefully as they can be susceptible to fungal and bacterial conditions if the environment is not suitable.

However, once hardened and developed into a size that will survive in the ground, they may be transferred from their pots into their final position. This is best done in autumn or spring so that they have time to establish a good root system prior to the hot temperatures of summer. Plants may also be planted out in summer but will need regular watering until autumn/winter unless summer rainfall is sufficient.

When planting out potted plants, water well at the time of planting and for at least the first month afterwards.

Growing cultivars from seed, as already mentioned, will produce variant plants which cannot be claimed to be representative of the original plant. Two well-known cultivars *L. angustifolia* 'Munstead' and *L. angustifolia* 'Hidcote' are notorious for being grown from seed in many nurseries around the world. Because of this it can now prove difficult to find an originally sourced plant.

Species lavenders such as *L. minutolii* and *L. pubescens* can be grown from seed, providing the parent plant has been kept separate from other lavenders, and bees have not cross-pollinated it with other species. Likewise subspecies such as *L. stoechas* subsp. *pedunculata* are sometimes collected from the wild and grown into mature plants. However, even when sourced from their natural habitat, seedlings will show some natural variation.

Seed can be sown in a gritty, well-drained seed mix, covered slightly and kept damp but not wet, and left to germinate. Germination is erratic and, depending on how fresh the seed is, may take any time from two weeks to one year.

It is much more convenient to purchase well-grown and correctly named plants from a reputable grower and leave breeding and seed sowing to professional growers who have years of experience of the lavender cultivar market and know whether they have a significantly different plant. The marketplace, not to mention the public, is already confused over commonly available plants such as the seed-grown versions of 'Hidcote' and 'Munstead'. Often people bring me a plant under a cultivar name, wanting to purchase more plants of the same name. Frequently I have to say that they have bought a seed-grown plant, show them what it ought to look like and send them home disappointed. Hence my warning about buying seed-grown plants or trying to grow your own from seed.

Plants bought from a grower must have a bushy top and good root system. Avoid spindly, weedy specimens, as they are likely to snap off in the wind once planted in the ground. Plants should be hardened enough to withstand local conditions. Lush-growing plants can sometimes be an indicator of being too soft (not hardened enough) and/or overfeeding. Such plants will need to be acclimatised gradually before planting out. A well-grown plant will look 'in tune' with its environment.

PESTS AND DISEASES

Pests and diseases affecting lavender vary depending on country, climatic conditions and temperature, etc. In general, lavender is a very hardy, healthy plant and the impact of disease is minimal, especially when grown in light, well-drained soil with adequate air movement.

General hygiene is important when pruning any plants, and lavender is no exception. Cutting equipment is best cleaned with an anti-viral solution (available as a liquid or in powder form) after cutting back individual bushes or between pruning cultivars. This is vital between groups of cuttings. Your local veterinarian will generally use an anti-viral wash before and after handling animals, and may be a helpful person to ask about suitable brands.

Spiders occasionally spin webs over lavender spikes, but they cause no harm to the plant.

Other suggestions for sterilising secateurs include soaking them in strong soapy (Sunlight soap) water for at least 15 minutes. A diluted solution of chlorine or bleach will also be effective, but tends to rust the equipment over time. You will probably find that you need a couple of pairs of secateurs.

Other good husbandry practices include regular weeding and pruning and removal of dead or diseased material.

Spittle bugs, cuckoo spit, frog hoppers (*Philaenus spumarius*)

Spittle bug usually appears in early spring as small green frog-like insects amongst the foliage. They are easily detected by the spittle exuded as camouflage. As an adult, the spittle bug turns into a hopping insect and is a little harder to contain. The damage caused is minimal but looks unsightly on plants, particularly those used for cut flowers. Damage is usually confined to twisting and some deformation of stems and leaves.

Spittle bugs are best removed with a systemic spray (in spring) or, if only on a few bushes, remove them with a paintbrush and place them in a jar of water. Spraying the hose over the bush and washing the insects off may also be temporarily effective, but this needs to be done on a regular basis to have a lasting effect.

Lady birds, lady bugs (*Coccinella* spp.)

Lady birds frequently overwinter in lavender bushes and can be seen on the plants in early spring. They do no harm to the plants; in fact, they can be beneficial by keeping the aphid population to a minimum. So if spraying with insecticide, be aware that both bees and lady birds may be affected.

Aphids (*Myzus* spp.), sage hoppers (*Eurypteryx melissae*), mealy bugs (*Planococus* sp.) and caterpillars

Aphids and sage hoppers can be seen on plants during spring, summer and autumn. They cause mottling on *L. stoechas* cultivars and some unsightliness with severe infestations. Aphids, particularly the clover aphid, are responsible for transmitting the alfalfa mosaic virus (AMV). Insecticides generally available on the market will clear plants of these insects. An aphid-specific spray can be used for treating plants without killing bees or other insects.

Stem mealy bugs can sometimes affect plants, causing bent stems. Once again a systemic insecticide will control this type of infestation.

Various species of caterpillars may attack and chew leaves or whole plants, but their existence is largely dependent on the predators present in a particular location.

There are probably other insects worldwide which cause leaf or plant damage — I have mentioned only the more common ones.

Rabbits

Young plants are most susceptible to rabbits, which tend to dig up newly transplanted lavender plants and leave them lying on the surface. Rabbits will occasionally dig around the roots of older, more established plants but do not seem to nibble the tops.

Weedmatting can be effective as can small circles of chicken wire placed over the young plants to protect them. An alternative solution is to reduce the rabbit population, as rabbit-repellent spray is effective only for a short period.

WINDBURN

Certain lavenders are more susceptible to windburn than others. Symptoms are similar to rust, but in fact it is not a fungal disease at all. The leaves eventually rejuvenate and are perfectly green again for the following spring.

FUNGAL DISEASES

Phoma species can affect lavender plants but usually as a secondary infection after plants have been damaged. Where there has been excessively high rainfall in the area and drainage is poor, then stress, infection and *Phoma* may set in. Symptoms include greying and loss of foliage, die-back and general malaise, often found with plants suffering from *Phytophora* or root rot.

Shab (*Phoma lavandulae*) is a specific *Phoma* species that causes wilting and yellowing of affected branches, followed by leaf fall, eventual die-back of that area and ultimately death to the plant. Shab was reputed to be one of the diseases that affected the Mitcham lavender industry in England, causing die-back of plants and subsequent death of much of the stock in the late 1880s. The infection spread quickly via cutting equipment, hence the reminder to sterilise cutting equipment regularly. Shab is not present in all countries and does not seem to cause problems in garden situations. It is much less likely to affect lavender grown in light, well-drained soils and sunny, well-ventilated areas. *Lavandula angustifolia* cultivars do not seem to be affected by shab.

Phytophora occurs in both wet and dry conditions where soil is compacted, although it is probably more likely in plants that have suffered overwatering or very poor drainage. Affected parts of a bush or individual stems may die off and can easily be pulled out of the ground due to the rotting of roots. Spores are spread from plant to plant by raindrops, water sprayer or cutting equipment. To combat the problem, the ground needs to be saturated with a fungicide — consult your local agricultural inspector. It can be quite demoralising to see a beautiful patch of lavender wilt, but it may be treatable if diagnosed early enough. The unfortunate problem with this disease is that it may take two years to become apparent, by which time it may be too late to save existing plants.

Plants suffering from these two fungal diseases (including the roots) and any material around them should be dug out and burned.

Lavender leafspot (*Septoria lavandulae*) is prevalent where watering and humidity are constant, and can often be seen in nursery situations where plants receive regular watering. Leafspot causes spotting of the leaves and occasionally leaf fall, and is generally more unsightly than serious. A fungicide may be applied but plants will recover on their own, providing they do not receive further overwatering.

BACTERIAL BLAST (*PSEUDOMONAS SYRINGAE*)

More prone in damper areas, this disease causes die-back of young shoots in spring. Sprays may be used to control it, but it is not generally a threat to lavender.

ALFALFA MOSAIC VIRUS (AMV)

One of the few recognised viruses, AMV has no doubt been quite common in the lavender world but, because it exhibits seasonal symptoms, it may often go unnoticed.

Symptoms are a bright yellow mottling in a mosaic pattern, mostly on the leaves, but occasionally on stems and spikes. The yellowing is quite different from that of stress or underfeeding (see opposite).

The virus is primarily transmitted by the clover aphid (*Myzus persicae*) or by cutting tools or unwashed hands. AMV may also be transmitted by other common aphids, such as the ornate aphid (*Myzus ornatus*) and up to 11 other types of aphid, but probably not by the leaf hopper or spittle bug.

There is no cure for AMV; infected plants need to be removed and destroyed by burning. If plants are not removed, the infection will spread. Affected foliage tends to become stunted and slightly deformed and flower production is diminished.

Symptoms are most noticeable in spring and early summer and again in late autumn. They may well disappear in the hotter temperatures over summer. However if the weather remains cooler, symptoms may also persist over the summer.

The virus spreads through the plant more quickly in cooler weather. Cuttings taken from the unaffected parts of the plant may remain virus-free. However it is good husbandry practice to always take cuttings only from strong, healthy, disease-free stock.

Alfalfa mosaic virus is a common virus occurring on many wild and ornamental plants in the garden and on clover and lucerne. Infection, once transmitted, is immediate. It is possible to have only one plant affected out of all the lavender in the garden and, once that plant is removed, there is usually no recurrence.

Alfalfa mosaic virus (AMV) causes yellow mottling on leaves, and occasionally on stems and spikes.

YELLOW DECLINE

Yellow decline is one of the most publicised diseases of lavender in France. It is considered a threat to healthy plants in Europe as it can reduce the life of a lavender crop to three or four years. Although many lavenders and lavandins may be affected, *L.* x *intermedia* 'Grosso' is one of the few that is not. The disease is caused by a mycoplasm (something between bacteria and a virus) that is spread by a leaf hopper, *Hyalethes obsoletus*. Fortunately some countries do not have either the hopper or the mycoplasm. Check with local agricultural officers.

THE BOTANY
OF LAVENDER

MEASUREMENTS

Both qualitative and quantitative measurements are used in this book. Quantitative measurements are mostly subjective, being dependent on climatic and soil conditions. The measurements used are taken from field-grown lavenders experiencing dry conditions. A wetter climate will produce more exaggerated results as will pot-grown plants, which are generally better fed and watered. For example, one cultivar measured in dry conditions had a spike 9cm long in dry conditions, but in wetter conditions this measurement changed to 15cm on the new spikes produced.

L. 'Raycott'   Qualitative measurements provide a better comparison for plants grown in similar conditions. Where reference plants are available, comparative measurements can then be made for any conditions. Common cultivars have been used for reference where possible.

DENSITY OF FOLIAGE

Foliage density differs between lavenders, but efficient pruning will keep an otherwise open-foliaged plant quite compact over the summer months.

SECTION *LAVANDULA*

Open	*L. angustifolia* 'Twickel Purple'
Semi-open	*L.* x *intermedia* 'Alba'
Dense	*L.* x *intermedia* 'Grey Hedge'

Open	*L.* 'Pippa White'
Semi-open	*L.* 'Marshwood'
Dense	*L.* 'Pippa'

LEFT

L. angustifolia —
general outline of spike

RIGHT

L. 'Marshwood' —
general outline of spike

HEIGHT OF PLANTS

The heights described represent three-year-old or mature plants, and assume that the plants have been pruned once a year during that time and not left to grow tall or woody in the centre. Old lavender bushes will grow very large if uncared for, and while this may look impressive in a garden, they may be practically impossible to rejuvenate due to the amount of old wood in the centre. Some lavenders such as

L. x *intermedia* 'Alba' and *L.* x *intermedia* 'Grey Hedge' do have a natural inclination to grow tall and woody, so need to be kept in check while still in pots.

Measurements used are for plants in full flower.

Small	up to 50cm in flower; bushes may be only 30–40cm
	e.g. *L. angustifolia* 'Lady' and *L.* 'Evelyn Cadzow'
Medium	up to 70cm in flower; bushes may be only 40–50cm
	e.g. *L. angustifolia* 'Hidcote' and *L.* 'Plum'
Semi-tall	up to 80cm in flower; bushes may be only 50–60cm
	e.g. *L. angustifolia* 'Bosisto' and *L.* 'Helmsdale'
Tall	80cm to over 1m in flower; bushes may be only 50–80cm
	e.g. *L.* x *intermedia* 'Grey Hedge' and *L.* 'Marshwood'

The width of a lavender plant is usually equal to the height but in some cultivars may be one and a half times the height.

SHAPE OF LAVENDER PLANT IN FLOWER

The overall shape and width of a lavender plant are best determined in summer when in full flower. There are three general categories of shape used in the descriptions in this book.

SECTION *LAVANDULA*

Spreading	*L. angustifolia* 'Lady'
Bushy	*L. angustifolia* 'Munstead'
Spherical/rounded	*L. angustifolia* 'Twickel Purple'

SECTION *STOECHAS*

Spreading	*L.* 'Pippa White'
Bushy	*L.* 'Pippa'
Upright bushy	*L.* 'James Compton'

To ascertain the shape of a lavender plant without inflorescences, view it in early spring before the plant begins flowering.

LEAF SHAPE AND MARGINS

Most lavender has linear or linear lanceolate leaves, with some of the rarer forms having pinnate and bipinnate outlines.

Leaf margins are mostly entire (smooth) but some lavenders have dentate (toothed) or partly dentate edges.

LEFT

Foliage colour in
Section *Lavandula*

GREY
L. x *intermedia* 'Grey Hedge'

GREY–GREEN
L. angustifolia 'Hidcote Pink'

LIGHT GREEN
L. angustifolia 'Rosea'

MID-GREEN
L. angustifolia 'Lady'

RIGHT

Foliage colour in
Section *Stoechas*

LIGHT GREEN
L. 'Evelyn Cadzow'

BRIGHT GREEN
L. 'Somerset Mist'

GREY–GREEN
L. 'Marshwood'

FOLIAGE COLOUR

Generally leaf colour of *L. angustifolia* and *L.* x *intermedia* cultivars is green in early summer, changing to grey–green in late summer/autumn and grey in winter. The primary (first) leaves tend to be green because they are more sparsely covered in hair, whereas the next stage of new growth is densely covered, producing a greyish tinge. As the leaves age, they tend to lose their hair cover but pruning in autumn promotes new growth giving an overall grey appearance in winter.

Because there are varying degrees of green and grey within the colour spectrum, the following guide may assist when comparing foliage colour. Comparisons are best made in late spring to mid-summer.

Light green	*L. angustifolia* 'Rosea'
Mid-green	*L. angustifolia* 'Lady'
Grey–green	*L. angustifolia* 'Hidcote Pink'
Grey	*L.* x *intermedia* 'Grey Hedge'

The foliage of *L. lanata* x *L. angustifolia* cultivars is a velvety, silver–grey colour, similar to their common parent, *L. lanata*. There is little difference between the young and older leaves.

Lavandula stoechas cultivars do not tend to change their leaf colour as much throughout the season as do Section *Lavandula* lavenders. However the colours between plants vary, indicated in the following comparative guide.

Light green	*L.* 'Evelyn Cadzow'
Bright green	*L.* 'Somerset Mist'
Mid-green	*L.* 'Helmsdale'
Grey–green	*L.* 'Marshwood'

Foliage colour in other lavenders also ranges from green to grey.

PEDUNCLE LENGTH

The peduncle is the stalk bearing the inflorescence. The length of peduncles varies considerably between plants. Measurement of the peduncle is from the base of the spike to the start of the foliage. In some cultivars there may be an odd pair of leaves halfway up the spike, e.g. *L.* x *intermedia* 'Grey Hedge', but the measurement is still made to the main foliage line. The following examples may be used for comparison (illustrated on page 28).

SECTION *LAVANDULA*

Short	*L. angustifolia* 'Lady' (6–13cm)
Medium	*L. angustifolia* 'Hidcote' (12–22cm)
Long	*L.* x *intermedia* 'Grey Hedge' (16–28cm)

SECTION *STOECHAS*

Short	*L.* 'Swan River Pink' (2–4.5cm)
Short–medium	*L.* 'Rocky Road' (3–5cm)
Medium	*L.* 'Pippa' (5–7cm)
Long	*L.* 'Marshwood' (12–21cm)

PEDUNCLE WIDTH

Like peduncle length, the width is just as variable and does not obviously relate to the length. For instance, a short peduncle is not necessarily thin nor a long peduncle broad. The best way to compare differences is once more with standards.

TOP LEFT

Width of peduncles in
Section *Lavandula*

BROAD OR THICK
L. angustifolia 'Twickel Purple'

MEDIUM
L. angustifolia 'Hidcote'

NARROW OR THIN
L. angustifolia 'Lady'

Length of gaps between
whorls in Section *Lavandula*

LONG
L. angustifolia 'Twickel Purple'

MEDIUM
L. angustifolia 'Hidcote'

SHORT/COMPACT
L. angustifolia 'Lady'

TOP RIGHT

Width of peduncles in
Section *Stoechas*

BROAD/THICK
L. 'Southern Lights'

MEDIUM
L. 'Helmsdale'

THIN/NARROW
L. 'Evelyn Cadzow'

BOTTOM LEFT

Peduncle lengths in
Section *Lavandula*

LONG
L. x *intermedia* 'Grey Hedge'

MEDIUM
L. angustifolia 'Hidcote'

SHORT
L. angustifolia 'Lady'

BOTTOM RIGHT

Peduncle lengths in
Section *Stoechas*

SHORT
L. 'Swan River Pink'

SHORT/MEDIUM
L. 'Rocky Road'

MEDIUM
L. 'Pippa'

LONG
L. 'Marshwood'

Section *Lavandula*

Narrow/thin	*L. angustifolia* 'Lady' (1mm)
Medium	*L. angustifolia* 'Hidcote' (1.5mm)
Thick/broad	*L. angustifolia* 'Twickel Purple' (2–3mm)

Section *Stoechas*

Narrow/thin	*L.* 'Evelyn Cadzow' (1–1.5mm)
Medium	*L.* 'Helmsdale' (2mm)
Thick/broad	*L.* 'Southern Lights' (3mm)

Peduncle widths are included only if outside the norm (i.e. thin or broad).

Hair on the peduncle

The amount of hair on peduncles of *L. stoechas* cultivars is quite an important distinguishing characteristic. Differences occur not only in the amount and type of hair (pubescent, tomentose or hirsute), but also in the degree of hairiness immediately below the spike. The placement, type and shape of hair on the peduncle may give a hint as to the parentage of the cultivar in question (illustrated on page 30).

Section *Stoechas*

Finely/sparsely pubescent	*L.* 'Major'
Hair of medium length — may be sparse	*L.* 'Helmsdale'
Long hair, plentiful	*L.* 'Marshwood'

Pubescence on stems of Section *Lavandula* cultivars is a less distinctive feature. Most are finely pubescent and not distinctly different to the human eye. Grey–green stems result from fine tomentose covering. This characteristic in other Section lavenders is included in individual descriptions.

Peduncle colour

Peduncle colour is a more important characteristic in Section *Stoechas* cultivars than in Section *Lavandula* cultivars.

Section *Stoechas*

Light green	*L.* 'Evelyn Cadzow'	Bright green	*L.* 'Pippa White'
Mid-green	*L.* 'Helmsdale'	Red–green	*L.* 'James Compton'
Grey–green	*L.* 'Marshwood'		

LEFT

Degree of hairiness on peduncles in Section *Stoechas*

LONG/PLENTIFUL
L. 'Marshwood'

MEDIUM LENGTH
(may be sparse)
L. 'Helmsdale'

LITTLE/FINELY PUBESCENT
L. 'Major'

RIGHT

Colour of peduncles in Section *Stoechas*

BRIGHT GREEN
L. 'Pippa White'

RED
L. 'James Compton'

MID-GREEN
L. 'Helmsdale'

GREY–GREEN
L. 'Marshwood'

Most peduncles in Section *Lavandula* cultivars tend to be mainly mid-green or grey–green.

One difference apparent in some cultivars is coloration on the edges of the peduncle. Occasionally a cultivar will display either dark green or reddish-purple tinges, which make it quite distinctive, e.g. *L. angustifolia* 'Mystique' and *L.* x *intermedia* 'Grey Hedge'.

GROWTH HABIT OF PEDUNCLES

Peduncles tend to grow in a variety of ways. Some are upright; others tend to spread out, even to the point of touching the ground. The positioning of the peduncles and the bush shape give the lavender its overall effect in flower. Peduncles may also be bent or wavy, sometimes with noticeable curves in the profile. Others may be straight or semi-wavy.

L. stoechas and *L.* x *intermedia* cultivars generally have quite straight peduncles.

SECTION *LAVANDULA*

Upright	*L. angustifolia* 'Bosisto'
Semi-upright	*L. angustifolia* 'Hidcote'
Sprawling/splayed	*L. angustifolia* 'Twickel Purple'

Degree of waviness in peduncles

Straight	*L. angustifolia* 'Hidcote'
Semi-wavy	*L. angustifolia* 'Munstead'
Wavy	*L. angustifolia* 'Rosea'

LATERAL BRANCHING

Branching is present in all lavenders to some degree, occurring within the foliage, many naturally and others from the point of the previous year's pruning. Peduncles sent from the point of pruning can occasionally have three separate branches topped by flowering spikes.

Lateral branching of peduncles, the length of these axillary stems and the frequency or degree to which they branch are important distinguishing characteristics between species and cultivars.

Branching on the peduncle itself is also an important characteristic. It can range from sessile (stalkless) arrangement of flowers on either side of the peduncle to short-stalked or very long branching with well-formed, though smaller spikes.

Many lavenders, particularly in Section *Stoechas*, produce one main peduncle only (e.g. *L. stoechas* 'Marshwood'), but in some cases branching of the main stem may occur in the axils of the primary (initial) leaves just above the main foliage line. Others such as *L. stoechas* 'Clair de Lune' naturally branch very freely in the foliage. When comparing plants, distinguish between lavenders that naturally branch and those that produce branches from their previous year's pruning.

In *L.* x *intermedia* cultivars, branching along the peduncle is often a feature and may vary, depending on the cultivar, from one pair of opposite stems up to three pairs arranged alternately up the stem (illustrated on page 33).

The type of lateral branching varies; for instance, there may be only one lateral on one side and a pair further up, or vice versa. The pair of laterals may not be of even length. One-sided branching is common in *L. angustifolia* cultivars.

Lateral branches on *L.* x *intermedia* cultivars are terminated in small but well-formed spikes; *L. angustifolia* cultivars do not form small heads on their lateral branches in the same way. Usually they are either single flowers, or flowers in sets of three to four on either side of the stem, sometimes horizontally. Larger groups of three to six may form a misshapen clump on the end of a stalk. The arrangement of the flowers in this axillary branching differs. Sometimes there will be one flower only on one side of the stem, or four flowers on one side and two on the other, or three plus three. It is possible for a single bush to show all variations, particularly the longer-branching cultivars.

The percentage and type of lateral branching on a peduncle of a particular plant are probably dependent on which part of the parent plant the cutting was taken from. For instance, a cutting taken from a double-branched stem of a *L.* x *intermedia* cultivar may result in a plant with a higher percentage of double branching than is usual. This can also occur in *L. angustifolia* cultivars, where cuttings taken from the same bush may result in some plants with little or no branching, and some with a high percentage of short or axillary branching. This explains why sometimes it is possible to find one out of ten plants that has predominantly one-sided branching, whereas the others may be single or mixed.

A comparison of lateral branching follows, with Section *Lavandula* as an example:

Semi-stalked	Little if any stalk, 1–3mm	*L. angustifolia* 'Hidcote'
Short-stalked	1–2cm stalk	*L. angustifolia* 'Munstead'
Semi-long	2–6cm stem	*L. angustifolia* 'Twickel Purple'
Long	over 6cm	*L.* x *intermedia* 'Grosso'

See illustration on page 34.

Inflorescence shape

The inflorescence is the spike, which in lavender consists of a single main axis bearing a number of single sessile (stalkless) or short-stalked flowers in an alternate or spiral arrangement. The youngest flowers are near the apex of the spike.

Lavender spikes come in a range of different shapes — from long, narrow spikes like *L.* x *intermedia* 'Jaubert' to the short, compact head of *L. angustifolia* 'Lady'.

Determining shapes can be quite difficult, so a general guide follows:

Narrow-conical	shaped like a cone with the widest part at the base and two long tapering sides forming an apex or sharp point, e.g. *L.* x *intermedia* 'Grey Hedge'
Broad-conical	as for narrow-conical but shorter and broader, e.g. *L.* x *intermedia* 'Grosso'
Truncate-conic	similar to conical except that both the tip and base appear to have been sharply cut off, e.g. *L.* x *intermedia* 'Hidcote Giant'
Cylindric	shaped like a cylinder with a rounded top and base, e.g. *L.* x *intermedia* 'Dutch White'
Fusiform	spindle-shaped with widest part in the centre of the spike, e.g. *L. angustifolia* 'Munstead'
Fusiform-conic	mostly fusiform in shape with the widest part in the lowest third, giving a slightly plumper look, e.g. *L.* x *intermedia* 'Yuulong'

See illustration on page 35.

Distance between whorls

A whorl is defined (for lavender) as an arrangement of flowers at the same level and same axis in an encircling ring around the peduncle.

Lateral branching in
Section *Lavandula*
BRANCHING BELOW FOLIAGE
L. angustifolia 'Lady'

BRANCHING ABOVE FOLIAGE
L. x intermedia
'Impress Purple'

RIGHT
Lateral branching in
Section *Stoechas*
SINGLE/NO BRANCHING
L. 'Marshwood'

BRANCHING ABOVE FOLIAGE
L. 'Clair de Lune'

BRANCHING ABOVE AND
WITHIN FOLIAGE
L. 'Van Gogh'

All lavender spikes are composed of whorls of flowers around the central stem. This arrangement of whorls determines the length and shape of the spike. They may be 'interrupted', with either even or uneven gaps between whorls, or 'uninterrupted' or compact, with little space if any between whorls.

A short fat spike may be composed of many different whorls of flowers packed tightly together, whereas a long narrow head may have as many whorls but spaced a long distance apart.

When plants are adequately watered, spikes will be longer and gaps in an interrupted spike also longer. In very dry conditions spikes tend to be stunted and more difficult to identify (see illustration on page 28).

Uninterrupted/compact	*L. angustifolia* 'Lady'
Unevenly interrupted	*L. angustifolia* 'Hidcote'
Interrupted/long and mostly even	*L. angustifolia* 'Twickel Purple'

LEFT

Type/length of
lateral branching in
Section *Lavandula:*

medium/long

short

semi-stalked

RIGHT

Long lateral branching
in Section *Lavandula:*

triple

single

double

A base whorl that is somewhat removed from the main spike may occur in some cultivars. They may be 1–6cm below the main spike, but are included in the overall length as they are part of the spike itself.

Spike length and width

Spike dimensions are one of the characteristics, like peduncle length, that alter dramatically with conditions. Spike length differs between plants in a Section and also between Sections. The measurement in plants with sterile bracts is taken from the base of the spike to the top, excluding the sterile bracts. Other lavenders include the base whorl, which may be lower down the peduncle, as part of the length. The length measurement is given first, followed by the width measurement.

Section *Lavandula*

Short	*L. angustifolia* 'Lady' (2–3cm x 2cm)
Medium	*L. angustifolia* 'Hidcote' (3–7cm x 2cm)
Long	*L. angustifolia* 'Twickel Purple' (8–19cm x 2cm)

Section *Stoechas*

Short	*L.* 'Evelyn Cadzow' (1–2cm x 1–1.5cm)
Medium	*L.* 'Major' (2.5–4cm x 1.5–2cm)
Long	*L.* 'Pippa White' (4–5cm x 1–1.5cm)

Length and shape of the spike are more important features than the width, therefore width of spikes has been included only where it is considered a distinguishing characteristic. See illustrations on page 36.

Spike shapes

TRUNCATE-CONIC
L. x *intermedia*
'Hidcote Giant'

FUSIFORM
L. angustifolia
'Munstead'

NARROW-CONICAL
L. x *intermedia*
'Grey Hedge'

CYLINDRIC
L. x *intermedia*
'Dutch White'

FUSIFORM-CONIC
L. x *intermedia*
'Yuulong'

BROAD-CONICAL
L. x *intermedia*
'Grosso'

FLOWERS

The flower of a lavender consists of a corolla or petals, which in lavender are fused together, and a calyx or sepals which are also fused together. The part seen 'in bud' is the calyx. The corolla tube emerges through the calyx to display a dilated end that is five-lobed — two at the top and three at the bottom. See next chapter for more detail.

The upper part of the calyx may have a secondary, small attachment which can be seen with the human eye or magnifying glass. Descriptions of Section *Stoechas* cultivars include the colour but not the shape of these appendages.

COLOUR OF COROLLAS AND STERILE BRACTS

All colours of corollas have been measured against the Royal Horticultural Society colour charts (RHS) under strictly controlled light-box conditions. Where applicable, RHS colours are in brackets but the written description is that seen by eye. The colours were measured when the corollas were freshly and fully open — they tend to become darker or occasionally fade with age or on harvesting. The calyces also tend to be lighter-coloured in bud and darken when the flower has opened.

The problem with using the RHS colour range is that there is an unfortunate lack of variation in the violet–blue range and some of the colours, as in the case of the *L. lanata* x *L. angustifolia* cultivars, do not exactly match the RHS shade.

As the home gardener may not have access to these colours, a list of like-coloured lavenders has been included in Appendix 1. When determining corolla or sterile bract colour by eye, always view on an overcast day, as bright light will wash out the colours and give a false impression. Colours that appear pink to the human eye are often revealed to be more purple when compared to colour charts. However, the human eye is capable of placing colours in better perspective than the RHS colour chart and is more reliable when the choice of a cultivar for the garden is made.

LEFT
Length of spikes in
Section *Lavandula*

LONG
L. angustifolia 'Twickel Purple'

MEDIUM
L. angustifolia 'Hidcote'

SHORT
L. angustifolia 'Lady'

RIGHT
Length of spikes in
Section *Stoechas*

LONG
L. 'Pippa White'

MEDIUM
L. 'Major'

SHORT
L. 'Evelyn Cadzow'

FERTILE BRACTS

All lavenders have fertile bracts in some shape or form. They are basically modified protective leaves which, in the case of lavender, subtend or partially subtend the buds of the inflorescence. They appear to be as unique to lavender as fingerprints are to humans.

The general shape of bracts in Section *Lavandula* is broadly ovate to obovate, acute to acuminate and sparsely pubescent, but the shape, length and width of the bracts vary between cultivars. Detailed descriptions of fertile bracts are provided for species lavenders and Section *Stoechas* and Section *Dentata* cultivars, but have been kept very simple for the cultivars. The following examples can be used for comparison when observing bracts in Section *Lavandula* cultivars. Quantitative measurements in brackets show length followed by width.

SECTION *LAVANDULA*

Small and narrow	*L. angustifolia* 'Lady' (3–4mm x 3–4mm)
Intermediate	*L. angustifolia* 'Hidcote' (4–5mm x 4–5mm)
Broad	*L. angustifolia* 'Twickel Purple' (4–5mm x 3–7mm)
Long and narrow	*L.* x *intermedia* 'Grey Hedge' (5–6mm x 3–4mm)

Section *Stoechas* lavenders have very large fertile bracts that subtend or almost subtend the calyces. Both shape and colour vary between cultivars.

Fertile bracts provide an important diagnostic tool for classification in lavenders (illustrated on page 38).

BRACTEOLES

Like bracts, bracteoles are another important distinguishing feature between Section *Lavandula* cultivars, giving some insight into the possible parentage of the plant. They are small, leaf-like organs, mostly linear in shape, which may be seen between the fertile bract and the calyx. The length, width, shape and degree of branching of bracteoles differ between cultivars and, together with fertile bracts, provide important diagnostic tools in the identification of species and cultivars in Section *Lavandula*. Quantitative measurements in brackets show length followed by width.

Insignificant, tiny or not present	*L. angustifolia* 'Hidcote' (if present, only 0.5mm)
Thin, small	*L. angustifolia* 'Twickel Purple' (0.5–1.5mm x 0.5–0.2mm)
Long, thin, plentiful	*L.* x *intermedia* 'Grey Hedge' (2–3mm and 0.2–1mm)

See illustration on page 38.

Bracteoles are present in the intersectional hybrids but not in any other Section of lavenders.

STERILE BRACTS

At one time referred to as 'coma' bracts, sterile bracts are described as a tuft of leaves or, in lavender, bracts terminating the spike. They are present in Section *Stoechas* and Section *Dentata* lavenders and are very obvious, giving the spike its main focus of colour. The range of colour varies from violet through to pink and white.

Length and width of sterile bracts
Length of sterile bracts is included in individual descriptions but widths may be determined by the shape of the sterile bracts (illustrated on page 39). The shape of both sterile and fertile bracts is only approximate in descriptions, as it can vary slightly on a spike and occasionally between spikes.

Shape of sterile bracts
Sterile bract shapes are as variable as their colours. The illustration on page 39 details shapes and the Glossary lists terms used to describe outlines of sterile bracts.

Number of sterile bracts
Generally a flower spike will have four sterile bracts, either of equal size or with two longer than the others.

Occasionally a semi-double bracted (four or more) or double-bracted (eight or more) spike will arise. Such spikes are immediately appealing and the cultivars are worth acquiring for their purely ornamental and picturesque value.

Degree of undulation of sterile bracts
The amount of undulation or degree of waviness along the margins of the sterile bracts ranges from weak or non-existent to very strong. In the case of strong undulation, it is

often difficult to determine the shape of the sterile bract itself due to the bract folding inwards on itself. The degree of undulation may be slight, moderate or strong.

GENERAL CONCISE DESCRIPTION OF *LAVANDULA*

The *Lavandula* species is a perennial herb, subshrub or shrub, which is aromatic, erect and pubescent (covered in short, soft hair). The stems are woody and often, but not always, branched. Stems are rectangular or square displaying occasional ribbing. Leaves are opposite, simple, entire, dentate, pinnate or bipinnate. Hair on the leaves is usually branched, often with stalked or sessile glands.

The inflorescence is a terminal spike, either simple or branched, dense and compact or long and loose (i.e. the distance between whorls is short or long). Fertile bracts are opposite, alternate or spiral, imbricate or arranged in vertical tiers. The colour of the bracts may be green, red–purple, white or membranous. Coma or sterile bracts form a large feather or plume-like structure above the spike (e.g. Section *Stoechas*). Bracteoles are present in Section *Lavandula* and in the intersectional hybrids such as *L.* x *allardii*, *L.* x *heterophylla* and *L.* 'Goodwin Creek Grey'. Flowers are sessile or on short stems (pedicellate). Corollas are tubular and either just subtend the calyces or are extended by half their length beyond the calyx. The outermost part of the tube is dilated with five lobes that are rather short, nearly equal or more obviously two-lipped.

Variation in sterile bract number, colour and shape

The upper lip has two upright lobes and the lower lip has three horizontal to reflexed lobes. The colour of corollas ranges from white, purple, dark blue or violet through to pink and light blue. Calyces are tubular, 8-, 13- or 15-nerved, and 5-toothed with the posterior tooth often enlarged and appendiculate (forming an appendage over the corolla before it opens) in some of the Sections.

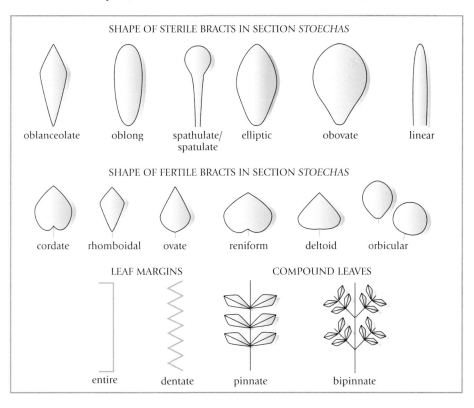

SHAPE OF STERILE BRACTS IN SECTION *STOECHAS*

oblanceolate   oblong   spathulate/ spatulate   elliptic   obovate   linear

SHAPE OF FERTILE BRACTS IN SECTION *STOECHAS*

cordate   rhomboidal   ovate   reniform   deltoid   orbicular

LEAF MARGINS

entire   dentate

COMPOUND LEAVES

pinnate   bipinnate

USES OF LAVENDER

Although this section is not botanical in nature, a brief list of uses, intended as a guide only, is included after each description.

Lavender is one of the most versatile of all herbs and has many purposes, with new uses being developed all the time. This is a brief and simple guide to how lavender may be used. For a more detailed account, there are many interesting books listed in the bibliography with chapters on lavender recipes and craft.

Ornamental planting

Grow lavender in the garden as a specimen or border plant or formally as hedging or topiary. Plants may be used as a centrepiece, colour coordinated with other plants in the garden, or planted en masse for stunning effect.

Smaller plants may be suitable for long-term pot growing, providing they are regularly repotted, fed and watered. Larger plants can be grown in containers until two years old before being transplanted to the garden.

Colour in ornamental planting

Lavender with light blue flowers such as *L. angustifolia* 'Irene Doyle' and *L. angustifolia* 'Bosisto' tends to stand out in the garden because of its translucent quality. Tall lavandins such as *L.* x *intermedia* 'Nicoleii' and *L.* x *intermedia* 'Yuulong' also attract immediate attention in a border. *Lavandula* x *intermedia* 'Old English' grows into a most beautiful architecturally shaped bush and is effective planted either side of a pathway or as a feature plant for an entrance or back-of-border.

Vivid or bright blue-flowered cultivars such as *L. angustifolia* 'Pacific Blue' and *L.* x *intermedia* 'Bogong' have a special appeal and are just as effective planted en masse or as individual plants.

Long-flowered lavenders are picturesque, with cultivars such as *L. angustifolia* 'Twickel Purple' and *L. angustifolia* 'Tasm' continuing to flower indefinitely in long cascading peduncles like miniature fountains in the midst of the garden.

Grey- and silver-leaved plants such as *L.* x *intermedia* 'Grey Hedge', *L.* 'Sawyers' or *L.* 'Molten Silver' make spectacular hedges and complement other plants in the garden. Use them as feature plants for effect.

Most of the dark-flowered cultivars such as *L. angustifolia* 'Hidcote' or *L. angustifolia* 'Blue Mountain' tend to be later flowering than their lighter-flowered counterparts. They are beautiful on their own but particularly appealing mixed with different coloured lavenders, e.g. pink or white, either as a hedge or en masse. Dark-flowered lavenders planted along the top of a wall at eye level are most attractive or give effective contrast around white- or yellow-flowered plants. The larger cultivars such as *L.* x *intermedia* 'Grosso' and *L.* x *intermedia* 'Impress Purple' can be planted with *L.* x *intermedia* 'Alba' or *L.* x *intermedia* 'Dutch White'.

Pink-flowered cultivars are displayed to their very best when grown against a background of dark-flowered lavender. Likewise white-flowered lavenders can be very elegant plants either on their own or mingled with other colours.

Section *Stoechas* and Section *Dentata* cultivars may be grown singly or massed for effect. *Lavandula stoechas* cultivars, in particular, display a diverse range of coloured sterile bracts, with a shade to match the colour scheme of most gardens.

Fragrance
Section *Lavandula* contains the most suitable cultivars for fragrant crafts and use, ranging from pot pourri, lavender bags and sachets through to inclusion of flowers or spikes in soaps and candles. Lavender oil is used in products such as hair shampoos, deodorants, soaps, candles, face creams and moisturisers.

Oil
Many lavenders are suitable for the distilling of oil. Some oil is more suited for use in disinfectants, soaps, candles and deodorants, etc, while the most fragrant oil is used for the perfume industry, aromatherapy and culinary pursuits.

Culinary use
Only some lavenders are suitable for culinary purposes, e.g. for making biscuits, cakes, ice cream and flavoured icing sugar. Two examples are *L. angustifolia* 'Avice Hill' and the true form of *L. angustifolia* 'Munstead'.

Hedging
Most lavender can be shaped into hedging but some cultivars are better suited than others. For spacing between plants, see page 8.

ORIGIN OF PLANTS
Where possible, the breeder, country of origin and approximate date have been included.

HISTORY, CLASSIFICATION AND LAVENDER SPECIES

BRIEF HISTORY

Lavender has long been used for its cosmetic, cleansing and healing qualities, with the first recorded history dating back to ancient Greek and Roman times. Dioscorides, a Greek physician, described lavender as having slender twigs and hair similar to thyme, only longer. The Greeks apparently used mainly *L. stoechas* medicinally, making wines and vinegars from the spikes and foliage. The Romans used it to scent their baths and relieve their aching limbs. It may be that the Romans distinguished between *L. stoechas* and *L. vera*, using the first for wine-making and the second for their exotic perfumes. However this is not clear.

It is generally assumed that the Romans introduced lavender to England but it may well have been introduced earlier. No records exist to confirm this. During the Dark Ages, monks recorded their herbal knowledge and lavender thrived in their monastery gardens. Abbes Hildegarde (1098–1180), a learned female botanist, made a study of lavender and wrote of her findings. Subsequently herbalists such as Turner and Gerard (16th century) attributed lavender with an ability to heal anything from colds and headaches to limb paralysis and neurosis, as well as with use as both a tonic and a laxative. *Lavandula stoechas* was referred to as 'Sticadore' and was one of the main ingredients of 'Four Thieves vinegar' used to combat the plague during the Middle Ages. The spikes of *L. stoechas* were still being used medicinally until the middle of the eighteenth century. Even today in France and Spain, fresh spikes of *L. stoechas* and *L. dentata* are suspended in water in closed bottles placed in the sun, for use as a haemostatic or for cleansing wounds.

Apart from *L. stoechas*, it appears the Romans may also have known *L. pedunculata* and *L. dentata*, but possibly included them under the name *L. stoechas* or other names. During the Middle Ages, lavender was divided into two separate genera, *Stoechas* consisting of *L. stoechas*, *L. pedunculata* and *L. dentata*, and *Lavandula* containing *L. spica* (now known as *L. latifolia*). Linnaeus in his works of 1753 combined all known lavenders into one genus, later including *L. multifida*. His son added *L. pinnata* in 1790. Unfortunately Linnaeus failed to differentiate between true lavender (*L. angustifolia*) and spike lavender (*L. latifolia*) and called both of them *L. spica*. Botanists, realising the difference between the two, later renamed true lavender *L. officinalis* and subsequently *L. vera*. In 1930, according to the rules of botanical nomenclature, the name *L. spica* was withdrawn from public use in order to avoid confusion. *Lavandula spica* was renamed *L. latifolia*, and *L. angustifolia* replaced the names *L. vera* and *L. officinalis*. Unfortunately few nurserymen have taken note of this, and the misnaming of lavenders continues to plague the marketplace, with plants still being sold under the old names *L. spica*, *L. officinalis* or *L. vera*.

In 1826, Baron Frederic Charles Jean de Gingins-Lassaraz, a Swiss botanist, was able to describe 12 species, dividing them into three sections. By 1948, two more species and another section had been added to make a total of 18 species and four sections. Then, in 1937 Miss Chaytor wrote her well-researched monograph on the genus *Lavandula* in which she listed 28 species, including a new section, bringing the total to five sections altogether.

Another section was added in 1996, placing one of the existing species into a new division of its own. Likewise a couple of species have been reclassified, increasing the number of species now known to over 30. Perhaps in the future there will be further, as yet unknown, species added to the list.

Miss Edna Neugebauer, a well-known horticulturist and garden writer who lived in California, United States of America, made it her life's work to collect as many lavender species as possible. She succeeded in collecting 17 species, most of which are rare in cultivation. Nowadays Joan Head, editor of the international lavender journal *The Lavender Bag*, has approximately 25 species in her private collection and hopes to have grown, or at least tried growing, the remainder of the species during her lifetime.

Apart from the lavender species, there are also numerous cultivars that have proved enormously popular with gardeners worldwide.

For a more detailed account of the historical uses, folklore and history associated with lavender, readers are directed to further reading material in the bibliography.

CLASSIFICATION AND LAVENDER SPECIES

Lavenders belong to the Labiatae (Lamiaceae) family which contains square (or rectangular) stemmed plants such as thyme (*Thymus* spp.), mint (*Mentha* spp.) and sage (*Salvia* spp.).

The genus *Lavandula* consists of over 30 species of small shrubs or herbs. The botanical name is derived from the Latin verb 'lavare' meaning 'to wash', a reference to the use of water perfumed by oils of members of the genus.

The natural habitat of these plants is in the countries bordering the Mediterranean Sea. Some are also found in the general Sahara region extending westwards to the Macronesian Islands and eastwards to Arabia and India.

Genus *Lavandula* is divided into six sections: Section *Lavandula* (formerly *Spica*; mostly native to the Mediterranean region, in particular France); Section *Stoechas* (Mediterranean region); Section *Dentata* (Mediterranean, Macronesia and southwards to Arabia); Section *Pterostoechas* (North Africa and Macronesia); Section *Chaetostachys* (Peninsula of India); and Section *Subnuda* (Arabian Peninsula and adjacent parts of Africa). Of these, Section *Lavandula* contains the most commonly grown and hardiest of the lavender genus.

A general description follows of the Sections comprising genus *Lavandula* and corresponding species.

SECTION *LAVANDULA*
(synonym: **Section *Spica***)

Formerly known as Section *Spica*, this section was recently renamed Section *Lavandula*. Hopefully with this change, use of the old name *Spica* will finally be eradicated.

Cultivars in this section are shrubs growing to 1 metre or more in height. Leaves are linear, linear-lanceolate or spathulate with entire, often revolute (turned over) margins, usually grey when young, and turning greener with age as the hair on the leaves becomes more sparse. Spikes are mostly cylindric, conic or occasionally fusiform, with bracts and flowers arranged in whorls, which are interrupted (a long distance apart) or uninterrupted (very compact). Fertile bracts are mostly uniform and opposite. There may be two or more bracteoles per flower. Flowers are sessile (no stem) or short-stemmed (pedicellate). The calyx is 8- or 13-nerved, 5- or 8-toothed with the posterior tooth large and appendiculate, covering the tip of the flower bud. The two posterior lobes of the corolla are larger and more upright than the three lower ones and the corolla tube may be nearly twice the length of the calyx.

Species are mostly confined to the north-west Mediterranean region. The former name *spica* refers to the spike-like inflorescence. This group of lavender is commonly referred to as 'English lavender' and contains the most fragrantly scented examples of the genus.

LAVANDULA ANGUSTIFOLIA
(synonyms: *L. vera* in part, *L. officinalis*, *L. spica* in part)

A shrub, 60–70cm, with linear leaves and revolute margins. The younger leaves are greyer than the older leaves, with primary (initial) leaves about 6cm in length and hairless. The smaller leaves may have short, branched, stellate (star-shaped) hairs. The peduncles are either unbranched or have short lateral branches. Branching may occur under the foliage line. Peduncles are of varying length but shorter than *L. latifolia*. Spikes are compact or interrupted, often with the basal whorl separated from the main spike by 2–4cm. Fertile bracts, although green when the flowers are in bud, tend to become brown once the flowers have fully opened. They are strongly veined, broadly ovate to obovate, acute to acuminate and sparsely pubescent (little hair). Bracteoles are small and linear or occasionally broad and branched (0.5–2mm). Calyces are 13-nerved, 4–5mm long with small teeth and a broad ovate or suborbicular appendage. The fertile bracts are shorter than the calyces and covered in hair. The corolla is 10–12mm long, and light blue to violet. The two broad and rounded upper lobes are larger and more upright than the three lower ones. The corolla tube is up to twice the length of the calyx.

Lavandula angustifolia is native to the Pyrenees in southern France (above 500–600m), north-east Spain, Switzerland and northern Italy. The name *angustifolia* means narrow-leaved. *Lavandula angustifolia* has more sweetly scented inflorescences than *L. latifolia* and *L. lanata* and commences flowering in early summer.

The species is divided into two subspecies:

Lavandula angustifolia subsp. *angustifolia*

Fertile bracts cover one-third to one-half of the calyx and the calyx appendage is difficult to see. Peduncles are about 16–20cm with a 4–6cm spike. The habit of the plant is bushy and dense (illustrated on page 48).

Lavandula angustifolia subsp. *pyrenaica*

This subspecies differs from *L. angustifolia* in having much larger, broader and longer fertile bracts which extend along two-thirds of the calyx or almost to the top. The pubescence is confined to the veining of the fertile bracts and the calyx appendage is remote. Peduncles are 12–23cm and the spikes are 4–5cm and generally more compact than *L. angustifolia* subsp. *angustifolia*. Bracteoles, where present, are 2mm and up to

1mm wide. Corollas are a vibrant violet (88A) and calyces are green, lightly suffused with dark violet (86A). The plant is bushy with moderately dense foliage and grows to 50cm. It is native to the east Pyrenees in France and north-east Spain. A rare find in a collection (illustrated on page 48).

LAVANDULA ANGUSTIFOLIA SUBSP. ANGUSTIFOLIA VAR. DELPHINENSIS

Possibly a controversial division under the heading *L. angustifolia*, but an interesting one. Miss Chaytor in her monograph on lavenders describes what was then termed *L. delphinensis* as a robust, larger-growing plant than *L. angustifolia* reaching 50cm (bush only). The leaves are lanceolate to oblong with slightly revolute margins. Spikes are long, cylindric and evenly interrupted with longer peduncles than *L. angustifolia*. Miss Chaytor went on to say that many intermediate forms between *L. angustifolia* and *L. delphinensis* existed but that it was better to describe the two extremes first. The natural habitat of *L. delphinensis* is Switzerland, France and Italy.

In my experience of growing this plant from wild collected seed, I have found the resulting seedlings and plants remarkably similar in all characteristics. They are robust, dense-foliaged plants (70cm) with long, upright, thin peduncles (20–25cm). Only one plant had any significant bracteoles, which were very small (0.5–1mm). Spikes are cylindric, long (6–8cm) and interrupted.

These plants could simply be described as another cultivar of *L. angustifolia* but, for the present time at least, I shall keep these plants separate from *L. angustifolia* cultivars.

A problem with the name *L. delphinensis* has been its use in the past as a synonym for the true, elusive *L. angustifolia* 'Alba'. This poses an interesting query. I have several plants named *L. delphinensis* 'Alba' from different sources. They are white-flowered seedlings, one similar to *L. angustifolia* 'Nana Alba' and the other different from anything else I have grown, with broad, dense, mid-green leaves and very white corollas on cylindric, occasionally fusiform spikes (2–3cm). Bracteoles are 1–2mm, with occasional short-stemmed lateral branching and three to four flowers (illustrated on page 48).

LAVANDULA LATIFOLIA
(synonym: *L. spica* in part)

Leaves are linear to oblanceolate or occasionally narrow elliptic (8cm long), covered in short grey hairs which tend to become sparser on larger leaves. Peduncles are long (at least 40–50cm) with many lateral branches and spikes (illustrated on page 49). Spikes may be short and compact (4–5cm), or long and interrupted (5–10cm). Fertile bracts are lanceolate with acute or pointed tips, and covered with hair. Bracteoles are long and linear (4–6mm), occasionally broader and branched. The calyx is grey with violet tips (86A) and tomentose, 13-nerved, about 5mm with small rounded teeth. The appendage on the calyx is elliptic to broad ovate. Corollas are 8mm long, and

mauve to bright violet–blue (90A), being darker on the outside of the corolla and lighter in the centre. The corolla is less than twice the length of the calyx with broad, oblong or rounded lobes.

The bush itself is not large, approximately 40cm at maturity, but with the flowering stems may reach over 1m. This species tends to be prone to lavender leafspot, dislikes damp, wet and humid conditions, and is less hardy than *L. angustifolia*. *Lavandula latifolia* is not a long-lived plant and is not widely available.

It is commonly called 'spike lavender' because of its habit and its previous name *L. spica*. The fragrance of the spikes, although much harsher than *L. angustifolia*, is not unpleasant. The oil from *L. latifolia* (oil of aspic) is often used in ceramic paint, in the preparation of varnishes and in soaps, disinfectants and shampoos. The name *latifolia* means 'broad leaf'.

Lavandula latifolia is found in southern Europe, in France, Spain, Italy and the Balkan Peninsula, growing at a lower altitude (below 600m) than *L. angustifolia*. The flowering time is also later than other lavenders, usually late summer. Where both *L. angustifolia* and *L. latifolia* intermingle, natural hybridisation occurs between the two populations, giving rise to hybrids or what the French term 'lavandins'. Botanically these hybrids are given the collective name *L.* x *intermedia* in recognition of their common parentage. Their characteristics tend to be intermediate between the two species and they are always sterile.

Over the centuries much confusion in naming has occurred, particularly over the names *L. angustifolia* and *L. latifolia*. See page 44 for details.

Lavandula lanata

A large shrub (at least 80cm in flower) with white, woolly, tomentose leaves and stems. Leaves are 3–5cm long, oblong-lanceolate to linear-spathulate. The spikes are 2–10cm long with 25–40cm peduncles. Corollas are a deep, vibrant violet–purple. The strongly pubescent calyces are 8-nerved and 8-toothed, and green suffused with dark violet. The upper tooth has an elliptic appendage. Fertile bracts are linear or lanceolate, usually equalling or exceeding the calyx. Bracteoles are 2–5mm but not as plentiful as *L. latifolia*. It flowers in late summer (illustrated on page 50).

Lavandula lanata is native to southern Spain (up to 1800m) growing on dry calcareous slopes. In a garden situation *L. lanata* is best grown in very well-drained conditions and

LEFT
Two varieties of *L. latifolia* —
one with a short spike,
the other with a long spike

RIGHT
Whole peduncle and
foliage of *L. latifolia*

dislikes transplanting. Although not common in cultivation, it will always be sought after for its beautiful silver–grey, dense foliage. The whole plant, even the spikes and peduncles, has a soft, velvety texture and a unique fragrance. The name *lanata* refers to the long matted hair on the foliage. Often referred to as 'Woolly lavender'.

NATURAL HYBRIDS IN SECTION *LAVANDULA*

Miss Chaytor, in her monograph on lavender *A Taxonomic Study of the Genus Lavandula* (1937), stated that most if not all of the garden forms of lavender are probably hybrids between *L. latifolia* and *L. angustifolia*, as most show

characteristics of one or the other. I agree that many of the plants found and named in cultivation are indeed hybrids but most tend to be either seedlings from self-pollinated plants or hybrids between the cultivars of *L. angustifolia*, rather than between *L. latifolia* and *L. angustifolia*. One of the reasons for this is that many of the plants I have examined show the characteristics displayed by the *L. angustifolia* parent with no characteristics of *L. latifolia*. The other reason is that *L. latifolia* is rare in gardens, and flowers later, often after the *L. angustifolia* cultivars have been cut back. It is difficult to breed a *L.* x *intermedia* cultivar unless the two parent plants are growing close together and the flowering period coincides, or the plants are deliberately hand-pollinated. It can and does happen but is not a common occurrence. It is more likely to happen in the wild. All cultivars listed under *L. angustifolia* are fertile whereas *L.* x *intermedia* cultivars are sterile.

Occasionally it is possible to find a *L. angustifolia* cultivar with perhaps one characteristic that is similar to *L. latifolia*, yet its lineage may be descended from *L. angustifolia* parents. Such a case is the small-growing lavender *L. angustifolia* 'Crystal Lights', which has long, broad, branched bracteoles and wider leaves than is usual for a *L. angustifolia* cultivar. It seems possible that its ancestry may have included *L. latifolia* at some stage and the characteristic for larger bracteoles has presented itself in the progeny. This may explain longer lateral branching seen in some *L. angustifolia* cultivars, such as 'Twickel Purple', which otherwise displays all the characteristics of *L. angustifolia*.

SECTION *STOECHAS*

Prior to the nineteenth century, Section *Stoechas* was placed in another genus. Linnaeus recognised similarities with the other lavenders he knew at the time and placed them all in one genus, *Lavandula*.

The word *stoechas* is derived from the Greek name for a group of islands (Stoechades) just off the Mediterranean coast of France and now called Iles de Hyeres.

Section *Stoechas* consists of shrubs to about 1 metre or more in height. Leaves are entire and the inflorescence a dense spike with mostly unbranched peduncles.

The sterile bracts, formerly known as coma bracts, are enlarged, forming what are commonly called 'rabbit's ears', and can be of varying colours. Fertile bracts are broad and arranged in vertical rows, each subtending two to seven flowers. The amount and type of hair on the margins of the fertile bracts differ between species and subspecies. Flowers may have short stalks (pedicellate) with 13-nerved, enlarged calyces with posterior tooth and an orbicular to reniform appendage covering the mouth of the calyx in bud. When the corolla appears, this appendage becomes upright. The corolla tube is

slightly longer than the calyx, and occasionally is twice the length. Corolla lobes are somewhat equal.

Most of the species are found in the Mediterranean region with some in the Azores, Asia Minor, North Africa and Algeria.

Lavenders from Section *Lavandula* have been cultivated and well known since the Middle Ages (at least), but it seems that only the lavenders of Section *Stoechas* were known and used by the Romans and Greeks of classical times (particularly as an antiseptic).

Although Section *Stoechas* lavenders may have been distilled for oil in the past, lavenders from Section *Lavandula* are now used for that purpose, in particular *L. angustifolia* and *L.* x *intermedia* cultivars.

LAVANDULA STOECHAS SUBSP. STOECHAS

A bushy shrub, 30–60cm, with linear to oblong-lanceolate, entire and tomentose leaves. The spikes are dense and short (2–3cm) and mostly truncate-conic with short peduncles (3–4cm), which occasionally have a purplish tinge just under the spike. The fertile bracts are rhombic-cordate, covered in hair and membranous suffused with red–purple. The colour of the fertile bracts is green with the upper half purple. There is pubescence on both the bracts and margins. The corolla is dark purple but not as dark as the corollas of *L. stoechas* subsp. *caesia*. The calyx is pubescent, 13-nerved and 4–6mm long with the upper tooth having a purple, obcordate appendage. Sterile bracts are purple, 1–5mm, and oblong-obovate with only slightly undulating margins.

This subspecies is common to the Mediterranean region, Portugal, North Africa, Madeira and Tenerife, where it is found growing in mostly acid soils, and is often called Italian, French or Spanish lavender. The leaves and spikes are used to perfume linen and to deter moths. In ancient times, it was used as a medicinal plant.

LAVANDULA STOECHAS SUBSP. CAESIA

Similar to *L. stoechas* subsp. *stoechas* except that it grows into a much larger plant (60–70cm). The foliage is greyer and the plant is more upright than *L. stoechas* subsp. *stoechas*. Peduncles are short (1–2cm) and spikes are short, compact (1–2mm) and truncate-conic. Fertile bracts are dark red–purple, pubescent, rhombic-cordate and acute. The bracts are the same length as the calyx. Corollas are almost one-half to one-third extended beyond the calyx and very noticeable. Calyces are green, with two-thirds purple and pubescent. The calyx appendage is dark purple. Sterile bracts are 2–9mm, more obovate and a darker, richer purple–violet (86A to 88A) than *L. stoechas* subsp. *stoechas*.

Native to Spain and Portugal, but appears to be uncommon in cultivation.

The cultivar known as **'Bella Signora'** is very similar in most respects except that the fertile bracts are slightly greener and the corollas and sterile bracts may be a lighter shade. This cultivar appears to be the result of natural seed variation, possibly from *L. stoechas* subsp. *caesia*, because in habit, foliage colour, etc, it is identical to the subspecies.

LAVANDULA STOECHAS SUBSP. PEDUNCULATA
(synonym: *L. pedunculata*)

Leaves are linear or lanceolate, with revolute margins. There may be a group of leaves together with a larger, more lanceolate leaf subtending. The fine-leaved foliage is a lighter green than the other subspecies. Stems, leaves and spikes have short-branched, stellate hairs. Peduncles are long (16–23cm), broad and green with slightly reddish edges. Spikes are medium (2–6cm), more truncate-conic than cylindric (see below). The fertile bracts cover the calyx and are broadly obovate to suborbicular, acute or rounded and slightly dentate. The colour is mostly green with red–purple margins and slightly pubescent on the bract itself with longer hair on the margins. The calyx is narrower in *L. stoechas* subsp. *pedunculata* than *L. stoechas* subsp. *stoechas* with acute-shaped teeth and broad but small, red–purple, obovate appendage. The colour of the calyx is green, with the upper half red–purple and the appendage red–purple. Fertile bracts cover the calyx. Corolla lobes are broad and rounded with the tube scarcely exceeding the calyx. The corolla is dark blue (103A). The sterile bracts are red–purple to violet–purple (83B) or mauve; they are elliptic or linear-lanceolate, 10–30mm, with quite undulated margins.

The subspecies grows in mostly calcareous soils in the Atlantic Islands, Spain, Portugal, North Africa, South Balkan Peninsula and Asia Minor, and is occasionally given the common name 'Spanish lavender'. The name *pedunculata* refers to the peduncle (with its much longer length compared to *L. stoechas* subsp. *stoechas*).

LAVANDULA STOECHAS SUBSP. CARIENSIS

Similar to *L. stoechas* subsp. *pedunculata* but there is less hair on the foliage and more on the peduncles, particularly beneath the spike. The calyx appendage has crenate margins compared to entire margins. Sterile bracts are paler in colour and the corolla tube is 1mm longer than the calyx. Occasionally the peduncle may have a fertile bract two-thirds from the base.

Native to West Anatolia and north of Istanbul.

LAVANDULA STOECHAS SUBSP. LUSITANICA

The foliage is grey–green with a bushy, more open, spreading habit. Peduncles are long (16–22cm), broad and mid-green with purple edges. The broad spike is compact (3–5cm) and cylindric or broad-conical (illustrated on page 52). The fertile bracts are red–purple and suborbicular to slightly deltoid, covering approximately two-thirds of the calyx. The calyces are green with the upper-half purple and pubescent, with a red–purple appendage. The corollas are dark blue (103A) and partly extended beyond the calyces. Sterile bracts are obovate or elliptic, 10–30mm, and red–purple to dark violet–purple (83A) with moderately undulating margins.

Grows on sandy soils in central and southern Portugal.

LAVANDULA STOECHAS SUBSP. LUISIERI

A plant of upright bushy habit with semi-open, grey–green foliage. Peduncles are short (2–3cm) and mid-green with slight red edges. Spikes are medium (2–4cm) and either cylindric or truncate-conic (illustrated on pages 52 and 57). Fertile bracts are green suffused with some red–purple, occasionally deltoid (more or less) or suborbicular, and mostly acute, covering one-half to two-thirds of the calyx. They have a crinkled appearance with prominent veining and sparse pubescence covering the calyx. Corollas are dark blue (103A) and are partly extended beyond the calyces. The colour of the calyx is a mixture of green and red–purple with patches of brown. The small purple calyx appendage is mostly entire. The vivid violet (88A) sterile bracts are spathulate or obovate, 10–18mm, with strongly undulating margins.

Native to the loamy schist soils of central and southern Portugal.

LAVANDULA STOECHAS SUBSP. SAMPAIANA

Taller than *L. stoechas* subsp. *pedunculata* but with similar light-green foliage and upright, bushy, semi-open habit. Very long, thick peduncles (20–30cm) are mid-green with very purple edges. Spikes are compact (3–5cm), broad and mostly cylindric (illustrated on pages 52 and 57). Fertile bracts are red–purple and deltoid or suborbicular, acute or apiculate, either completely covering or covering two-thirds of the calyx. Hair cover over the bract is finely pubescent with longer hair on the margins. The colour of the fertile bracts is red–purple with patches of brown. Corollas are dark blue (103A) and calyces are green with red–purple tips and pubescent. The calyx appendage is small and purple. Sterile bracts are linear to elliptic or slightly obovate and vibrant red–purple (87A), 10–30mm, with moderately undulating margins.

Grows on granite soil in western Spain and northern and central Portugal.

I am not familiar with the next two subspecies, which are rare in cultivation.

LAVANDULA STOECHAS SUBSP. ATLANTICA

A smaller bush than *L. stoechas* subsp. *pedunculata*, growing to 20–30cm. The leaves, young stems and peduncles are covered in hair. Peduncles are 3–10cm. Fertile bracts are rotund-ovate or reniform with entire or dentate margins. The corolla is violet and the calyx has an appendage. Fertile bracts above the basal pair may be petiolate. The pale violet sterile bracts are 20–30mm, lanceolate and acuminate. Leaves are similar to *L. stoechas* subsp. *pedunculata*.

Native to Spain and Morocco.

LAVANDULA STOECHAS SUBSP. MADERENSIS

This subspecies differs from *L. stoechas* subsp. *pedunculata* in the type of hair covering the leaves, peduncles and young stems. The sterile bracts are spathulate, oblanceolate and pale violet. Fertile bracts are shorter than *L. stoechas* subsp. *pedunculata* but are similar in shape, and the margins of the bracts are densely tomentose.

Grows in the Atlantic Islands, the Azores and Madeira.

Most of the subspecies have sparsely hairy peduncles except *L. stoechas* subsp. *sampaiana*, which has a denser covering. All of the subspecies are suitable for ornamental planting and some of the smaller lavenders, like *L. stoechas* subsp. *stoechas*, will form a dense low-growing hedge.

LAVANDULA STOECHAS FORMA LEUCANTHA

Previously called *L. stoechas* var. *albiflora*, this is a small plant (40–50cm) of rounded bushy habit and dense grey–green foliage. Peduncles are short (2–3.5cm), dull green and thin with fine pubescence. Spikes are globular and cylindric (1.5–3cm). The corollas and short sterile bracts are white. The fertile bracts are membranous with green veining and very finely pubescent all over. Calyces are green and also very finely pubescent with a tiny green appendage (illustrated on page 155).

Found in 1925 in the East Pyrenees, near Villefranche, France, it has also been sold under the name *L. stoechas* 'Snowman', and makes a fine low hedge.

LAVANDULA VIRIDIS

A large shrub to 1m with light green, sparsely haired leaves with reticulated (netted) veins. Peduncles are short to medium (5–8cm) broad, light green and pubescent. Spikes are more loosely arranged than in other species, 4–5cm, and mostly cylindric

(illustrated on page 52). Corollas are white to greenish-white with a tendency to go brown in the sun. The corolla tube is partly extended beyond the calyx. Fertile bracts are light green (148B), elliptic and apiculate, and completely cover the calyx. The green calyx has a large suborbicular, acute, entire upper-toothed appendage and is densely covered in hair. The sterile bracts are 8–20 mm and greenish (150C). Their shape is elliptic and apiculate. Leaves and stems are quite glandular, sticky to touch and very strongly scented.

Lavandula viridis is native to south-west Spain, southern Portugal and Madeira. The name *viridis* refers to the green pigmentation, hence its common name 'Green lavender'.

SECTION *DENTATA*

Until recently, *L. dentata* was considered to be part of Section *Stoechas*, but in 1996 it was placed in a section of its own. This would seem very appropriate since the plants are quite distinct from their *L. stoechas* relatives. Some of the different characteristics are a dentate (toothed) leaf margin and an inflorescence that has reduced sterile bracts compared with Section *Stoechas* plants. I have never seen *L. dentata* hybridise with any plants in Section *Stoechas*, yet *L. stoechas* cultivars are notorious for hybridising among themselves.

LAVANDULA DENTATA VAR. DENTATA

Leaves are linear to narrow oblong, 2–3cm long with dentate, revolute margins. Both leaves and shoots are green compared to the grey leaves of *L. dentata* var. *candicans*. The dull green peduncles are medium to long (10–20cm). The medium spikes (3–5cm) are cylindric, and not particularly dense, while the sterile bracts are mauve, ovate-lanceolate to nearly elliptic, and 5–10mm (illustrated on page 60). A transition occurs between fertile and sterile bracts. Fertile bracts are similar in shape to the sterile bracts. The calyx is tubular and tomentose with a very broad purple appendage. Corollas are light blue–violet (97C) and strongly pubescent with the tube slightly exceeding the calyx. Calyces are mostly green suffused with some violet. The sterile bracts are mauve to light violet (92A).

The bush is small to medium and very frost-tender compared to its larger relative *L. dentata* var. *candicans*.

A dark-flowered form of *L. dentata* var. *dentata* also exists and has been sold for some years in New Zealand. The sterile bracts are purple–violet (90A) and corollas also violet (94A). It has slightly shorter spikes (2–4cm) than its lighter-coloured counterpart (illustrated on page 60). The calyces are bright green and the fertile bracts are suffused with violet. Likewise the French have a dark form which is slightly broader in the spike. The cultivar known as *L.* 'Monet' is identical to the New Zealand dark form. Both forms grow to 60–70cm.

Lavandula dentata var. *dentata* is native to Spain and North Africa.

LAVANDULA DENTATA VAR. CANDICANS

The most commonly grown form of *L. dentata* is *L. dentata* var. *candicans*. It is a much larger bush, in excess of 1m by 1.5m wide, and is hardier than *L. dentata* var. *dentata*. It has very tomentose leaves, young stems and peduncles. Spikes are 4–5cm and broad-conical to truncate-conic (illustrated on pages 60, 62 and 63). Peduncles are long, 10–30cm or longer. Sterile bracts are lavender–violet (91A), similar to the lighter-flowered form of *L. dentata* var. *dentata*. Corollas are light violet–blue (97A) and darker around the edges; calyces green with violet tips. The habit of this plant is mostly upright and bushy, making it highly suitable for hedging and as an ornamental plant in warmer areas. Grow it on the sunny side of the house if in an area that experiences mild frosts. Specimens will flower for most of the year with short rest intervals in-between.

I have another specimen which is lower growing, 90cm–1m and 1.5m wide, with much greyer leaves, spreading habit and darker-coloured sterile bracts (90B and C). The fertile bracts are a deeper violet than *L. dentata* var. *dentata* or *L. dentata* var. *candicans*.

Native to North Africa, Madeira and Cape Verde Islands.

LAVANDULA DENTATA VAR. BALEARICA

Spikes are shorter and the sterile bracts more prominent in this form. Leaves are also smaller and less hairy. Native to the Balearic Islands.

Lavandula dentata (though which form?) was well known in Roman times. It is commonly called 'French lavender' or 'Toothed lavender'. The name *dentata* refers to the toothed leaf margins and the name *candicans* refers to the hairiness of the foliage.

Fresh or dried, the spikes are suitable for arrangements or pot pourri. and the plants are attractive ornamentals.

INTERSECTIONAL HYBRIDS

LAVANDULA X ALLARDII

A large shrub up to 1.5m in height and width with semi-open, grey–green foliage, *L.* x *allardii* is assumed to be a hybrid between *L. latifolia* and *L. dentata*. It was discovered as a seedling in a French garden in the 1890s. The 'x' is placed between *Lavandula* and *allardii* to signify that the plant is of hybrid origin and that the parents are known.

Leaves are linear to oblong-spathulate with some entire leaves, although most show dentate margins towards the apex (illustrated on page 63). The peduncles are long, 15–25cm, sometimes longer. Occasionally long lateral branching can occur with well-formed spikes. The green–grey pubescent fertile bracts are broadly lanceolate and long. There is no enlarged sterile bract terminating the inflorescence but there are plenty of long, broad-shaped bracteoles. Spikes are narrow-conical, very long, 12–20cm or longer, and interrupted. The base whorl may be 2–5cm below the main spike. The length of the spike differs depending on what conditions the plants are grown under, being longer and more interrupted where there is adequate water supply. Differences can also be observed in cutting grown material. Fertile bracts are green with some purple around the margins and splashes of purple inside the bract. Corollas are bright violet–blue (90A). Large bracteoles are present and calyces are green with a touch of dark violet (86A).

A most spectacular plant, particularly en masse, it is best used as an ornamental or for cut flowers. It has a scent halfway between the two parents. It tends to succumb to medium or heavy frosts, particularly towards the end of the winter, so is better suited to a warmer environment or one with only mild frosts. If moderate frost damage does occur, affected areas can be cut out and the plant will reshoot from the base.

A form with larger, longer spikes, called 'African Pride,' is sometimes available. Another larger-growing plant, called 'Devantville', can frequently be seen growing along the Mediterranean coast of Spain and France.

LAVANDULA X HETEROPHYLLA

Discovered in France and Italy in the early 1800s, this hybrid's parentage is presumed to be *L. dentata* and *L. angustifolia*. It is smaller growing than *L.* x *allardii*, about 80cm–1m, and has a semi-open, darker-green foliage. Even with the semi-open nature of the foliage it is a more compact plant than *L.* x *allardii*. Most leaves are linear or elliptic with entire margins. Near the base, however, leaves are partially dentate in the centre or towards the apex of the leaf. Peduncles are medium (7–15cm) and the spikes are cylindric and less interrupted than in *L.* x *allardii*, with an occasional base whorl 4–6 cm below the main spike (illustrated on page 63). Fertile bracts are ovate and acute. The corolla is small and a vibrant violet (94C) and calyces are green with a touch of dark violet (86A). There are no sterile bracts. Bracteoles are large and plentiful. Like its *L. angustifolia* parent, this plant tends to be much hardier than *L.* x *allardii* but will still not withstand a hard frost.

Both plants may be susceptible to sooty mildew in wetter, damper weather but otherwise are well suited for ornamental planting or planting en masse.

SECTION *PTEROSTOECHAS*

These species are herbs or subshrubs with heavily branched stems. Leaves are generally pinnate or bipinnate, less commonly with dentate or entire margins. The spike is compact, interrupted or loose, mostly cylindric or basically square. All bracts are fertile and the flowers (usually one to each bract) have no stems. The calyx is 15-nerved and 5-toothed, with the posterior two being somewhat enlarged. The corolla is two-lipped with the upper lip lobes longer, and the tube twice the length of the calyx.

The natural distribution of the species is in the temperate and tropical Atlantic Islands, northern tropical Africa from Somaliland to Nigeria, and in the Mediterranean regions (excluding the Balkans and Asia Minor). The species seem to intermingle and hybridise in intervening regions. All are frost-tender and have quite a different fragrance from that associated with Section *Lavandula* lavenders. The name *pterostoechas* means 'winged spike'.

Some of the species currently in cultivation are listed below. There are approximately 15 species in this section.

LAVANDULA BUCHII

Until recently this species was described as a variety of *L. pinnata*, but in 1996 it was given the status of a separate species.

It is similar to *L. pinnata* but has shorter fertile ovate bracts and smaller, slightly obovate leaves. The terminal lobe of the leaf is rhomboidal. *Lavandula buchii* is native to Tenerife.

Lavandula buchii var. *gracile* has graceful, narrow cut leaves. The lobes are linear. A most elegant grey-leaved plant, it grows to 1m in its natural surroundings, Tenerife (illustrated on page 64).

LAVANDULA CANARIENSIS

A large shrub to 1.5m with much branched, hairless stems. Leaves are pubescent, bipinnate and light green in colour. Spikes are 8–10cm, and branched at the base. Fertile bracts are ovate-lanceolate, acuminate, hairless, and tinged blue towards the apex. Calyx is 15-nerved with no appendage on the upper tooth (illustrated on page 64).

Native to the Canary Islands. The name *canariensis* simply means 'of the Canary Islands'.

LAVANDULA MINUTOLII

Stem and leaves are covered in hair. The leaves themselves are pinnate with oblanceolate lobes. The fertile bracts are equal to or longer than the calyces. A most attractive blue-flowered lavender, 80cm–1m (illustrated on page 64).

Native to Gran Canaria.

LAVANDULA MULTIFIDA

Subshrub, 0.5–1m. Stems are erect and branched with mostly bipinnate and occasionally irregular, sparsely haired leaves. Spikes are 2–7cm, often branched at the base. Small fertile bracts are cordate-ovate and acuminate. The calyx is 15-nerved, and very hairy with no appendage on the upper tooth. Corollas are blue–violet with large lobes (illustrated on page 64).

Native to the western Mediterranean, Portugal and North Africa. The name *multifida* means 'much divided', referring to the leaves.

LAVANDULA PINNATA

Shrub to 1m with branched stems. The whole plant is covered in short white hairs, giving a grey felt-like appearance. Leaves are pinnate with broad lobes. Peduncles are long, 20–30cm. Spikes also long (7–9cm), either single or branched at the base. The fertile bracts are tinged blue–purple, lanceolate and shorter than the calyces. The calyx itself is 15-nerved and does not have an appendage.

Found in the Canary Islands and Madeira. The name *pinnata* refers to the shape of the leaves.

LEFT

L. dentata var. *candicans*

RIGHT

L. 'Goodwin Creek Grey'
L. x *heterophylla*
L. x *allardii*

LAVANDULA PUBESCENS

The leaves of *L. pubescens* are green and very fern-like and the plant itself grows quite upright. The spikes are long with blue flowers (illustrated on page 64).

Native to Egypt, Syria, Palestine and Arabia. The name *pubescens* means downy.

TOP

L. buchii var. *gracile*
L. buchii
branched seedling
L. multifida
L. minutolii

BELOW

L. 'Sidonie'
L. canariensis
L. pubescens
L. aristibracteata
L. 'Blue Canaries'

LAVANDULA ROTUNDIFOLIA

A herb of sprawling habit and rounded, bright green leaves with irregularly dentate edges. The spikes are broad and have delightful pink corollas. Possibly the only groundcover lavender.

Native to the Cape Verde Islands.

SECTION *CHAETOSTACHYS*

Herbaceous plants with branched peduncles and spikes. Stems are thick and many leaved. The fertile bracts are arranged either alternately or in spirals with a single flower in the axil of each. The calyx is 15-nerved.

The two species *L. bipinnata* and *L. gibsonii* are native to central and southern India and rare in cultivation.

SECTION *SUBNUDA*

Herbaceous plants with alternate or spiral arrangement of the fertile bracts. Stems display varying degrees of branching either from the base as in *L. subnuda*, or throughout their entire length. Leaves may be almost entirely absent in adult plants.

The eight species are native to South Arabia and tropical Africa, and are rare in cultivation. One species in cultivation is *L. aristibracteata* which grows in the Surudi Hills in northern Somalia. It has large, broad, pinnate leaves and spinescent fertile bracts which, growing longer than the calyx, give the spike the appearance of a thistle (illustrated opposite).

The main difference, according to Miss Chaytor, between Section *Chaetostachys* and Section *Subnuda* is plant habit — the abundance and size of the leaves, the branching of the spikes and the size and shape of the areole of the nucule. Furthermore the species are totally separated from each other; no apparent hybridising has been noted.

Both sections differ from Section *Lavandula*, Section *Stoechas* and Section *Pterostoechas* in the alternate and spiral arrangement of the bracts.

CULTIVARS OF
Lavandula angustifolia

Lavandula angustifolia cultivars resemble *L. angustifolia* in their characteristics and height, and are the hardiest and most fragrant of all lavender cultivars.

Lateral branching of the peduncle is uncommon in *L. angustifolia* cultivars, compared to other cultivars belonging to Section *Lavandula*. When present, branching is mostly confined to semi-stalked (1–10mm) or short-stemmed (1–2cm) laterals with one to six flowers on the terminal end, none of which bears any resemblance to a spike. Most of the branching is single (i.e. a pair of branches on opposite sides of the peduncle) or one-sided. Some cultivars occasionally have longer stems or double branching and, where relevant, this is mentioned in the descriptions.

In this group most spikes are interrupted, with obvious gaps between the whorls, and most have base whorls a short distance from the main spike. Some, though, are only slightly interrupted and others are quite compact. Spike length is measured from the apex to the base whorl.

The corolla size varies considerably between cultivars and can be a distinguishing feature. Large corollas tend to give an inflorescence a much bolder look.

Bracteoles are less prominent in *L. angustifolia* cultivars and are described in the text as 'insignificant' when they are either not present or difficult to see without a magnifying glass.

Peduncles may be bent (wavy) or semi-bent rather than straight, a characteristic that is more common with *L. angustifolia* cultivars. The peduncle length is measured from the base of the bottom whorl to the main foliage line (excluding primary leaves).

Lavenders that appear pink to the human eye are often closer to lilac or purple when measured against RHS colour charts.

Lavandula angustifolia cultivars flower earlier than *L.* x *intermedia* cultivars, at the beginning of summer, and if pruned lightly immediately following the first flowering, they will often flower a second time before autumn. The majority are very fragrant, and can be used for fresh or dried flowers, fragrant products, and ornamental, hedging or container purposes. It is only the sweeter members of this group that are suitable for culinary purposes and oil production.

LAVANDULA ANGUSTIFOLIA 'ALBA' (synonym: **'Blue Mountain White'**)

A medium plant (60cm) of busy habit with semi-open to dense, mid-green foliage. Peduncles are medium (12–18cm), mid-green and semi-upright. Semi-stalked lateral branches may be present, terminated with one to three flowers. Spikes are medium (3–5cm), cylindric and interrupted, with the base whorl 1–2cm below the main spike. Fertile bracts are broad. Bracteoles are narrow (0.5–1mm). Corollas are white, and buds and calyces are densely pubescent and green (194A).

This particular plant was not the one described by Miss Chaytor in her monograph on lavender but it has been available in New Zealand for over 50 years and gave rise to the cultivar 'Blue Mountain'. It was raised by Stan Hughes at Blue Mountain Nursery in New Zealand and possibly would have been better called 'Blue Mountain White', but the name 'Alba' has perpetuated.

L. angustifolia 'Alba'
L. angustifolia 'Crystal Lights'
L. angustifolia 'Celestial Star'
L. angustifolia 'Nana Alba'

'Alba' is an attractive white form suitable for ornamental, fragrant and hedging purposes. The name *L. angustifolia* 'Alba' is often confused with *L. x intermedia* 'Alba' but, apart from the white flowers, the plants are nothing alike. Heightwise, 'Alba' is between the other white cultivars 'Crystal Lights' and 'Celestial Star'.

LAVANDULA ANGUSTIFOLIA 'AMANDA CARTER'

A rounded, semi-tall plant (70cm) with open grey–green foliage. Peduncles are long (11–32cm), broad, mid-green and splayed. There may be infrequent semi-stalked laterals terminated with one to four flowers. Spikes are long (9–14cm), cylindric and mostly evenly interrupted, with the base whorl 1–6cm below the main spike. Fertile bracts are very broad. Bracteoles are insignificant. Corollas are dark lavender–violet (92A), calyces are reasonably pubescent and dark violet (86A). The buds are slightly more blue (illustrated on page 70).

Raised in New Zealand by Peter Carter in the mid-1990s, 'Amanda Carter' is similar to 'Twickel Purple' in habit and can be used for ornamental, mass planting or fragrant purposes.

LAVANDULA ANGUSTIFOLIA 'ASHDOWN FOREST'

A small to medium plant (50–60cm) with bushy habit and dense mid-green foliage. Peduncles are short (7–10cm), very thin and semi-upright. Spikes are short to medium (2–4cm), cylindric and slightly interrupted, with the base whorl 1cm below the main spike. Fertile bracts are small to broad. Bracteoles are insignificant (0.5mm). Corollas

are very bright violet–blue (90A), calyces are finely pubescent and green suffused with dark violet–blue (93A).

Raised in the United Kingdom in 1985 by Nutlin Nursery, 'Ashdown Forest' is a smaller plant suitable for low hedging, container growing or ornamental use.

LAVANDULA ANGUSTIFOLIA 'AVICE HILL'
(synonym: **'Impression'**)

A medium bush (60–70cm) of beautiful spherical habit with semi-open, grey–green foliage. The peduncles are long (16–30cm), grey–green and splay outwards like a fountain. There are some short to medium-stemmed laterals present, terminated with one to four flowers. Spikes are long (8–10cm), mostly cylindric and evenly interrupted, with the base whorl 2–4cm below the main spike or occasionally one-third of the way down the peduncle. Fertile bracts are small to intermediate. Bracteoles are narrow (0.5–1mm). The corollas are large and violet–blue (90C), calyces are pubescent and dark violet (86A). The buds are similar in colour to the corollas.

This cultivar was raised by Avice Hill, a well-known New Zealand herb and lavender enthusiast, in 1980 from 'Munstead' seed and selected because of its fragrance. It was subsequently named after her by Virginia McNaughton in 1997. Because of the even arrangement of spikes across the bush, 'Avice Hill' is well suited for ornamental and hedging purposes. It also has culinary, fragrant and oil qualities. The flowering time is later than many other *L. angustifolia* cultivars, being on or about Christmas Day in the Southern Hemisphere.

ABOVE
L. angustifolia 'Avice Hill'

RIGHT
L. angustifolia 'Fring'
L. angustifolia 'Sachet'
L. angustifolia 'Cedar Blue'
L. angustifolia
'Backhouse Purple'
L. angustifolia 'Tarras'

LAVANDULA ANGUSTIFOLIA 'BACKHOUSE PURPLE'
(synonyms: **'Backhouse'**, **'Backhouse Nana'**)

Habit is upright, bushy and medium (60–70cm), with semi-open, mid-green foliage. Peduncles are grey–green, medium to long (16–23cm), and semi-upright. Semi-stalked laterals terminated with two to 20 flowers are frequent. Spikes are medium (3–7cm), fusiform or cylindric and slightly interrupted, with the base whorl 1–3cm below the main spike. Fertile bracts are small to intermediate. Bracteoles are insignificant (0.5–1mm). Corollas are violet–blue (90C), calyces are pubescent and dark violet (86A).

Introduced by Mr Backhouse in the United Kingdom before 1962, 'Backhouse Purple' is suitable for ornamental and hedging purposes or as individual plants along a pathway.

LAVANDULA ANGUSTIFOLIA 'BEECHWOOD BLUE'

A medium plant (60cm), spherical in shape with moderately dense, mid-green foliage. There may be infrequent semi-stalked laterals, terminated with one or two flowers arranged either singly or one-sided. Peduncles are broad, long (18–24cm), mid-green and semi-upright. Spikes are long (8–10cm), slightly fusiform and mostly evenly interrupted, with the base whorl 1–4cm below the main spike. Fertile bracts are small. Bracteoles are insignificant (0.5mm). Corollas are bright violet–blue (90A), calyces are pubescent and dark violet (86A). The buds are similar in colour to the corollas (illustrated on page 72).

Raised in the United Kingdom by Beechwood, 'Beechwood Blue' is an attractive rounded bush suitable for ornamental, fragrant, culinary or hedging purposes.

LEFT

L. angustifolia
'Hidcote' Plant B

L. angustifolia
'Fiona English'

L. angustifolia 'Blue Bun'

L. angustifolia 'Coconut Ice'

L. angustifolia
'Beechwood Blue'

RIGHT

L. angustifolia 'Blue Bun'

LAVANDULA ANGUSTIFOLIA 'BLUE BUN'
(synonym: 'M1')

Habit is small (50cm) and spherical with dense grey–green foliage. Peduncles are mid-green, medium (16–19cm), upright and sometimes broad. Semi- to short-stalked laterals are present, terminated with one to three flowers. Spikes are medium (3–4cm), compact, cylindric and slightly interrupted, with the base whorl 1–1.5cm below the main spike. Fertile bracts are small. Bracteoles are insignificant (0.5–1mm). Corollas are bright violet–blue (90A), calyces are pubescent and green with dark violet tips (86A). Buds are green.

Named in New Zealand by Peter Smale, formerly of Crop and Food Research, New Zealand, in the mid-1990s, 'Blue Bun' is a small compact plant suitable for ornamental, low hedging and fragrant uses.

LAVANDULA ANGUSTIFOLIA 'BLUE CUSHION'
(synonym: 'Schola')

A small bushy plant (50cm) with dense mid-green foliage. Peduncles are medium (15–17cm), mid-green, thin and semi-upright. There may be occasional semi-stalked laterals terminated in one to three flowers, arranged either singly or one-sided. Spikes are medium (4–7cm), cylindric, sometimes fusiform and interrupted, with the base whorl 1–3cm below the main spike. Fertile bracts are broad. Bracteoles are narrow (1–2mm). Corollas are bright violet–blue (90B), calyces are pubescent and green with a tinge of slightly darker violet–blue (90A).

Introduced in the United Kingdom by Blooms of Bressingham in 1992, 'Blue Cushion' is a delightful, small compact plant suitable for container growing, hedging, ornamental and fragrant purposes.

LAVANDULA ANGUSTIFOLIA 'BLUE MOUNTAIN'

LEFT

L. angustifolia 'Princess Blue'

L. angustifolia 'Granny's Bouquet'

L. angustifolia 'Loddon Pink'

L. angustifolia 'Blue Cushion'

L. angustifolia 'Heacham Blue'

RIGHT

L. angustifolia 'Blue Cushion'

A medium plant (60cm) of bushy habit with dense grey–green foliage. Peduncles are short to medium (10–17cm), thin, grey–green and upright. There are occasional semi- to medium-stemmed laterals terminated with one to four flowers. Spikes are medium (5–7cm), cylindric and slightly interrupted, with the base whorl 1–5cm below the main spike. Fertile bracts are large. Bracteoles are tiny (0.5–1mm). Corollas are vibrant violet (88A), calyces are densely pubescent and dark violet (86A) (illustrated on pages 70 and 74).

Raised by Stan Hughes in New Zealand in the mid-1950s, 'Blue Mountain' was originally a seedling from the cultivar 'Alba', described earlier. Frequently used in landscaping, 'Blue Mountain' has proved a very popular dark-flowered cultivar, suitable for ornamental use, hedging and container growing because of its naturally compact form. It is one of the most fragrant of the dark-flowered cultivars and can be used for culinary purposes.

LAVANDULA ANGUSTIFOLIA 'BOSISTO'
(synonyms: **'Bosisto's'**, **'Bosisto's Variety'**)
A semi-tall plant (70–80cm) of upright bushy habit and dense grey–green foliage. Peduncles are long (16–22cm), mid-green and semi-upright. There may be an occasional semi-stalked lateral terminated with one to four flowers. Spikes are medium (4–5cm) and cylindric, with the base whorl 1–4cm below the main spike. Fertile bracts are large and broad. Bracteoles are thin or broad and branched (1–2mm). Corollas are large and dark lavender–violet (92A), calyces are densely pubescent and green suffused with dark violet (86A). The buds are much greener.

Raised in Australia and named after Joseph Bosisto in the 1920s, 'Bosisto', being a taller cultivar, may be used for a larger hedge or as an ornamental or fragrant plant.

L. angustifolia 'Blue Mountain'

LAVANDULA ANGUSTIFOLIA 'BOWLES EARLY'
(synonyms: **'Bowles'**, **'Bowles Early Dwarf'**, **'Bowles Variety'**,
'Miss Dunnington', **'Miss Donnington'** in part)
A small to medium plant (60cm) of upright bushy habit with dense mid-green foliage. Peduncles are soft grey–green, medium (14–18cm) and upright. There may be occasional semi-stalked laterals, terminated with one to five flowers. Spikes are short (2–3cm), cylindric, occasionally fusiform and interrupted, with the base whorl 1–2cm below the main spike. Fertile bracts are intermediate. Bracteoles are narrow (1–2mm). Corollas are bright violet–blue (90A) with similar-coloured, pubescent calyces (illustrated on page 76).

Introduced in the United Kingdom by Amos Perry about 1913, 'Bowles Early', with its compact upright growth, is suitable for low hedging and ornamental uses.

LAVANDULA ANGUSTIFOLIA 'BUDAKALASZI'
Habit is medium to semi-tall (60–70cm) and spherical with dense grey–green foliage. Peduncles are long (16–26cm), mid-green, semi-upright and occasionally broad. There may be infrequent semi-stalked laterals, terminated with one to three flowers. Spikes are medium to long (4–9cm), cylindric and interrupted, with the base whorl 2–3cm below the main spike. Fertile bracts are intermediate. Bracteoles are mostly insignificant (0.5–1mm). Corollas are a bright, vibrant violet–blue (90A), calyces are pubescent and dark violet (86A). In bud, though, the calyces are darker and appear to be more purple (illustrated on pages 77 and 81).

Raised from Hungarian seed by Virginia McNaughton in 1992, 'Budakalaszi' means 'spike of Buda' (as in Budapest). The plant may not be a true representation of its namesake but it is, nevertheless, a stunning plant with dark spikes evenly arranged across the bush and is suitable as a feature or an ornamental plant.

LEFT

L. angustifolia 'Bosisto'

CENTRE

L. angustifolia 'Rosea'
L. angustifolia 'Munstead'
L. angustifolia
'Hidcote Pink'
L. angustifolia 'Bosisto'
L. angustifolia
'Violet Intrigue'

RIGHT

L. angustifolia 'Bosisto'
at rear:
L. angustifolia
'Budakalaszi'

LAVANDULA ANGUSTIFOLIA 'BUENA VISTA'

A medium plant (50–70cm) of bushy habit with mid-green foliage. Peduncles are medium (14–20cm), semi-upright and mostly thin. There may be occasional semi-stalked laterals terminated with one to five flowers. Spikes are long (7–12cm), cylindric and mostly evenly interrupted, with the base whorl 1–4cm below the main spike. Fertile bracts are intermediate. Bracteoles are insignificant (0.5mm). Corollas are large and a vibrant violet–blueberry (89C). Calyces are pubescent and dark violet–blue (93A) (illustrated on page 70).

Raised by Dr Don Roberts in the United States, 'Buena Vista' is a striking plant with picturesque long interrupted spikes that give the plant a certain grace. Suitable for fragrant craft work or as an ornamental plant.

LAVANDULA ANGUSTIFOLIA 'CEDAR BLUE'

(synonym: **'Hidcote'** in part)

Habit is upright and bushy but small (50–60cm), with dense grey–green foliage. Peduncles are short to medium (10–17cm), very thin and upright. There may be infrequent semi-stalked laterals terminated with one to three flowers, arranged either singly or one-sided. Spikes are short (2–3cm), mostly cylindric and interrupted, with the base whorl 1–3cm below the main spike. Fertile bracts are medium. Bracteoles are insignificant (0.5mm). Corollas are violet–blue (90C), calyces are pubescent and green with dark violet tips (86A) (illustrated on page 71).

'Cedar Blue' resembles a miniature 'Bosisto' in form and is suitable for container growing, ornamental and low hedging purposes. It was named in 1994 by Muntons Microplants Ltd, United Kingdom.

LAVANDULA ANGUSTIFOLIA 'CELESTIAL STAR'

A semi-tall plant (70cm), upright and bushy in habit with dense mid-green foliage. Peduncles are long (18–30cm), upright and mid-green with darker edges. There may be an occasional short-stemmed lateral with one to three flowers present. Spikes are mid-green, long (7–12cm), cylindric and interrupted, with the base whorl 1–5cm below the spike. Fertile bracts are broad. Bracteoles are narrow (0.5–2mm). Corollas are white, calyces are densely pubescent and green (illustrated on pages 69 and 78).

Found mislabelled as *L. latifolia* in a Christchurch garden, 'Celestial Star' was renamed by Virginia McNaughton, New Zealand, in the early 1990s. It is a bold, vase-shaped cultivar, makes quite a striking hedging or ornamental plant, and is suitable for fragrant crafts.

LAVANDULA ANGUSTIFOLIA 'COCONUT ICE'

Habit is small (50cm) and bushy with semi-open to dense grey–green foliage. Peduncles are long (20–24cm), mid-green and upright. There may be an occasional semi-stalked lateral terminated with one to four flowers. Spikes are medium to

L. angustifolia 'Budakalaszi'

long (4–9cm), mostly cylindric and interrupted, with the base whorl 1–4cm below the main spike. Fertile bracts are small to intermediate. Bracteoles are thin (0.5–1mm). Corollas are dark mauve–pink (75A) or white, calyces are green tinged with dark red–purple (71A). Buds are pale green (illustrated on pages 66, 72 and 79).

Raised in New Zealand by Virginia McNaughton in 1994, 'Coconut Ice' has both pink and white flowers on the same spike and is suitable for ornamental planting, low hedging, fragrant use or container growing.

LAVANDULA ANGUSTIFOLIA 'COMMON'

Habit is bushy to almost spherical and medium (60–70cm) with dense mid-green foliage. Peduncles are medium to long (17–23cm), mid-green and mostly semi-upright. There may be occasional semi- to short-stemmed laterals present terminated with one to three flowers. They are either arranged singly or one-sided. Spikes are medium to long (6–10cm), fusiform or cylindric and interrupted, with the base whorl 1–3cm below the main spike. Fertile bracts are very broad. Bracteoles are thin (1–2mm). Corollas are dark lavender–violet (92A), calyces are densely pubescent and rich violet–blue (89A). The buds tend to be bright violet–blue (90A) (illustrated on page 80).

Referred to as 'Common' probably because it was brought to New Zealand during the nineteenth century as seed, it is a compact fragrant, ornamental or hedging plant.

LAVANDULA ANGUSTIFOLIA 'CRYSTAL LIGHTS'

A very small plant (40cm) of bushy to rounded habit and dense, mid-green to light green foliage. Peduncles are light green, short (8–10cm), thin to medium, and semi-upright. There may be a rare semi-stalked lateral, terminated in one to three flowers. Spikes are medium (4–6cm), quite compact, cylindric, mostly evenly interrupted with an occasional base whorl 1cm below the main spike. Fertile bracts are broad. Bracteoles are thin (1–2mm). Corollas are white, calyces are finely pubescent and green (193A) (also illustrated on page 69).

Raised by Virginia McNaughton, New Zealand, in the mid-1980s, 'Crystal Lights' is slightly taller and more compact than 'Nana Alba'. Peduncles and spikes tend to be even in length with distribution across the plant, giving it an almost spherical shape. Suitable for pot growing, ornamental purposes, low hedging or for fragrant crafts. Also effective when planted beside other small darker-flowering cultivars such as 'Blue Cushion', 'Thumbelina Leigh' or 'Lavenite Petite'.

ABOVE
L. angustifolia 'Crystal Lights'

BELOW
L. angustifolia 'Celestial Star'

LAVANDULA ANGUSTIFOLIA 'EGERTON BLUE'

A semi-tall to large plant (70–90cm) of bushy habit, and semi-open to dense grey–green foliage. Peduncles are medium (15–22cm), mid-green and semi-upright. There are frequent semi- to medium-stemmed laterals, terminated with one to three flowers. Spikes are medium to long (6–10cm), cylindric and interrupted, with the base whorl 1–5cm below the main spike. Fertile bracts are intermediate to broad and long.

Bracteoles are tiny (0.5–1mm). Corollas are very bright violet–blue (90A) and calyces are dark violet (86A) (illustrated on page 81).

'Egerton Blue', formerly known as *L. angustifolia* 'Vera', was raised in Australia by Rosemary Holmes and Edythe Anderson in the early 1980s. Following a selection process and in order to avoid further confusion, it was decided in 1997 that the name 'Egerton Blue' should replace the selected form of 'Vera'. It is suitable as an ornamental, fragrant and oil plant.

LAVANDULA ANGUSTIFOLIA 'FIONA ENGLISH'

Habit is bushy and medium (60–70cm) with dense mid-green foliage. Peduncles are medium (15–19cm), mid-green and semi-upright. Occasional semi- to short-stemmed laterals terminated with one to five flowers, either single or one-sided, may occur. Spikes are medium (4–6cm), cylindric, occasionally fusiform and interrupted, with the base whorl 1–2cm below the main spike. Fertile bracts are very broad. Bracteoles are narrow (1–2mm). Corollas are dark lavender (94C), calyces are pubescent and a much brighter violet–blue (90A) (illustrated on page 72).

Named by Peter Carter, New Zealand, in the early 1990s, 'Fiona English' is suitable for hedging, fragrant or ornamental purposes. Like the cultivar 'Common', this plant has been in New Zealand for many years.

LEFT

L. angustifolia 'Nana
Atropurpurea' Plant B

L. angustifolia 'Nana
Atropurpurea' Plant A

L. angustifolia
'Thumbelina Leigh'

L. angustifolia 'Common'

L. angustifolia 'Royal Purple'

RIGHT

L. angustifolia 'Common'

LAVANDULA ANGUSTIFOLIA 'FOLGATE'
(synonyms: **'Folgate Blue'**, **'Folgate Dwarf'**, **'Folgate Variety'**)
A medium plant (60–70cm) of bushy habit with dense mid-green foliage. Peduncles are medium (17–22cm), mid-green and upright. There are frequent semi- to short-stemmed laterals, terminated with one to four flowers, arranged either singly or in double pairs. Spikes are medium (3–8cm), mostly cylindric and slightly interrupted, with the base whorl 1–4cm below the main spike. Fertile bracts are broad. Bracteoles are broad and branched or narrow (1–2mm). Corollas range from soft violet–blue to bright violet–blue (90A). Calyces are reasonably pubescent and green with dark violet tips (86A).

Like many other cultivars, the identity of 'Folgate' has been confused over the years. I have seen various plants sold under this name. Released before 1933, 'Folgate' was imported to New Zealand in the early 1960s.

LAVANDULA ANGUSTIFOLIA 'FOVEAUX STORM'
A medium plant (60–70cm) of bushy habit and dense grey–green foliage. Peduncles are medium (14–19cm), grey–green with darkened edges and semi-upright. There are frequent semi-stalked laterals terminated with one to four flowers, either singly or one-sided. Spikes are medium (4–7cm), cylindric and slightly interrupted, with the base whorl 1cm below the main spike. Fertile bracts are intermediate. Bracteoles are insignificant (1–2mm). Corollas are dark vibrant violet (88A), calyces are densely pubescent and very dark violet–purple (83A). Buds are a slightly different violet from the flowers (also illustrated on page 82).

Raised in New Zealand by Geoff and Adair Genge in the early 1990s, 'Foveaux Storm' is the darkest of the dark violet-flowered cultivars and although slow-growing is one of the most spectacular in flower. It is suitable as a feature or ornamental plant, or for hedging.

CENTRE

L. angustifolia
'Egerton Blue' and
Achillea seedling

RIGHT

L. angustifolia
'Egerton Blue'

L. angustifolia
'Mystique'

L. angustifolia
'Pacific Pink'

L. angustifolia
'Budakalaszi'

L. angustifolia
'Foveaux Storm'

LAVANDULA ANGUSTIFOLIA 'FRING'

(synonyms: **'Fring Favourite'**, **'Fring A'**)

An attractive spherical plant of medium height (60–70cm) with semi-open to open grey–green foliage. Peduncles are grey–green, long (20–27cm) and splayed. There are frequent semi-stalked laterals terminated with one to six flowers, either single or one-sided. Spikes are long (7–9cm), cylindric or fusiform, mostly evenly interrupted with the base whorl 4–6cm below the main spike. Fertile bracts are small to intermediate. Bracteoles are insignificant (1–2mm). Corollas are bright violet–blue (90A), calyces are pubescent and a darker violet–blue (illustrated on pages 71 and 82).

A field variety raised at Norfolk Lavender, United Kingdom, 'Fring' is a particularly attractive cultivar suitable as an ornamental or feature plant. It requires hard pruning.

LAVANDULA ANGUSTIFOLIA 'GRANNY'S BOUQUET'

A very small plant (40cm), round and compact with dense mid-green foliage and masses of flower spikes. Peduncles are very thin, mid-green, short to medium (10–14cm), and semi-upright. There may be occasional semi-stalked laterals terminated with one flower, either single or one-sided. Spikes are short to medium (2–6cm), compact, cylindric and interrupted, with the base whorl 2–4cm below the main spike. Fertile bracts are small. Bracteoles are insignificant (0.5mm). Corollas are large and vibrant violet (88A). Calyces are pubescent and green with a tinge of bright violet–blue (90A) (illustrated on pages 73 and 82).

Raised by Virginia McNaughton and Dennis Matthews, New Zealand, in the mid-1990s, 'Granny's Bouquet' is a very compact lavender suitable for container growing, low hedging or ornamental purposes. Its name derives from its unusual fragrance.

LAVANDULA ANGUSTIFOLIA 'GRAY LADY'

Habit is medium (60–70m) and bushy with dense grey–green foliage. Peduncles are medium (15–22cm), mid-green and semi-upright. There may be short-stemmed laterals terminated with one flower, arranged either singly or as a double pair. Spikes are medium (5–6cm), cylindric and slightly interrupted, with the base whorl 1–1.5cm below the main spike. Fertile bracts are intermediate. Bracteoles are insignificant (0.5mm). Corollas are bright violet–blue (90A), calyces are densely pubescent and a slightly darker violet–blue.

Possibly of United States origin, the version of 'Gray Lady' grown in New Zealand is very similar to 'Hidcote' (Plant A) in habit.

LAVANDULA ANGUSTIFOLIA 'HEACHAM BLUE'
(synonym: **'G4'**)

A medium plant (60–70cm) of bushy habit and semi-open to dense mid-green foliage. Peduncles are mid-green, long (22–28cm) and splayed. There may be an occasional semi-stalked lateral terminated with two to three flowers. The arrangement is mostly one-sided. Spikes are medium to long (6–12cm), mostly cylindric, occasionally fusiform and interrupted, with the base whorl 2–3cm below the main spike. Fertile bracts are large and broad. Bracteoles are insignificant (0.5mm). Corollas are bright violet–blue (90A), calyces are pubescent and dark violet (86A) (illustrated on pages 73 and 84).

Raised as a field variety at Norfolk Lavender, United Kingdom, 'Heacham Blue' is an attractive blue-flowered cultivar suitable as an ornamental or hedging plant.

LAVANDULA ANGUSTIFOLIA 'HELEN BATCHELDER'

A medium plant (60–70cm) of bushy habit with dense grey–green foliage. Peduncles are medium (12–23cm), thin, grey–green and semi-upright. Spikes are medium (3–4cm), cylindric and interrupted, with the base whorl 1–3cm below the main spike.

Fertile bracts are small to intermediate and broad at the base. Bracteoles are short and broad (0.5–1mm). Corollas are bright violet–blue (90A), calyces are pubescent and a lighter violet–blue (93C).

Raised in the United States, 'Helen Batchelder' is suitable for ornamental and fragrant purposes.

LAVANDULA ANGUSTIFOLIA 'HIDCOTE'
(synonyms: 'Hidcote Blue', 'Hidcote Purple', 'Hidcote Variety')
For many years, the true identity of 'Hidcote' has remained one of the most confused in the lavender world. Unfortunately 'Hidcote' continues to be grown from seed and sold to an unsuspecting public. Plant A represented here has been maintained as a cutting source for over 50 years, while Plant B seems to have appeared in the marketplace during the 1990s, also proclaimed to be the true 'Hidcote'.

PLANT A
A medium bushy plant (60–70cm) with dense grey–green foliage. Peduncles are medium (12–22cm), mid-green and semi-upright. There are semi-stalked laterals terminated with one to three flowers, mostly single, but sometimes double. Spikes are medium (3–7cm), cylindric and slightly interrupted, with the base whorl 1–2cm below the main spike. Fertile bracts are intermediate. Bracteoles are insignificant (0.5mm). Corollas are vibrant violet (88A), calyces are densely pubescent and dark violet (86A) (illustrated on page 84).

Plant A appears to be the traditional type of 'Hidcote' that has become so well loved by gardening enthisiasts. Two other similar cultivars are 'Gray Lady' and 'Tom Garbutt'. Likewise 'Imperial Gem' bears a resemblance, but was bred many years after 'Hidcote'.

PLANT B (synonym: 'Peter Pan')
A medium bushy plant (60cm) with dense grey–green foliage. Peduncles are mid-green, medium (10–15cm) but shorter than Plant A, and semi-upright. There may be semi- and short-stemmed laterals terminated in one to three flowers, and these are usually one-sided. Spikes are medium and compact (3–5cm), with an occasional base whorl 1cm below the main spike. Fertile bracts are intermediate. Bracteoles are thin (1–2mm). Corollas are violet–blue (90C), calyces are densely pubescent and bright violet–blue (86A). Buds are more violet (90A) (illustrated on page 85).

Plant B is different from Plant A in having much plumper spikes and slightly denser foliage.

'Hidcote' was raised by Major Lawrence Johnston in the United Kingdom before 1950 and is a wonderful dark-flowered cultivar for ornamental use, hedging or feature plants and can be spectacular when planted en masse.

LAVANDULA ANGUSTIFOLIA 'HIDCOTE PINK'

A medium plant (70cm) of bushy to spherical habit possessing attractive dense grey–green foliage. Peduncles are medium (15–19cm), thin and semi-upright. There may be a rare short-stemmed lateral terminated with one to three flowers. Spikes are mostly fusiform, occasionally cylindric and medium to long (6–8cm), with the base whorl 1–2.5cm below the main spike. Fertile bracts are intermediate. Bracteoles are insignificant (0.5–1mm). Corollas are a mixture of mauve–pink (69B) and lavender–pink (69C). Calyces are densely pubescent and green suffused with bright red–purple (70A) (also illustrated on page 75).

Introduced by Major Lawrence Johnston, United Kingdom, before 1958, 'Hidcote Pink' is densely and evenly covered in spikes, and is one of the best pink-flowered cultivars for ornamental or hedging purposes. Quite striking when planted en masse, 'Hidcote Pink' has quite pink flowers when they open but they fade quickly. However, this does not detract from its overall effect.

LAVANDULA ANGUSTIFOLIA 'IMPERIAL GEM'
(synonym: **'Nana 1'**)

Habit is bushy and medium (60–70cm) with dense grey–green foliage. There may be occasional semi-stalked laterals terminated with one to three flowers. The arrangement is either single or one-sided. Peduncles are medium (10–19cm), mid-green to grey–green, and semi-upright. Spikes are medium (4–6cm), mostly cylindric and interrupted, with

the base whorl 1–2cm below the main spike. Fertile bracts are intermediate to broad. Bracteoles are insignificant (0.5mm). Corollas are vibrant violet (88A), calyces are densely pubescent and dark violet (86A) (illustrated on page 88).

Raised in the United Kingdom by Norfolk Lavender in the late 1960s, 'Imperial Gem' is very similar to 'Hidcote' Plant A. It differs slightly in having wider peduncles and being a better-formed bush. It can be used for similar purposes.

LAVANDULA ANGUSTIFOLIA 'IRENE DOYLE'

Habit is small to medium (50–60cm) and bushy with dense mid-green to grey–green foliage. Peduncles are short (8–12cm), dark green and semi-upright. There are frequent semi- to short-stemmed laterals terminated with one to eight flowers, which may be single or double. Spikes are short to medium (3–4cm), mostly cylindric and slightly interrupted, with the base whorl 2–4cm below the main spike. Fertile bracts are intermediate. Bracteoles are insignificant (0.5mm). Corollas are dark violet–blue (93B), calyces are finely pubescent and green with deep purple tips (79A) (illustrated on pages 86 and 91).

Raised in the United States by Tom DeBaggio in 1983, 'Irene Doyle' is a popular blue-flowered cultivar suitable for fragrant or ornamental purposes, low hedging or container growing. It is sometimes called 'Two Seasons lavender' because of its ability to flower twice in one season, a trait shared with many other *L. angustifolia* cultivars.

L. angustifolia 'Irene Doyle'

LAVANDULA ANGUSTIFOLIA 'JEAN DAVIS'

A medium plant (60–70cm) of upright habit and dense grey–green foliage. Peduncles are thin, medium to long (12–25cm), and semi-upright. Spikes are medium (5–7cm), cylindric, occasionally fusiform and interrupted, with the base whorl 1–4cm below the main spike. Fertile bracts are small. Bracteoles are insignificant (0.5–1mm). Corollas are soft lavender–pink (69C) with shades of mauve–pink (69B). Calyces are densely pubescent and green tinged with red–purple (64A) (illustrated on page 76).

Uses are similar to those for 'Rosea'.

LAVANDULA ANGUSTIFOLIA 'LADY'
(synonyms: **'Atlee Burpee'**, **'Burpee'**, **'Lavender Lady'**)

A small bushy plant (40–50cm) with open mid-green foliage. The peduncles are short (6–13cm) and thin with mostly semi-stalked laterals bearing one to three flowers. Spikes are also short (1–3cm) and globular-cylindric or sometimes fusiform, with the occasional base whorl 1–2cm below the main spike. Fertile bracts are small and narrow. Bracteoles are small (0.5–1mm). Corollas are bright violet–blue (90A) with lighter throats, calyces are finely pubescent and dark violet (86A) (illustrated on page 88).

'Lady' was raised in the United States at W. Atlee Burpee and Company in 1993 and promoted as an annual bedding plant due to its ability to flower in the first year from seed. While this trait is not uncommon among lavenders, because of this publicity 'Lady' has continued to be produced from seed (instead of cuttings) by many nurseries, resulting in some interesting variations on the market. To keep its compact form, 'Lady' needs to be pruned hard in autumn to avoid its tendency to split open. It is suitable as an ornamental or low hedging plant, or can be added to pot pourri. It is occasionally incorrectly called 'Lavender Lady'.

LAVANDULA ANGUSTIFOLIA 'LAVENITE PETITE'

Habit is small (40–50cm) and bushy with dense mid-green foliage. Peduncles are medium (12–19cm), mid-green, very broad, and semi-upright to upright. There may be an occasional semi-stalked lateral, terminated with one to three flowers. Spikes are medium (5–8cm), cylindric and mostly evenly interrupted, with the base whorl 1–2cm below the main spike. Fertile bracts are intermediate. Bracteoles are thin or broad and branched (1–2mm). Corollas are vibrant violet–blue (90A/88A). Calyces are densely pubescent and a bright violet–blue (90A), whereas the buds tend to be darker (93A) (illustrated on page 76).

Raised by Virginia McNaughton in New Zealand in the late 1980s, 'Lavenite Petite' has a compact form suitable for container growing, low hedging and ornamental purposes.

LAVANDULA ANGUSTIFOLIA 'LITTLE LADY'
(synonym: **'Batland'**)
A small plant (40–50cm) of bushy habit with dense grey–green foliage. Peduncles are short (5–7cm), mid-green and semi-upright. Spikes are short to medium (2–4cm) and cylindric. Fertile bracts are small. Bracteoles are insignificant (0.5mm). Corollas are vibrant violet–blueberry (89C), calyces are mostly green with a touch of dark violet–purple (83A).

The cultivar **'Little Lottie'** (synonym: **'Clarmo'**), with pink corollas, is similar in habit to 'Little Lady'. Both are suitable for container or ornamental growing.

LAVANDULA ANGUSTIFOLIA 'LODDON BLUE'

A medium (60cm), more rounded bush with dense grey–green foliage. Peduncles are medium (14–18cm), mid-green to grey-green with darker green edges, and semi-upright. There are frequent semi- to short-stemmed laterals terminated with one to four flowers. These are usually arranged singly but occasionally as a double pair. Spikes are medium (4–7cm) and cylindric or occasionally fusiform and interrupted, with the base whorl 1–3cm below the main spike. Fertile bracts are intermediate. Bracteoles are thin (1–2mm). Corollas are bright violet–blue (90B), calyces are densely pubescent and dark violet (86A). Buds are deeper violet–blue (illustrated on page 90).

Introduced by Thomas Carlile, United Kingdom, before 1963, 'Loddon Blue' can be used as an ornamental plant, for hedging or craft work. Although considered a dark-flowered form, it is not as dark as 'Hidcote'.

L. *angustifolia*
'Twickel Purple'

L. *angustifolia*
'Hidcote' Plant A

L. *angustifolia*
'Lady'

L. *angustifolia*
'Imperial Gem'

L. *angustifolia*
'The Colour Purple'

LAVANDULA ANGUSTIFOLIA 'LODDON PINK'

Habit is medium (50–60cm) and bushy with dense mid-green foliage. Peduncles are long (19–28cm), mid-green and semi-upright. There may be an occasional semi-stalked lateral terminated with one to five flowers. Spikes are medium to long (6–10cm), fusiform or cylindric and interrupted, with the base whorl 3–4cm below the main spike. Fertile bracts are small to intermediate. Bracteoles are thin (0.5–1mm). Corollas are pink (69A) and mauve–pink (69B), calyces are densely pubescent and mostly green with dark red–purple tips (71A) (illustrated on page 73).

Introduced before 1950 by Thomas Carlile, United Kingdom, 'Loddon Pink' is one of the darker pink cultivars with upright growth used for its ornamental and fragrant qualities.

LAVANDULA ANGUSTIFOLIA 'LULLABY'
(synonym: **'Lullaby Pink'**)

A medium plant (60–70cm) of bushy habit and dense grey–green foliage. Peduncles are medium (15–19cm), mid-green and semi-upright. There are occasional short-stemmed laterals terminated with one to three flowers which are mostly single, sometimes one-sided. Spikes are long (8–11cm), mostly cylindric or occasionally fusiform, with the base whorl 2–6cm below the main spike. Fertile bracts are small to intermediate. Bracteoles are insignificant (0.5–1mm). Corollas are large and pale with a slight tinge of lavender–pink (69C), calyces are densely pubescent and green with a touch of red–purple (72A) (illustrated on pages 70 and 91).

Formerly released as seed by Watkins Seed Company, New Zealand, in the mid-1990s, 'Lullaby' can be used for similar purposes as for other pink-flowered cultivars.

LAVANDULA ANGUSTIFOLIA 'LULLABY BLUE'

Habit is bushy and medium (60cm) with dense mid-green foliage. Peduncles are mid-green, medium (13–19cm), semi-upright and occasionally broad. There may be occasional semi-stalked laterals terminated with two to six flowers. Spikes are medium (4–5cm), cylindric or occasionally fusiform and interrupted, with the base whorl 2cm below the main spike. Fertile bracts are small. Bracteoles are insignificant (0.5mm). Corollas are lavender–violet (91A), calyces are densely pubescent and green with violet–blue tips (94B) (illustrated on page 70).

Raised in New Zealand by Peter Carter in the mid-1990s, this cultivar is a blue form of 'Lullaby' and an attractive small plant suited to container growing, and ornamental or fragrant use.

LAVANDULA ANGUSTIFOLIA 'MAILLETTE'

A medium plant (60–70cm) of bushy habit with semi-open, mid-green foliage. Peduncles are long (18–25cm), mid-green and upright. There are usually medium-stemmed laterals terminated with one to three flowers. Spikes are long (12–18cm), cylindric and mostly evenly interrupted, with the base whorl 1–7cm below the main spike. Fertile bracts are large and quite long. Bracteoles are thin (1–2mm). Corollas are violet–blue (93C), calyces are finely pubescent and green, with the upper half dark violet (86A) (illustrated on page 91).

A very attractive cultivar raised in France and introduced by Pierre Grosso, 'Maillette' is suitable for ornamental, fragrant and oil purposes.

LAVANDULA ANGUSTIFOLIA 'MARTHA RODERICK'

A small plant (50cm) of bushy habit and dense grey foliage. Peduncles are short (10–13cm), mid-green and semi-upright. There may be semi- and short-stemmed laterals terminated with one to three flowers, mostly single and occasionally one-sided. Spikes are medium (3–6cm), cylindric and interrupted, with the base whorl 1–3cm below the main spike. Fertile bracts are intermediate to broad. Bracteoles are tiny (0.5–1mm). Corollas are bright violet–blue (90B), calyces are densely pubescent and green suffused with a little dark violet–purple (83A) (illustrated on page 91).

Raised in the United States, 'Martha Roderick' makes a good container and smaller ornamental and fragrant plant.

LAVANDULA ANGUSTIFOLIA 'MAUSEN DWARF'

A medium plant (60–70cm) of bushy habit with semi-open to dense mid-green foliage. Peduncles are long (15–30cm), mid-green and semi-upright. Short to medium-stemmed laterals may occur terminated with one to two flowers, arranged either singly or as a double pair. Spikes are medium to long (6–13cm), fusiform or cylindric and interrupted,

L. angustifolia 'Okamurasaki'

L. angustifolia 'Sharon Roberts'

L. angustifolia 'Loddon Blue'

L. angustifolia 'Sarah'

L. angustifolia 'Tom Garbutt'

with the base whorl 1–6cm below the main spike. Fertile bracts are broad. Bracteoles are thin (1–2mm). Corollas are dark lavender (94C), calyces are pubescent and dark violet (86A).

The name 'Mausen Dwarf' has resulted from a case of mistaken identity. Originally it was a plant being trialed at the former Redbank Research Station, New Zealand, as part of its selection of 'Munstead'. A nursery misinterpreted the name 'Munstead Dwarf', calling it 'Mausen Dwarf' instead. It is quite different from its supposed namesake, but the name 'Mausen Dwarf' has stayed with the plant in the marketplace and is probably now impossible to eradicate. It is an impressive plant in full flower, growing larger than 'Munstead'.

A good hedging plant with fragrant and ornamental uses.

LAVANDULA ANGUSTIFOLIA 'MELISSA'
A medium plant (60–70cm) of upright bushy habit and dense grey–green foliage. Peduncles are medium (14–23cm), very thin, mid-green and semi-upright. Spikes are medium (3–4cm), cylindric or fusiform and interrupted, with the base whorl 1–3cm below the main spike. Fertile bracts are small to medium. Bracteoles are insignificant (0.5–1mm). Corollas are soft lavender–pink (69C) fading slightly darker, calyces are densely pubescent and mostly green with bright red–purple tips (illustrated on page 76).

Raised in the United States by Andrew Van Hevelingen, 'Melissa' is a delicate pink-flowered cultivar suitable for ornamental or hedging purposes.

LAVANDULA ANGUSTIFOLIA 'MIDHALL'
Habit is small (40–50cm) and bushy with semi-open, mid-green foliage. Peduncles are medium (13–23cm), grey–green with darkened edges, very thin and semi-upright. There may be occasional semi-stalked laterals terminated in one or two flowers, arranged singly

RIGHT
from front:

L. angustifolia
'Lullaby'

L. angustifolia
'Irene Doyle'

L. angustifolia
'Nana Atropurpurea'
Plant A

BELOW LEFT

L. angustifolia
'Maillette'

BELOW RIGHT

L. angustifolia
'Purple Pixie'

L. angustifolia
'Martha Roderick'

L. angustifolia
'Maillette'

L. angustifolia
'Tucker's Early Purple'

L. angustifolia
'Otago Haze'

or one-sided. Spikes are medium (4–7cm), cylindric or occasionally fusiform and slightly interrupted, with the base whorl 2cm below the main spike. Fertile bracts are small to intermediate. Bracteoles are insignificant (0.5mm). Corollas are dark lavender–violet (92A), calyces are densely pubescent and green with the upper half a dark lavender–violet (92A) like the corollas.

'Midhall' was discovered in a New Zealand nursery in the 1950s and is not commonly available. A small plant suitable for ornamental uses.

LAVANDULA ANGUSTIFOLIA 'MISS KATHERINE'

A semi-tall plant (70cm) of bushy habit and dense grey–green foliage. Peduncles are long (26–30cm), mid-green and upright. There may be an occasional short-stemmed lateral terminated with one to six flowers. Spikes are long (7–11cm), fusiform and occasionally cylindric, mostly evenly interrupted with the base whorl 4–6cm below the main spike. Fertile bracts are intermediate and long. Bracteoles are insignificant (0.5–1mm). Corollas are soft lavender–purple (76A) with a touch of vibrant red–violet (88C). Calyces are pubescent and grey–green with a tinge of red–purple (72A) (also illustrated on page 76).

LEFT AND RIGHT

L. angustifolia 'Miss Katherine'

Raised by Norfolk Lavender, United Kingdom, 'Miss Katherine' is a lilac–pink cultivar that has a beautiful form and can be easily seen from a distance. Use in borders as a feature, or as an ornamental plant or hedge.

LAVANDULA ANGUSTIFOLIA 'MITCHAM GRAY'
(synonym: **'Mitcham'**)
A small to medium plant (60–70cm) of bushy habit with semi-open grey foliage. Peduncles are medium (16–22cm), very thin, grey–green and upright. There may be semi-stalked laterals terminated with one to three flowers. Spikes are medium (3–6cm), cylindric and mostly evenly interrupted, with the base whorl 1–2cm below the main spike. Fertile bracts are intermediate. Bracteoles are narrow or broad (0.5–1mm). Corollas are bright violet–blue (90A), calyces are quite pubescent and deep purple (79A). In bud, the calyces are darker violet (86A) (illustrated on page 70).

Similar to 'Hidcote' in its uses.

LAVANDULA ANGUSTIFOLIA 'MUNSTEAD'
(synonyms: **'Dwarf Munstead'**, **'Munstead Blue'**, **'Munstead Dwarf'**, **'Munstead Variety'**)
Habit is bushy and medium (60–70cm) with dense mid-green foliage. Peduncles are mid-green, medium (14–23cm) and semi-upright. Occasional short to medium-stemmed laterals, terminated with one to four flowers, do occur. Spikes are medium to long (6–13cm), fusiform or cylindric and interrupted, with the base whorl 1–5cm below the main spike. Fertile bracts are intermediate. Bracteoles are thin (1–2mm). Corollas are dark lavender–violet (92A), calyces are finely pubescent and a rich violet–blue (89A). Buds are dark violet (93A) (illustrated on pages 75 and 95).

'Munstead' is reputed to have been raised by Gertrude Jekyll, United Kingdom. Introduced by Barr in 1916, it is well suited to hedging, and fragrant or ornamental use. Unfortunately, it continues to be grown from seed in many nurseries and there are now many variations available in the marketplace.

LAVANDULA ANGUSTIFOLIA 'MYSTIQUE'
(synonym: **'Bedazzled'**)
A small plant (40–50cm) of bushy habit with semi-open, mid-green foliage. Peduncles are medium (14–17cm), broad, mid-green with distinctive darkened edges and semi-upright. There may be occasional semi-stalked laterals terminated with three or four flowers, arranged either singly or one-sided. Spikes are long (5–15cm), cylindric and interrupted, with the base whorl 1–7cm below the main spike. Fertile bracts are intermediate. Bracteoles are small, broad and branched, occasionally narrower (1–2mm). Corollas are large and very vibrant violet (88A). Calyces are pubescent and green with a touch of dark violet (86A) (illustrated on pages 81 and 95).

Raised by Virginia McNaughton, New Zealand, in 1991, 'Mystique' is an unusual plant with vibrant-coloured corollas which are in striking contrast to the calyces. The peduncles also tend to be very wavy. It is best planted en masse for effect or to brighten up a corner.

LAVANDULA ANGUSTIFOLIA 'NANA'

The original plant described as 'Nana' was small (40–50cm) and similar to 'Hidcote' in appearance. However, the 'Nana' cultivar that is frequenting the marketplace is nothing like the original, being of medium height (60–70cm) with dark lavender flowers. I have not described it in detail, as it is not the true cultivar released under this name.

A further confusing factor is the synonyms for 'Imperial Gem' and 'Princess Blue', namely 'Nana 1' and 'Nana 2' respectively.

LAVANDULA ANGUSTIFOLIA 'NANA ALBA'
(synonyms: **'Dwarf White'**, **'Baby White'**)

Habit is bushy and very small (30–40cm) with dense grey–green foliage. Peduncles are short (6–12cm), mid-green to grey–green, semi-upright and thin. There may be occasional semi-stalked laterals, terminated with one to three flowers. Spikes are medium (4–5cm), cylindric and interrupted, with the base whorl 1–2cm below the main spike. Fertile bracts are intermediate. Bracteoles are narrow or slightly broader (1–2mm). Corollas are white, calyces and buds green (193A) and pubescent (illustrated on pages 69 and 96).

Raised in the United Kingdom before 1938 by Musgrave, 'Nana Alba' is the smallest white-flowered lavender and is suitable for pot growing, and ornamental or fragrant uses.

LAVANDULA ANGUSTIFOLIA 'NANA ATROPURPUREA'
(synonym: **'Atropurpurea'**)

'Nana Atropurpurea' was raised in the United Kingdom by Logan before 1923, but like some other lavender cultivars has been mistakenly identified over the years. The following two cultivars have both been proclaimed as the true plant.

PLANT A (synonym: **'Midnight Blues'**)

Habit is bushy and medium (60–70cm) with dense grey–green foliage. Peduncles are medium (14–20cm), slightly grey–green and semi-upright. There are frequent semi-stalked laterals terminated with one to five flowers which are mostly one-sided only. Spikes are medium to long (4–9cm), cylindric and mostly evenly interrupted, with the occasional base whorl 1cm below the main spike. Fertile bracts are very broad. Bracteoles are tiny (0.5–2mm). Corollas are vibrant violet (88A), calyces are densely pubescent and dark violet (86A).

This plant has been available in New Zealand under this name since the 1960s. It fulfils all the descriptions of a dark violet-flowered cultivar, very similar to 'Hidcote', which may in fact have given rise to 'Hidcote'. It is however a better specimen than 'Hidcote' (Plant A), having denser spikes and a more even and plentiful distribution of spikes across the bush (illustrated on pages 80, 91 and 96). This plant may also be sold under the name **'Purple Devil'**.

RIGHT

L. angustifolia 'Munstead'

BELOW

L. angustifolia 'Mystique'

Note the darkened edges of the stem — this characteristic is apparent in some plants but probably most notable in this cultivar.

PLANT B

A medium plant (60–70cm) of bushy habit and semi-open, grey–green foliage. Peduncles are medium to long (16–22cm), mid-green to grey–green with slightly darkened edges, and semi-upright. There are frequent semi-stalked laterals terminated with one to seven flowers, mostly one-sided. Spikes are long (9–16cm), cylindric and interrupted, with the base whorl 1–4cm below the main spike. Fertile bracts are very broad. Bracteoles are thin (0.5–1mm). Corollas are large and bright violet–blue (90A), calyces are densely pubescent and green with the upper half suffused with dark violet (86A) (illustrated on page 80).

Plant B was imported from Norfolk Lavender, United Kingdom, and is completely different from Plant A, having brighter but lighter-coloured flowers and more open foliage. It is also more fragrant than Plant A.

Both cultivars make wonderful ornamental, fragrant or feature plants.

LAVANDULA ANGUSTIFOLIA 'OKAMURASAKI'

A semi-tall plant (70cm) of bushy habit with semi-open, mid-green foliage. Peduncles are medium (14–20cm), mid-green and semi-upright. Spikes are medium to long (5–9cm), cylindric and interrupted, with the base whorl 1–5cm below the main spike. Fertile bracts are small but narrow and long. Bracteoles are insignificant (0.5–1mm). Corollas are very large and bright violet–blue (90A) with lighter throats, calyces are densely pubescent and dark violet (86A). The buds are lighter violet (illustrated on pages 90 and 98).

Meaning 'Purple Hill', 'Okamurasaki' was raised in Japan, and is a fragrant ornamental plant that attracts attention with its large flowers.

LAVANDULA ANGUSTIFOLIA 'OTAGO HAZE'

A small bushy plant (50cm) with dense grey foliage. Peduncles are short (9–11cm), thin, mid-green and upright. There may be semi- to short-stemmed laterals terminated with one to three flowers. The arrangement is usually single but may be one-sided. Spikes are short to medium (3–6cm), compact, cylindric and slightly interrupted, with the base whorl 1cm below the main spike. Fertile bracts are intermediate. Bracteoles are narrow or broad (1–2mm). Corollas are dark lavender–violet (92A) with white throats and prominent orange stamens. Calyces are finely pubescent and green with bright violet–blue tips (90A) (illustrated on page 91).

Named in the late 1990s by Jenny McGimpsey of Crop and Food Research, Redbank Research Centre, New Zealand, 'Otago Haze' is a charming compact plant, suitable for container growing, and for ornamental, hedging or fragrant purposes.

LAVANDULA ANGUSTIFOLIA 'PACIFIC BLUE'
(synonym: **'565/6'**)

A medium to semi-tall plant (60–70cm) of bushy to spherical habit with moderately dense mid-green foliage. Peduncles are long (26–32cm), mid-green and splayed. There are frequent semi- to long-stemmed laterals terminated with one to three flowers. Spikes are long (7–10cm), cylindric or fusiform and interrupted, with the base whorl 1–3cm below the main spike. Fertile bracts are intermediate. Bracteoles are insignificant (0.5mm). Corollas are bright violet–blue (90A), calyces are pubescent and dark violet–purple (83A). Buds are dark violet–blue (93A) (illustrated on page 100).

Imported from France to New Zealand, and named in the early 1990s by Peter Smale, formerly of Crop and Food Research, New Zealand, 'Pacific Blue' is a beautiful ornamental, hedging and oil plant.

LAVANDULA ANGUSTIFOLIA 'PACIFIC PINK'

Habit is bushy and medium (50–60cm) with moderately dense grey–green foliage. Peduncles are medium to long (19–22cm), thin, mid-green and upright. There may be occasional semi-stalked laterals terminated with two to four flowers. Spikes are medium (4–6cm), cylindric, occasionally fusiform and interrupted, with the base whorl 3–4cm below the main spike. Fertile bracts are small to intermediate. Bracteoles are insignificant (0.5mm). Corollas are mauve–pink (75A/B), calyces are pubescent and green with bright red–purple ribbing (70A) (illustrated on page 81).

Raised in New Zealand by Peter Carter in the mid-1990s, 'Pacific Pink' is a compact pink-flowered form of 'Pacific Blue', suitable for hedging or ornamental purposes.

L. angustifolia 'Okamurasaki'

LAVANDULA ANGUSTIFOLIA 'PRINCESS BLUE'
(synonym: **'Nana 2'**)

An upright bushy shrub, medium to semi-tall (70cm), with semi-open to dense mid-green foliage. Peduncles are medium (12–22cm), mid-green and upright. There may be infrequent short-stalked laterals terminated with one or two flowers, single or one-sided. Spikes are medium to long (6–10cm), mostly cylindric, occasionally fusiform and mostly evenly interrupted, with the base whorl 1–3cm below the main spike. Fertile bracts are small and narrow. Bracteoles are insignificant (0.5mm). Corollas are large and bright violet–blue (90A), calyces are finely pubescent and green with a touch of dark violet (86A) (illustrated on page 73).

Raised by Norfolk Lavender, United Kingdom, in the late 1960s, 'Princess Blue' is a lovely ornamental, feature and fragrant plant. With its upright habit, it is readily noticed in a garden.

LAVANDULA ANGUSTIFOLIA 'PURPLE PIXIE'
(synonym: **'982/6'**)

Habit is small to medium (50–60cm) and bushy with dense grey–green foliage. Peduncles are short (5–6cm), mid-green and semi-upright. Spikes are medium (5–6cm), cylindric and interrupted, with the base whorl 1–2cm below the main spike. Fertile bracts are intermediate. Bracteoles are narrow (1–2mm). Corollas are bright violet–blue (90A), calyces are densely pubescent and dark violet (86A) (illustrated on page 91).

Imported from France to New Zealand, and named in the mid-1990s by Peter Smale, formerly of Crop and Food Research, New Zealand, 'Purple Pixie' is suitable as an ornamental or container plant, or for hedging.

LAVANDULA ANGUSTIFOLIA 'ROSEA'
(synonyms: **'Nana Rosea'**, **'Pink'**)

A medium plant (60–70cm) of upright bushy habit and dense, light green foliage. Peduncles are mid-green, medium to long (16–23cm), and upright. There may be an occasional short-stemmed lateral terminated with one to four flowers, arranged either singly or as a double pair. Spikes are medium to long (5–9cm), cylindric and interrupted, with the base whorl 1–6cm below the main spike. Fertile bracts are small to intermediate. Bracteoles are tiny (0.1–1mm). Corollas are mauve–pink (69B), calyces are densely pubescent and green suffused with bright red–purple (70A) (illustrated on pages 75 and 100).

The traditional pink lavender, introduced before 1937, 'Rosea' is a compact plant suitable for hedging, for use as an ornamental plant or for fragrant crafts. Pink lavenders are shown to perfection planted against any of the dark-flowered cultivars.

Lavandula angustifolia 'Royal Velvet'

A small to medium plant (50–60cm) of bushy habit with semi-open grey–green foliage. Peduncles are medium (9–20cm), mid-green and semi-upright. There may be semi-stalked laterals terminated with one to three flowers. Spikes are medium to long (7–9cm), cylindric and interrupted, with the base whorl 2–4cm below the main spike. Fertile bracts are broad. Bracteoles are narrow (0.5–1mm). Corollas are bright violet–blue (90A), calyces are pubescent and dark violet (86A).

A striking dark-flowered cultivar raised by Andrew Van Hevelingen in the United States, 'Royal Velvet' is suitable for ornamental and feature planting or for fragrant crafts.

Lavandula angustifolia 'Sachet'

A medium plant (60–70cm), bushy in habit with semi-open, mid-green to grey–green foliage. Peduncles are mid-green, short to medium (10–15cm), thin and semi-upright. There may be infrequent semi-stalked laterals terminated with one to three flowers, mostly single but occasionally one-sided. Spikes are short to medium (2–5cm), cylindric, occasionally fusiform and interrupted, with the base whorl 1–2cm below the main spike. Fertile bracts are small to intermediate. Bracteoles are insignificant (0.5mm). Corollas are large and bright violet–blue (90A/B) with lighter throats, calyces are finely pubescent and green with the upper half suffused with violet–blue (93A) (illustrated on page 71).

Raised in the United States by Dr Don Roberts, 'Sachet' can be used as a fragrant or ornamental plant.

Lavandula angustifolia 'Sarah'

Habit is small (50cm) and bushy with semi-open, mid-green to grey–green foliage. Peduncles are medium (15–20cm), thin, mid-green and semi-upright to splayed. There may be infrequent semi-stalked laterals terminated with one flower. Spikes are medium to long (5–10cm), cylindric and interrupted, with the base whorl 1–4cm below the main spike. Fertile bracts are intermediate. Bracteoles are insignificant. Corollas are bright violet–blue (90A), calyces are densely pubescent and dark violet (86A) (illustrated on page 90).

Another attractive cultivar raised in the United States, 'Sarah' is suitable for hedging, and for fragrant or ornamental use.

Lavandula angustifolia 'Sharon Roberts'

A medium, bushy plant (60–70cm) with semi-open, mid-green to grey–green foliage. There may be semi-stalked laterals terminated with one flower, arranged either singly or as a double pair. Peduncles are medium to long (18–23cm), broad, mid-green with dark

edges, and semi-upright to splayed. Spikes are medium to long (6-10cm), cylindric and mostly evenly interrupted, with the base whorl 1–3cm below the main spike. Fertile bracts are intermediate. Bracteoles are thin (1–2mm). Corollas are bright violet–blue (90A) and calyces the same colour and quite pubescent (illustrated on page 90).

Raised in the United States by Dr Don Roberts, 'Sharon Roberts' is a lovely fragrant plant that can be grown for ornamental, fragrant or culinary uses.

LAVANDULA ANGUSTIFOLIA 'SOUTH POLE'

A small to medium plant (50–60cm) of bushy habit and open grey–green foliage. Peduncles are short to medium (7–12cm), mid-green, and semi-upright to splayed. There may be semi-stalked laterals terminated with one to four flowers. Spikes are short to medium (2–4cm), cylindric and slightly interrupted, with the base whorl 1–2cm below the spike. Fertile bracts are intermediate. Bracteoles are quite broad (1–2mm). Corollas are the softest lavender–lilac (85D), calyces are pubescent and green with a touch of dark violet (86A).

Raised in New Zealand by Peter Carter in the mid-1990s, 'South Pole' has very attractive, almost ice-blue flowers and can be grown as an interesting feature plant. Keep well pruned.

LAVANDULA ANGUSTIFOLIA 'SUSAN BELSINGER'

A small to medium plant (40–50cm) of bushy habit with semi-open grey foliage. Peduncles are short (6–10cm), thin, grey–green and semi-upright. There may be semi-stalked laterals terminated with one to three flowers, arranged either singly or one-sided. Spikes are short to medium (2–4cm), compact, cylindric and slightly interrupted, with an occasional base whorl 1cm below the main spike. Fertile bracts are small. Bracteoles are small, branched or insignificant (0.5–1mm). Corollas are bright violet–blue (90A/B), calyces are finely pubescent and green suffused with deep purple (79A).

Raised by Tom DeBaggio in the United States, 'Susan Belsinger' is suitable as a container, ornamental, fragrant or hedging plant.

LAVANDULA ANGUSTIFOLIA 'TARRAS'

A medium (60cm), upright, bushy shrub with mid-green to grey–green foliage. Peduncles are medium (10–19cm), mid-green with darker edges, and upright. There may be occasional semi-stalked laterals terminated with one to five flowers. Spikes are mostly cylindric, medium (4–7cm) and interrupted, with the base whorl 1–2cm below the main spike. Fertile bracts are very broad. Bracteoles are narrow (0.5–1mm). Corollas are violet–blue (93C), calyces are densely pubescent and green with dark violet tips (86A) (illustrated on page 71).

Named by Joy Chapman, New Zealand, 'Tarras' can be grown as a fragrant ornamental or oil plant.

LAVANDULA ANGUSTIFOLIA 'TASM'

(synonym: **'Tasmanian'**)

A spherical bush covered in masses of flower spikes, similar to 'Twickel Purple'. Foliage is mid-green to grey–green and open in habit. Plant is medium to semi-tall (70–80cm). Peduncles are mid-green, long (19–24cm) and splayed. There may be occasional semi-stalked laterals terminated with one to three flowers. Spikes are medium to long (7–9cm), cylindric or fusiform and interrupted, with the base whorl 1–2.5cm below the main spike. Fertile bracts are intermediate to broad. Bracteoles are narrow (0.5–1mm). Corollas are violet–blue (90B/C), calyces are pubescent and green with a tinge of bright violet–blue (90A).

Tasm was introduced into New Zealand, possibly from Tasmania (hence the synonym), by the former Department of Scientific and Industrial Research. Similar to 'Twickel Purple' in outline but quite different in other characteristics, 'Tasm' has a definite second flowering period and has proved popular as an ornamental, hedging, fragrant and oil plant.

LAVANDULA ANGUSTIFOLIA 'THE COLOUR PURPLE'

Habit is bushy and medium (60cm) with dense grey–green foliage. Peduncles are medium to long (15–24cm), grey–green and upright. There may be an occasional semi-stalked lateral terminated with one flower. Spikes are medium (3–6cm), fusiform, occasionally cylindric and mostly evenly interrupted, with the base whorl 1cm below the main spike. Fertile bracts are broad. Bracteoles are broad or narrow (1–2mm).

Corollas are a dark vibrant violet (86A), calyces are densely pubescent and dark purple–blue (also illustrated on page 88).

Grown by the former Department of Scientific and Industrial Research, New Zealand, and named in the early 1990s, 'The Colour Purple' is a most striking cultivar in flower, suitable for ornamental, hedging or fragrant use.

LAVANDULA ANGUSTIFOLIA 'THUMBELINA LEIGH'

A very small plant (40cm) of spherical habit with moderately dense, mid-green foliage. Peduncles are short (8–11cm), thin to medium, and semi-upright. There may be occasional semi-stalked laterals terminated with one to three flowers, arranged either singly or one-sided. Spikes are short (2–3cm) and very compact, cylindric or occasionally fusiform. Fertile bracts are small. Bracteoles are tiny (0.5–1mm). Corollas are large and a mixture of bright violet–blue (90A) and dark lavender–violet (92A). Calyces are pubescent and dark violet (86A).

Raised by Elsie and Brian Hall, New Zealand, in the mid-1990s, 'Thumbelina Leigh' is suitable for ornamental use, low hedging, fragrant crafts and container growing.

LAVANDULA ANGUSTIFOLIA 'TOM GARBUTT'

(synonym: **'Hidcote'** in part)

Habit is bushy and medium (60–70cm) with dense grey–green foliage. Peduncles are medium (12–21cm), mid-green to grey–green, and semi-upright. There are frequent semi- to short-stemmed laterals terminated with one to two flowers. Spikes are medium (4–7cm), cylindric and interrupted, with the base whorl 1–3cm below the main spike. Fertile bracts are intermediate. Bracteoles are insignificant (0.5–1mm). Corollas are very bright violet–blue (90A), calyces are pubescent and dark violet (86A) (illustrated on page 90).

Although named in New Zealand, this cultivar is remarkably similar in form to 'Hidcote' (Plant A) and is being sold under both names. Corollas may be a slightly different shade, but this could be cutting variation only. Use as for 'Hidcote'.

LAVANDULA ANGUSTIFOLIA 'TROLLA'

A small plant (50cm) of upright bushy habit with dense mid-green foliage. The grey–green peduncles are short (8–12cm), very thin and upright. Spikes are short (1–3cm), cylindric and interrupted, with the base whorl 1–2cm below the main spike. Fertile bracts are very small. Bracteoles are insignificant (0.5mm). Corollas are vibrant violet–blue (90A), calyces are pubescent and dark violet (86A).

Raised by Ruth Bookman, New Zealand, in the mid-1990s, 'Trolla' is used as an ornamental or small hedging plant.

OPPOSITE

L. angustifolia
'The Colour Purple'

LEFT

L. angustifolia
'Thumbelina Leigh'

RIGHT

L. angustifolia
'Violet Intrigue'

LAVANDULA ANGUSTIFOLIA 'TUCKER'S EARLY PURPLE'

A small to medium plant (50–60cm) of bushy habit with semi-open, grey–green foliage. Peduncles are medium (8–22cm), mid-green and semi-upright. There may be occasional semi- to short-stemmed laterals terminated with two to four flowers, arranged singly or as a double pair. Spikes are medium (4–6cm), cylindric and interrupted, with the base whorl 1–2cm below the main spike. Fertile bracts are very broad. Bracteoles are tiny (0.5–2mm). Corollas are bright violet–blue (90A) to purple, calyces are similar in colour and finely pubescent (illustrated on page 88).

Raised in the United States, 'Tucker's Early Purple' may be used as an ornamental, fragrant or container plant.

LAVANDULA ANGUSTIFOLIA 'TWICKEL PURPLE'
(synonyms: **'Twickle Purple'**, **'Twinkle Purple'**, **'Twickel'**, **'Twickes Purple'**)
A beautifully shaped lavender in flower, spherical and semi-tall (70–80cm), with open, mid-green to grey–green foliage. Peduncles are broad, long (26–34cm), mid-green and splayed. There may be occasional short to medium-stemmed laterals terminated with one to six flowers. Spikes are long (8–19cm), cylindric and interrupted, with the base whorl 1–7cm below the main spike. Fertile bracts are narrow in young spikes, broader in older spikes and often still green in flowering spikes. Bracteoles are small and branched, almost insignificant (0.5–2mm). Corollas are bright violet–blue (90B) fading to a dark lavender–violet (92A). Calyces are pubescent and dark violet (86A). Buds are a brighter violet (90A) (illustrated on page 88).

Raised in the Netherlands before 1922, and similar to a cascading fountain in full flower, 'Twickel Purple' is well suited as an ornamental or fragrant craft plant because of its long spikes. It may also be used as a hedge where a sprawling effect is desired or planted individually to display its full effect. It needs to be pruned regularly to maintain its rounded shape.

The cultivar known in New Zealand as **'Royal Purple'**, originally imported from Norfolk Lavender, United Kingdom, is very similar to 'Twickel Purple' in most respects. Peduncles are long (23–30cm) but possibly more upright than those of 'Twickel Purple'. Spikes are also long (8–17cm), cylindric and interrupted, with the base whorl 1–7cm below the main spike. Corolla and calyx colour is likewise similar (illustrated on page 80). 'Royal Purple' was raised at Norfolk Lavender, United Kingdom, during the 1940s.

LAVANDULA ANGUSTIFOLIA 'VIOLET INTRIGUE'
An upright bushy, semi-tall plant (70–80cm) with dense mid-green foliage. There are frequent semi-stalked laterals terminated with one to five flowers. Peduncles are very long (30–35cm), broad, mid-green and very upright. Spikes are long (9–12cm), cylindric and mostly evenly interrupted, with the base whorl 1–4cm below the main spike. Fertile bracts are broad. Bracteoles are insignificant (0.5mm). Corollas are vibrant violet (88A), calyces are densely pubescent and rich violet–blue (89A) (illustrated on pages 75 and 103).

Raised in New Zealand by Virginia McNaughton and Dennis Matthews in 1995, 'Violet Intrigue' is an impressive plant in flower, being very upright with an even distribution of spikes across the bush. Suitable as an ornamental, hedging or feature plant or for mass planting.

LAVANDULA ANGUSTIFOLIA 'WALLER'S MUNSTEAD'
Habit is bushy and medium to semi-tall (60–70cm) with semi-open, grey–green foliage. Peduncles are short to medium (6–15cm), mid-green and semi-upright. Spikes are medium (4–6cm), cylindric and interrupted, with the base whorl 1cm below the main spike. Fertile bracts are intermediate to broad. Bracteoles are insignificant (0.5–1mm). Corollas are large and violet–blue (90C), calyces are densely pubescent and dark violet–purple.

Named in the United States, 'Waller's Munstead' is different from the true 'Munstead', having more compact and evenly interrupted spikes. It is also more fragrant and is suitable for ornamental, fragrant, hedging or culinary purposes.

LAVANDULA ANGUSTIFOLIA 'WINTON'
A medium to semi-tall plant (60–70cm) of spherical habit and semi-open, mid-green foliage. Peduncles are long (17–25cm), mid-green and semi-upright. There may be an

occasional semi-stalked lateral terminated with one to four flowers. Spikes are medium to long (7–9cm), mostly cylindric and interrupted, with the base whorl 1–3cm below the main spike. Fertile bracts are intermediate. Bracteoles are tiny (0.5–1mm). Corollas are violet–blue (90C), calyces are finely pubescent and green with dark violet tips (86A). Buds are a brighter violet–blue (90B) (also illustrated on page 70).

Named by Geoff and Adair Genge, New Zealand, in the mid-1990s, 'Winton' is an attractive ornamental, fragrant or hedging plant which can also be used for culinary purposes.

L. angustifolia 'Winton'

CULTIVARS OF
Lavandula x *intermedia*

Lavandula x *intermedia* cultivars (lavandins) are sterile hybrids between *L. angustifolia* and *L. latifolia*. The plants themselves are not necessarily large, perhaps only 40–50cm, but in flower they are much taller than *L. angustifolia* cultivars. Long lateral branching of the peduncle above the main foliage line is common, but not always present. The laterals are usually arranged singly (a pair), as a double (two pairs) or triple (three pairs).

This lateral branching is generally terminated with small to long, well-formed spikes, although occasionally, in a plant such as *L.* x *intermedia* 'Alba', there may be only a few flowers present, as seen in *L. angustifolia* cultivars.

All cultivars have calyces and peduncles covered in hair to a greater or lesser extent, but the degree of pubescence is more of a distinguishing feature on calyces than peduncles.

Spikes in lavandins are usually 1.5–2cm wide, depending on the length and shape of the head. Lengths of spikes, bracteoles and peduncles are given in parentheses. However, these are subjective measurements taken in dry conditions and will alter in plants grown in wetter conditions.

All bracts in lavandins are fertile. Bracts at the base of the spike are often longer and narrower than the bracts immediately above. Bracteoles may be broader and more branched at the base of the spike and longer and narrower towards the top.

Although not mentioned in every description, all lavandins can be used for fragrant purposes but some are better suited than others. The majority of lavandins have a strong but

less sweet fragrance than *L. angustifolia* cultivars. The scent is generally sweeter towards the end of flowering (for lavandins), when most of the flowers on the spike have withered. These cultivars have long peduncles and strong fragrance, which make many of them ideal for fragrant crafts, fresh or dried flowers, and oil production.

Lavandin flowering occurs later than in *L. angustifolia* cultivars by a couple of weeks to a month, but earlier than *L. latifolia*.

LAVANDULA X INTERMEDIA 'ABRIALII'
(synonyms: **'Abrial'**, **'Abrialis'**)
Habit is bushy and semi-tall (70–80cm) with dense grey–green foliage. Peduncles are broad, mid-green, long (23–30cm), and upright. Lateral branching is long, mostly single, double or occasionally one-sided. Spikes are narrow-conical and long (7–12cm) with the base whorl absent or 1–4cm below the main spike. Fertile bracts are intermediate. Bracteoles are long, broad, branched (3mm) and plentiful. Corollas are violet–blue (90D), calyces are pubescent and bright violet–blue (90A). Buds are green with a touch of bright violet–blue (90A).

Grown as a field variety in France and introduced before 1935, 'Abrialii' has well-shaped, elegant spikes and is popular as an oil, fragrant or ornamental plant.

LAVANDULA X INTERMEDIA 'ALBA'
(synonym: **'Hidcote White'**)
Habit is open to bushy and large (80cm), with mid-green to grey–green foliage. Lateral branching is rare and either short-stemmed towards the top of the peduncle or medium- to long-stemmed lower down. There is no spike formation at the end of these laterals, only a few flowers. Peduncles are mid-green with intermittent darkened edges, very long (25–32cm) and upright. Spikes are medium (4–5cm), mostly cylindric and interrupted, with the base whorl either absent or 1.5–3cm below the main spike. Fertile bracts are intermediate. Bracteoles are mostly long and narrow (2mm). Corollas are white; calyces are grey–green (194A) and pubescent, though less so than with 'Dutch White'.

Known to have been in existence before 1880, 'Alba' has a tendency to become woody with age, requiring regular pruning. It is nevertheless a very handsome plant en masse or planted against darker colours, and may be used for fragrant crafts. It is often confused with *L. angustifolia* 'Alba' which is a much smaller plant.

LAVANDULA X INTERMEDIA 'ARABIAN NIGHT'
See *L.* x *intermedia* 'Super' (Plant C) or 'Impress Purple'.

LAVANDULA X INTERMEDIA 'BOGONG'/'MISS DONNINGTON'
(synonyms: **'Bujong'**, **'Byjong'**, **'Bygong'**)

This cultivar is known as 'Bogong' in New Zealand and 'Miss Donnington' in Australia. The name 'Miss Donnington' seems to have arisen out of confusion with the *L. angustifolia* cultivar 'Bowles Early' which has 'Miss Donnington' as one of its synonyms. The true 'Bowles Early' was imported to Australia by Judyth McLeod and subsequently released to the public. Since then, misnaming has occurred and this lavandin has acquired the name of a *L. angustifolia* cultivar synonym.

A large plant (90cm) of spherical habit with moderately dense, mid-green foliage and masses of flower spikes. Lateral branching is long, single, double or triple, rarely absent. The peduncles are very long (29–36cm), semi-upright to upright, and mid-green with darkened edges, although these markings are not as strong as in 'Grosso'. Spikes are long (6–10cm), cylindric and mostly evenly interrupted, with the base whorl either absent or 1–3cm below the main spike. Fertile bracts are intermediate and long. Bracteoles are long and narrow with occasional branching (2–3mm). Corollas are a vibrant violet (88A), calyces are reasonably pubescent and dark violet (86A). The buds tend to be a brighter violet–blue (90A) (illustrated on page 110).

Although grown in Australia, 'Bogong' does not seem to have originated there. A very old bush growing in New South Wales was reputed to have been a cutting from a plant brought to Australia from Mitcham in the United Kingdom. There is indeed a description of a large bush lavender growing at Mitcham and it is possible that lavandins were growing alongside other lavenders at the time. It is used as an oil plant, and for ornamental, fragrant or hedging purposes. Because of its uniform spikes, it is suited to mass planting.

I have also seen this plant sold under the names *L.* x *intermedia* and *L.* x *intermedia* 'Vera'.

LAVANDULA X INTERMEDIA 'CHAIX'

In most respects this plant is similar to 'Grey Hedge', except that it produces fewer flower spikes than 'Grey Hedge', which flowers quite prolifically. The name 'Chaix' has led to some confusion in the lavender world. It is actually the name of a botanist who was responsible for the name *L. officinalis* (synonym for *L. angustifolia*), so it is highly unlikely that his name would have been used as a cultivar name.

This plant was imported from France by the former Department of Scientific and Industrial Research, New Zealand, in the late 1970s or early 1980s to trial for oil. However, there is no mention of such a plant in France and I suspect that it was imported as 'Grey Hedge' with subsequent confusion and misnaming. Since then, there have been two forms of 'Grey Hedge' available on the market in Australasia — one flowers well, and the other does not ('Chaix'). It seems that 'Chaix' may have started existence as a cutting variation of 'Grey Hedge', possibly from the base of the bush where little flowering occurs. However, the reduced flowering matters little in this specimen as the foliage is superb and has obvious ornamental and hedging uses.

LEFT

L. x *intermedia* 'Bogong'

L. x *intermedia* 'Grosso'

L. x *intermedia* 'Impress Purple'

L. x *intermedia* 'Yuulong'

L. x *intermedia* 'Fred Boutin'

RIGHT

L. x *intermedia* 'Bogong' / 'Miss Donnington'

LAVANDULA X *INTERMEDIA* 'DILLY DILLY'
See *L.* x *intermedia* 'Grosso'.

LAVANDULA X *INTERMEDIA* 'DUTCH'
(synonyms: **'Vera'**, **'Early Dutch'**, *L. vera* in part, *L. hortensis*)
Habit is bushy and large (80cm) with semi-open, grey foliage. Peduncles are broad,
mid-green, long (19–35cm) and upright. Intermittent dark edges can be seen on the
peduncle one-third of the way below the spike (similar to 'Alba'). Lateral branching is
short-stemmed, mostly single or absent. Spikes are narrow-conical and medium to long
(6–9cm), with an occasional base whorl 2.5–3cm below the main spike. The fertile
bracts are intermediate and long. Bracteoles are long and narrow (3mm), occasionally
broad and branched. Corollas are blue–violet (94B), calyces are finely pubescent and
green with the upper half a darker violet (86A) (illustrated on page 109).

'Dutch' was one of the names given to the common type of lavandin grown in Europe
prior to the 1920s. It may be a synonym for 'Grey Dutch' which was bred at the Herb
Farm in Seal, United Kingdom, although this is uncertain. Suitable for ornamental or
hedging purposes.

The name 'Vera', with which 'Dutch' is synonymous, has caused enormous misunder-
standing in the lavender world (see page 44).

LAVANDULA X *INTERMEDIA* 'DUTCH WHITE'

A medium plant (70cm) of bushy habit with semi-open, grey foliage. Any lateral branching is short- to medium-stemmed high on the peduncle, with incomplete spikes, or longer branched further down the stem with small spikes. The peduncles are mid-green, very long (34–43cm) and semi-upright. Spikes are medium (5–8cm), cylindric or occasionally fusiform and interrupted, with the base whorl 1–3cm below the main spike. Fertile bracts are broad and long. Bracteoles are very long or occasionally broad and branched (2–3mm). The corollas are white, calyces are pubescent and light grey–green (also illustrated on page 109).

'Dutch White' is quite different from 'Alba', being a shorter bush with longer peduncles and spikes. The calyx colour is a lighter green compared to the grey–green calyces of 'Alba'. Lower-growing and more compact, 'Dutch White' is suitable for ornamental, hedging and fragrant purposes.

LAVANDULA X *INTERMEDIA* 'FRAGRANT MEMORIES'
(synonym: **'Grove Ferry'**)

Large (80 cm) and bushy in habit with dense grey foliage. Lateral branching is medium to long, mostly single and occasionally one-sided. The peduncles are broad, upright, long (18–28cm), and mid-green with slightly darkened edges. Spikes are narrow-conical, medium (5–7cm) and mostly evenly interrupted, with the base whorl absent or 1–2cm below the main spike. Fertile bracts are long and narrow and the base bracts may still be green in flower. Bracteoles are long, narrow (2–3mm) and plentiful, and occasionally broad and branched. Corollas are dark lavender–violet (92A), calyces are pubescent and green with the upper half a vibrant violet (88A). Buds are green with dark lavender–violet tips (92A) (illustrated on page 70).

Named in 1994 by D. Kemp in the United Kingdom, 'Fragrant Memories' is quite similar to 'Grey Hedge'. Silver–grey foliage makes 'Fragrant Memories' suitable as an ornamental or hedging plant.

LEFT AND RIGHT
L. x *intermedia* 'Dutch White'

LAVANDULA X INTERMEDIA 'FRED BOUTIN'

A large lavender (80cm) of bushy habit with dense grey foliage. Peduncles are long (16–32cm), upright and grey–green with slight darkening of the edges. Lateral branching when present is single or double and/or one-sided. Spikes are medium (3.5–8cm), narrow-conical and mostly evenly interrupted, with the base whorl absent or 1–3cm below the main spike. Fertile bracts are narrow, small but long. Bracteoles are long and thin (2–3mm), and occasionally branched. Corollas are dark violet–blue (93C), calyces are pubescent and green with the upper half a dark violet (86A). Buds are green with a tinge of violet–blue (93C) (illustrated on page 110).

Named in the United States at Huntington Botanical Gardens, this cultivar is well suited for ornamental or hedging purposes.

LAVANDULA X INTERMEDIA 'GRAPPENHALL'
(synonyms: **'Grappenhall Variety'**, **'Giant Grappenhall'**, **'Gigantea'**)

A large bushy plant (90cm) with mid-green, moderately dense foliage. Peduncles are broad, mid-green with slightly darkened edges, very long (30–38cm), and semi-upright to upright. Spikes are medium to long (5–9cm), narrow-conical and interrupted, with the base whorl 1–3 cm below the main spike. The fertile bracts are intermediate and long. Bracteoles are plentiful, long and narrow, or occasionally broad and branched (3mm). Corollas are lavender–violet (91A), calyces are finely pubescent and green, lightly suffused with dark violet (86A) (illustrated on pages 109 and 115).

'Grappenhall' is an attractive lighter blue-flowered lavandin suitable for ornamental, fragrant and hedging purposes.

LAVANDULA X INTERMEDIA 'GREY HEDGE'

A large plant to over 1m, of bushy to spherical habit with dense grey foliage. Peduncles are long (16–28cm), upright and mid-green with occasional slight darkening of the edges. Lateral branching is infrequent and mostly single and long-stemmed with small spikes; or short-stemmed with a few flowers halfway up the peduncle. Spikes are long (5–11cm), narrow-conical and mostly evenly interrupted, with an occasional base whorl 1–4cm below the main spike. Fertile bracts are long and narrow. Bracteoles are large, broad and branched, or long and narrow (2–3mm). Corollas are dark lavender–violet (92A), calyces are finely pubescent and green suffused in dark lavender–violet (illustrated on pages 109 and 115).

An excellent hedging or ornamental plant, 'Grey Hedge' may have a tendency to turn woody if left to grow untended, but when kept regularly pruned, the silver–grey foliage will continue to give pleasure for many years.

TOP LEFT
L. x intermedia 'Grappenhall'

TOP RIGHT
L. x intermedia 'Grey Hedge'

BOTTOM LEFT
L. x intermedia 'Grosso'

BOTTOM RIGHT
L. x intermedia 'Grey Hedge'

Another cultivar **'Scottish Cottage'** is very similar, if not identical, to 'Grey Hedge'. It was imported to New Zealand in the early 1990s from the United Kingdom, but no such name appears to exist elsewhere.

LAVANDULA X INTERMEDIA 'GROSSO'
(synonyms: **'Dilly Dilly'**, **'Wilson's Giant'**)
The foliage is mid-green, turning grey towards the end of the season, and very dense. The plant is semi-tall (75cm) and spherical in habit. Peduncles are broad, very long (30–36cm), splayed and mid-green with darkened (almost black) edges. Lateral branching is long, single or occasionally double or one-sided. The spikes are compact, broad-conical and medium to long (5–9cm), with an occasional base whorl 1–3cm below the main spike. Fertile bracts are intermediate to long, and narrow. Bracteoles are short for a lavandin (1–3mm), broad and branched. Corollas are violet–blue (90C) with much darker violet (86A), finely pubescent calyces (also illustrated on page 110).

'Grosso' was discovered in France in 1972 and is resistant to the mycoplasm yellow decline, which destroyed the 'Abrialii' plantings. Due to its spherical shape and masses of flower spikes, 'Grosso' is used as an ornamental or hedging plant, as well as for fragrant and oil purposes. It is one of the most popular oil plants in the lavender world because of its high-yielding spikes.

LAVANDULA X INTERMEDIA 'HIDCOTE GIANT'
Foliage is grey–green, moderately dense and bushy, and large in habit (80cm). There is frequent short to long lateral branching which is mostly single or double, and occasionally triple or one-sided. Peduncles are very broad, mid-green, very long (28–47cm), and semi-upright to splayed. Spikes are medium (4–7cm), compact, very broad (2–2.5cm) and truncate-conic. Fertile bracts are intermediate. Bracteoles are plentiful, broad and branched (2–3mm). Corollas are bright violet–blue (90B), calyces are pubescent and suffused with dark violet (86A) (illustrated on page 116). The buds are a slightly deeper violet–blue (90A).

A most distinctive and unusual lavandin due to the shape of the spikes and width of the peduncles, 'Hidcote Giant' is an intriguing plant which would be a feature in any garden.

LAVANDULA X INTERMEDIA 'IMPRESS PURPLE'
(synonyms: **'41/70'**, **'Arabian Night'** in part, **'Arabian Nights'**, **'Arabian Knight'**)
A large plant (80cm) of bushy habit and moderately dense, mid-green to grey–green foliage. Lateral branching is long, mostly single, occasionally double, one-sided or absent. The spikes that terminate the lateral branches may be incomplete. Peduncles are very long (30–40cm), semi-upright and mid-green with darkened (almost black) edges. Spikes are medium to long (5.5–9cm), compact and broad-conical to truncate-conic.

LEFT

L. x intermedia 'Jaubert'

L. x intermedia 'Old English'

L. x intermedia 'Margaret'

L. x intermedia 'Hidcote Giant'

L. x intermedia 'Seal'

RIGHT

L. x intermedia 'Hidcote Giant'

The base whorl is either absent or 1–5cm below the main spike. Fertile bracts are intermediate and long and may still be green when the spike is in flower.

Bracteoles are large, broad and branched, occasionally long and narrow (2–3mm), and always plentiful. Corollas are bright violet–blue (90A), calyces are finely pubescent and dark violet (86A) (also illustrated on pages 106 and 110).

Of French origin, but subsequently named 'Impress Purple' by Peter Smale, formerly of Crop and Food Research, New Zealand, this is a striking dark-flowered lavandin suitable for ornamental, hedging, fragrant and oil purposes.

LAVANDULA X INTERMEDIA 'JAUBERT'

Foliage is grey–green, moderately dense and the plant is large (90cm) and bushy in habit. Peduncles are mid-green, very broad and long (30–40cm), and semi-upright to upright. Spikes are narrow-conical, possibly the longest of the lavandins (11–17cm), mostly evenly interrupted, with the base whorl absent or 1–4cm below the main spike. One spike was measured at 21cm. Fertile bracts are very broad and long. Bracteoles are plentiful, long, broad and branched, or long and narrow (3–4mm). Corollas are closest to violet–blue (90C), calyces are pubescent and green with a tinge of dark violet (86A).

Raised in France, 'Jaubert' is a most elegant and spectacular plant with beautifully shaped spikes suitable for ornamental and fragrant purposes.

LAVANDULA X INTERMEDIA 'LULLINGSTONE CASTLE'

A large plant (90cm) of bushy habit, with beautiful dense grey foliage, similar to 'Grey Hedge', but with strong lateral branching and much longer peduncles. Peduncles are grey–green, long (28–34cm), semi-upright and grey–green with slightly darkened edges.

Lateral branching is mostly single and short- to long-stemmed with well-formed spikes. Spikes are long (8–11cm), narrow-conical and mostly evenly interrupted, with the base whorl absent or 2cm below the main spike. Fertile bracts are intermediate but broad at the base. Bracteoles are plentiful, large, branched and occasionally long and narrow (2–3mm). Corollas are dark lavender–violet (92A), calyces are finely pubescent and suffused in dark blue–violet (96A). The buds are much greener with blue tips (illustrated on page 109).

Raised by Hopleys in the United Kingdom in the early 1990s, this is a most attractive plant suitable for ornamental and hedging purposes or as a feature plant.

LAVANDULA X INTERMEDIA 'MARGARET'
(synonym: **'Rocky Hall Margaret'**)
A large spherical plant (80cm), with moderately dense, mid-green foliage. Lateral branching is short to long, mostly single or double or occasionally one-sided. Peduncles are thin to broad, very long (29–40cm), semi-upright and mid-green with darkened (almost black) edges. Spikes are medium (5–7cm), cylindric and evenly interrupted, with the base whorl absent or 1–3cm below the main spike. Fertile bracts are very long and narrow. Bracteoles are also narrow and long (2–3mm). Corollas are violet–blue (94C), calyces are densely pubescent and bright violet–blue (90A). Buds are dark lavender–violet (94C).

Named in New South Wales, Australia, the whole plant has a soft velvety appearance and is suitable for fragrant, hedging and ornamental uses.

LEFT
L. x *intermedia*
'Impress Purple'

RIGHT
L. x *intermedia* 'Jaubert'

LAVANDULA X INTERMEDIA 'MISS DONNINGTON'
See *L.* x *intermedia* 'Bogong'.

LAVANDULA X INTERMEDIA 'NICOLEII'
A large plant (80cm) of bushy habit with moderately dense, grey foliage. Peduncles are broad, mid-green, very long (27–40cm) and upright. Lateral branching is rare, apart from occasional short stems bearing a few flowers. Spikes are long (7–11cm), cylindric, mostly evenly interrupted, with the base whorl absent or 2–4cm below the main spike. Fertile bracts are intermediate and long. Bracteoles are very long, thin and occasionally branched (2–4mm). Corollas are dark lavender (94C), calyces are densely pubescent and grey–green with a touch of dark violet (86A) (also illustrated on page 109).

Bred by Peter Carter, New Zealand, in 1992, 'Nicoleii' is one of the most attractive and fragrant of the light blue-flowered lavandins. Suitable as an ornamental plant and for fragrant purposes.

LEFT AND RIGHT
L. x *intermedia* 'Nicoleii'

L. x *intermedia* 'Old English'

LAVANDULA X INTERMEDIA 'OLD ENGLISH'

Foliage is dense, mid-green to grey–green; the plant is bushy to spherical in habit and large (1m). There may be occasional lateral branching of short to medium length, single or one-sided. Peduncles are very long (30–50cm), upright and mid-green with slightly darkened edges. Spikes are long (6–11cm), narrow-conical and interrupted, with the base whorl absent or 1–4cm below the main spike. Fertile bracts are long and narrow with a wide base. Bracteoles are plentiful, broad and branched (2–3mm). Corollas are lavender–violet (91A), calyces are finely pubescent and green with dark violet tips (86A). The buds are similar but with lighter-coloured tips (also illustrated on page 116).

'Old English' is a good architectural-type plant when kept pruned and watered to encourage optimum growth. Raised prior to the 1930s at the Herb Farm, Seal, United Kingdom, it is suitable for ornamental and hedging purposes.

I have, unfortunately, seen the name 'Old English' used as a general term to describe lavenders and lavandins for promotional and sale purposes.

LAVANDULA X INTERMEDIA 'SCOTTISH COTTAGE'

See *L.* x *intermedia* 'Grey Hedge'.

LAVANDULA X INTERMEDIA 'SEAL'

A large bush to over 1m with moderately dense, mid-green to grey–green foliage and bushy habit. Peduncles are very long (40–50cm), semi-upright and mid-green with darkened (almost black) edges. Long lateral branching may be single, double or

L. x intermedia 'Seal'

one-sided. Spikes are medium (5–8cm), cylindric or fusiform and interrupted, with the base whorl 1–6cm below the main spike. Fertile bracts are either small (similar to 'Lady'), or long and narrow. Bracteoles are mostly long, broad and branched (2–3mm). Corollas are bright violet–blue (90B), and calyces are green suffused with dark violet (86A) (also illustrated on page 116).

Raised at the Herb Farm, Seal, United Kingdom, before 1935, 'Seal' is an old favourite, often being used to make lavender bags, as the fragrance persists for at least two years. It is a fine ornamental or hedging plant.

LAVANDULA X INTERMEDIA 'SUMIAN'
A large plant (80cm) of bushy habit, with grey-green, moderately dense foliage. Lateral branching is long and mostly single. Peduncles are broad and long to very long (17–38cm) with darkened edges. Spikes are medium (5–8cm), cylindric or broad-conical and cylindric, with the base whorl absent or 1.5–3cm below the main spike. Fertile bracts are intermediate and long, the base bracts being long and narrow. Bracteoles are long and narrow, or broad and branched (2–3mm). Corollas are vibrant violet (88A), calyces are quite pubescent and green suffused with bright violet–blue (90A) (illustrated on page 109).

Sometimes used for oil, 'Sumian', which was raised in France, has a pleasant fragrance and could be used for other fragrant or ornamental purposes.

LAVANDULA X INTERMEDIA 'SUPER'
The true identity of this plant is proving to be rather elusive as there appear to be two cultivars with that name in France, as well as one that was imported to New Zealand many years ago. 'Super' is a French cultivar introduced about 1956. Three cultivars with this name are described here.

PLANT A
A large plant (80cm) of bushy habit and moderately dense, grey–green foliage. There is frequent long lateral branching, single, double or one-sided. Peduncles are very long (39–48cm), broad, mid-green and semi-upright. Spikes are long (6–12cm), narrow to broad-conical and interrupted, with the base whorl either absent or 1.5–4cm below the main spike. Fertile bracts are broad with longer, greener base bracts. Bracteoles are plentiful, long and branched (2–3mm). Corollas are violet–blue (90C), calyces are densely pubescent and green suffused with dark violet (86A). The buds are slightly lighter in colour (90B).

PLANT B
A semi-tall plant (70–78cm) of bushy habit with moderately dense, grey–green foliage. Peduncles are very long (24–34cm), broad, more grey–green than Plant A, and splayed

rather than semi-upright. Lateral branching is long and mostly single. Spikes are long (6–12cm), narrow-conical and interrupted, with the base whorl absent or 1–3cm below the main spike. Fertile bracts are small and narrow, with longer green bracts at the base of the spike. Bracteoles are short and narrow or long and narrow, and occasionally branched (2–3mm). Corollas are violet–blue (94C), calyces are pubescent and green with the upper half a dark violet (86A).

Plant A has larger corollas, much broader bracts and more pubescent calyces than Plant B. Peduncles are also longer and more upright in Plant A.

Plant C
(synonyms: **'Arabian Night'** in part, **'Arabian Nights'**, **'Arabian Knight'**)
A large (80–90cm), spherical bush with moderately dense, mid-green foliage. Peduncles are very long (26–33cm), semi-upright and mid-green with darkened edges. Lateral branching is long, single, occasionally double or one-sided (illustrated on page 122). Spikes are medium to long (6–9cm), narrow to broad-conical, and slightly interrupted. Fertile bracts are intermediate or narrow and long. Bracteoles are long, broad and branched (2–3mm). Corollas are a mixture of two shades of violet–blue (92A and 94C), calyces are finely pubescent and green suffused with dark violet (86A).

This plant was originally imported to New Zealand as 'Super' by the then Department of Scientific and Industrial Research.

LEFT
Lavandins in bud with
L. x intermedia 'Super' Plant C
in foreground

RIGHT
L. x intermedia 'Super' Plant C
showing distinct lateral
branching of peduncles

Another cultivar **'Sussex'** is similar in all characteristics except for slightly longer peduncles and spikes and fewer inflorescences overall. In all other respects it is identical to Plant C. I suspect that 'Sussex' may be an aberrant cutting from Plant C, as it is most unusual, although not impossible, to have two lavandins almost identical. All other lavandins have a number of features that distinguish them from each other.

All four plants returned oil analyses within the 'Super' range but at varying levels within that range. 'Sussex' matches 'Plant C' but the other two are different. All three 'Super' cultivars can be used for ornamental, fragrant and oil purposes.

LAVANDULA X INTERMEDIA 'SUSSEX'
See *L.* x *intermedia* 'Super' Plant C.

LAVANDULA X INTERMEDIA 'WALBERTON'S SILVER EDGE'
(synonyms: **'Tim's Variegated'**, **'Walvera'**)
A variegated bushy lavandin sporting leaves with grey–green centres and cream outer margins. Foliage is semi-open. Peduncles are long (13–23cm), upright and unbranched, at least in young plants, with an occasional pair of leaves halfway up the peduncle. Spikes are short, compact (2.5–4cm) and broad-conical, with the occasional base whorl

LEFT

L. x *intermedia* 'Super' Plant C

CENTRE

L. x *intermedia* 'Super' — Plant C, Plant A, Plant B

RIGHT

L. x *intermedia* 'Walberton's Silver Edge'

1–2cm below the main spike. Fertile bracts are narrow and small, but long. Bracteoles are narrow and branched, or medium and branched (3mm). Corollas are dark lavender–violet (92A), calyces are pubescent and soft green suffused with blue–violet (94B). Buds are similar with darker tips (also illustrated on page 109).

A sport discovered by Tim Crowther at Walberton Nursery in the United Kingdom, 'Walberton's Silver Edge' with its attractive foliage is suitable as an ornamental, hedging or back-of-border plant.

LAVANDULA X *INTERMEDIA* 'WILSON'S GIANT'
See *L.* x *intermedia* 'Grosso'.

LAVANDULA X *INTERMEDIA* 'YUULONG'
A large plant over 1m, with dense mid-green to grey–green foliage, and spherical habit. Lateral branching is usually long and single, and occasionally double, triple or quadruple on younger bushes. Peduncles are very long (34–41cm), upright and mid-green with slightly darkened edges. Spikes are short (3.5–5cm), fusiform-conic and slightly interrupted, with the base whorl 1cm below the main spike. Fertile bracts are small, similar to 'Lady'. Bracteoles are long and narrow, occasionally short and branched (1–2mm). Corollas are dark lavender–violet (92A), calyces are green suffused with dark violet (86A) (also illustrated on page 110).

Raised by Rosemary Holmes and Edythe Anderson in Australia and named by the Royal Botanic Gardens, Melbourne, in 1986, 'Yuulong' is a very striking plant en masse due to its vibrant inflorescences and large form. Used for fragrant, ornamental and hedging purposes.

CULTIVARS OF
Lavandula lanata x
Lavandula angustifolia

This range of cultivars are mostly hybrids between *L. lanata* and *L. angustifolia*. They have the most beautiful soft velvety, silver–grey leaves, a legacy from the *L. lanata* parent, and are prolific spike producers.

Bracteoles are long, broad (at least 1mm wide) and branched. All bracts are fertile. Spikes are mostly 1–1.5cm wide. Corolla colours are particularly difficult to place in the RHS charts. Most are in the vicinity of vibrant violet (88A) but may differ slightly in shade. Even though corolla colours may be similar, spike shape, plant habits and sizes are completely different. They are all fine specimens, very suitable as feature or general garden plants.

L. 'Molten Silver'

All cultivars have an unusual but pleasant perfume and can be used for fragrant or floral purposes. They must be grown in well-drained soil and, because of their foliage, are not suited to wet conditions. Smaller plants are well suited to rock gardens and larger plants to grey, silver or dry gardens.

LAVANDULA 'ANDREAS'
A small to medium plant (50–60cm) of bushy habit, with semi-open foliage. Occasional medium-stemmed laterals, either single or double, terminate in short spikes. The peduncles are grey–green, long (16–30cm) and semi-upright. Spikes are medium (5–7cm), broad-conical, cylindric or fusiform-conic, with an occasional base whorl 2–4cm below the main spike. Fertile bracts are intermediate to broad. Bracteoles are

broad and branched (1–2mm) but not as plentiful as in the other cultivars. Corollas are a vibrant violet (88A), calyces are densely pubescent and dark violet–blue (93A). Buds are lighter in colour (94A).

Raised in New Zealand in the early 1990s, 'Andreas' is suitable as a small hedging or ornamental plant. Keep compact by hard pruning in autumn.

LAVANDULA 'JOAN HEAD'

A semi-tall plant (60–70cm), with dense foliage and spherical habit. Occasional short-stemmed lateral branching does occur, terminated with one to three flowers. Peduncles are grey–green, long (19–30cm) and splayed. Spikes are medium (4–7cm), more cylindric than broad-conical and evenly interrupted, with base whorl absent or 1–2cm below the main spike. The fertile bracts are intermediate and long. Bracteoles are broad, branched (2–3mm) and plentiful. The corollas are vibrant violet (88A), but a slightly lighter shade than 'Andreas'. Both buds and calyces are densely pubescent and dark violet–blue (93A).

Raised by Peter Carter, New Zealand, in the mid-1990s, 'Joan Head' is suitable for ornamental or hedging purposes.

LAVANDULA 'MOLTEN SILVER'

One of the larger-growing cultivars (1m x 1.5m) in this group, with dense foliage and spherical habit. Frequent lateral branching is long, single or double, and occasionally triple or one-sided. Each lateral is terminated with a spike. Peduncles are broad, grey–green, very long (30–50cm) and splayed. Spikes are medium (5–8cm), slightly broad-conical to cylindric and interrupted, with a base whorl 1–2cm below the main spike. The fertile bracts are intermediate to broad, and long. The bracteoles are not as conspicuous as in other cultivars, being mostly long and narrow (2mm), occasionally broad, but not plentiful. Corollas are a vibrant violet (88A), and the densely pubescent buds and calyces are much lighter in colouring than the other cultivars (also illustrated on pages 124 and 128).

A hybrid between *L. lanata* and *L. angustifolia* 'Twickel Purple', 'Molten Silver' was named by Virginia McNaughton and Dennis Matthews, New Zealand, in 1996 and is a spectacular large ornamental or hedging plant.

LAVANDULA 'RICHARD GRAY'

A small plant (40cm) of bushy habit and moderately dense foliage. Peduncles are grey–green, medium (10–20cm), and semi-upright to upright. Spikes are short (3–4cm), cylindric or occasionally broad-conical and interrupted. Fertile bracts are small, narrow and long. The bracteoles are broad and short (1mm). Corollas are vibrant violet (88A)

LEFT
L. 'Molten Silver'
L. 'Andreas'
L. 'Joan Head'
L. 'Richard Gray'
L. 'Silver Frost'

RIGHT
L. 'Molten Silver' in bud

BELOW
L. 'Molten Silver'

though slightly brighter than other cultivars. Both buds and calyces are densely pubescent and dark violet–blue (94A).

Raised at the Royal Botanic Gardens, Kew, United Kingdom, in the 1980s, 'Richard Gray' is a charming low-growing cultivar that makes a statement with its small statuesque form, dark flowers and silver–grey leaves. Use as a low hedging or ornamental plant, or as a container-grown plant.

LAVANDULA 'SAWYERS'
(synonyms: **'Sawyers Hybrid'**, **'Conard Blue'**)
An attractive plant (50–60cm) of spherical habit with dense foliage. Peduncles are grey–green, long (19–34cm) and splayed. Spikes are medium to long (6–11cm), and narrow to broad-conical. The fertile bracts are intermediate to broad, and long. Bracteoles are broad, branched (1–3mm) and plentiful. Corollas are vibrant violet (88A) and smaller than corollas in other cultivars. The densely pubescent calyces are dark violet–blue (93A), slightly lighter in bud (94A).

Raised by Suffolk Herbs, Sudbury, United Kingdom, in the late 1980s and sold by Norfolk Lavender, 'Sawyers' is well suited to hedging or ornamental use, especially planted en masse.

LAVANDULA 'SILVER FROST'

A semi-open foliaged plant, of bushy habit and medium height (50cm). Occasional medium-stemmed laterals terminated with short spikes do occur. Peduncles are grey–green, long (15–30cm) and splayed outwards. Spikes are medium (4–6cm), broad-conical and evenly interrupted, with lower whorl absent or 1cm below the main spike. Fertile bracts are large and broad. Bracteoles are broad, branched (2–3mm) and plentiful. Corollas are very vibrant violet (88A), calyces are densely pubescent and dark blue–violet (94A) (illustrated on page 127).

Raised in the United States by Andrew Van Hevelingen, 'Silver Frost' is another attractive cultivar in this series, suitable for ornamental or hedging purposes.

CULTIVARS OF
Lavandula stoechas

These cultivars are mostly hybrids resulting from the cross-pollination of plants within Section *Stoechas*. Their spikes comprise both fertile and colourful sterile bracts. There are no bracteoles in this Section.

Apart from some of the naturally low-growing cultivars, many will reach 1 metre or more if left unpruned over several years. In the cultivar descriptions, heights are based on three-year-old plants that have been well maintained. Annual pruning will keep the majority of cultivars in trim, but where hard pruning is recommended in the following descriptions, two cutting-back sessions may be necessary over summer. These cultivars flower in spring, then have a short rest, often to flower again before the end of the season. To achieve this, prune lightly after their first flowering, which may encourage further spike formation; follow this with harder pruning, preferably in autumn and well before winter.

L. 'James Compton'

Although not included in the descriptions, fertile bracts may have entire, serrated, dentate or crenate margins. Likewise, all fertile bracts have some degree of hair on the margins and on the bracts themselves.

Unless otherwise stated, there are generally four sterile bracts in most cultivars. All spikes are compact, some more loosely than others. The width of the spikes is generally 1–1.5cm. Broader spikes may reach 2–2.5cm.

Any mention of 'bicoloured' spikes refers to a marked colour variation between the sterile bracts and the corollas on spikes, i.e. blue corollas and white or green sterile bracts.

Lateral branching referred to in Section *Stoechas* lavenders occurs in the axils of the primary leaves just above the main foliage line.

Section *Stoechas* cultivars do not have the fragrance of Section *Lavandula* cultivars but they are wonderful ornamental or feature plants in the garden.

LAVANDULA 'ATLAS'

A tall plant (80cm) of bushy habit with semi-open to open, bright green to grey–green foliage. Peduncles are very long (18–34cm), broad, finely pubescent and bright green with a reddish tinge. Spikes are medium (2.5–4cm), and truncate-conic to cylindric. Fertile bracts are finely pubescent and mostly red with green bases. The shape is cordate and acute or suborbicular. Corollas are rich violet–blue (89A). Calyces are finely pubescent, two-thirds green and one-third purple. Appendages are light purple. Sterile bracts (15–25mm) are a vibrant purple–violet (87A and 88C), elliptic or linear, with moderately undulating margins. The number of sterile bracts varies from four to six.

A spectacular cultivar in full flower and one not easily missed in the garden, 'Atlas' can be used as an ornamental or feature plant. Keep well pruned.

LEFT

L. 'Tickled Pink'
L. 'Somerset Mist'
L. 'Avonview'
L. 'Evelyn Cadzow'
L. 'Swan River Pink'

RIGHT

L. 'Ploughman's Purple'
L. 'Sugar Plum'
L. 'Atlas'
L. 'Helmsdale'
L. 'Roxlea Park'

LAVANDULA 'AVONVIEW'

A large plant (80cm) of bushy habit with dense bright green to grey–green foliage. Peduncles are medium to long (7–10cm) with reddish edges and finely pubescent. Spikes are medium (2.5–3.5cm) and conical or occasionally cylindric. Fertile bracts are rhombic-cordate, obovate and acute or suborbicular. They are membranous suffused with red–purple and finely pubescent. Corollas are dark blue (103A) and large. Calyces are finely pubescent and green, with the upper third red–purple. Appendages are purple. Sterile bracts (5–20mm) are elliptic or oblanceolate, and vibrant purple–violet (87A) with slightly undulating margins (see over).

'Avonview' was named by Ross King, New Zealand, in the early 1990s. The contrasting dark purple corollas and purple–violet sterile bracts are a feature of this plant. Recommended as a hedging or ornamental cultivar but also effective for mass plantings.

LAVANDULA 'BALLERINA'

A medium bushy plant (60cm) with semi-open, mid-green to grey–green foliage. Peduncles are medium (6–9cm), dull green and tomentose. Spikes are short (1.5–2.5cm), and truncate-conic to cylindric. Fertile bracts are mostly membranous with green veining and finely pubescent with denser hair on the margins. The shape is obovate or rhombic-cordate and acute. Corollas are bright violet–blue (90A); calyces are pubescent and green, with bright green appendages. Sterile bracts (15–30mm) are obovate, elliptic or oblanceolate, with slightly undulating margins (illustrated on page 134). Their colour changes from white through to purple–pink (70C).

'Ballerina' was raised by Peter Carter, New Zealand, in 1997. Its main feature is the spike with its dainty, changeable sterile bracts that resemble butterflies fluttering in the breeze. An appropriate cultivar to have planted around a feature such as a statue or a bird bath. Keep well pruned.

LAVANDULA 'BLUEBERRY RUFFLES'

A medium plant (60–70cm), upright and bushy in habit with semi-open, mid-green to grey–green foliage. Peduncles are medium (6–10cm), dull green, occasionally with a reddish tinge halfway down the stem. The hair is denser immediately under the spike. Occasional lateral branching occurs. Spikes are medium (2–4cm), truncate-conic or cylindric. Fertile bracts are membranous suffused with green and red–purple, and pubescent. The bract shape is rhombic-cordate or obovate and acute. Corollas are dark blue (103A). Calyces are two-thirds green and one-third purple, and pubescent. Appendages are purple. Sterile bracts (5–20mm) are elliptic, linear or oblong, with strongly undulating margins (illustrated on page 134). The colour is a vibrant light blueberry (89D to 88D).

Raised in 1997 by Virginia McNaughton and Dennis Matthews in New Zealand, 'Blueberry Ruffles' is of botanical interest with its almost horizontal arrangement of ruffled sterile bracts. Suitable for ornamental or hedging purposes.

LEFT

L. 'Avonview' with
Rosmarinus officinalis
'Genges Gold',
Santolina 'Lemon Fizz',
Rosa 'Graham Thomas'
and *Cynara cardunculus*

BELOW LEFT

L. 'Southern Lights'
L. 'Bower's Beauty'
L. 'Ballerina'
L. 'Willowbridge Wings'
L. 'Lumiere'

BELOW RIGHT

L. 'Provocatif'
L. 'Plum'
L. 'Regal Splendour'
L. 'Pippa Pink'
L. 'Blueberry Ruffles'

LAVANDULA 'BOWER'S BEAUTY'

An upright, semi-tall to tall plant (70–80cm), with very open, bright green foliage. Peduncles are medium to long (8–10cm), broad, bright green and pubescent. Spikes are medium (3.5–4cm) and cylindric. Fertile bracts are green, suborbicular and covered in short dense hair. Corollas are rich violet–blue (89B); calyces are pubescent and green, with green appendages. Sterile bracts (10–18mm) are oblanceolate or elliptic, with strongly undulating margins. Their colour is white to creamy-white (158C).

Raised in the United Kingdom, 'Bower's Beauty' with its straggly open nature needs to be kept well pruned. Not a particularly attractive plant but can be used for ornamental purposes. Its interest lies in its upright habit and long bicoloured spikes.

LAVANDULA 'CLAIR DE LUNE'

Habit is bushy to spreading and small (50–60cm) with semi-open, grey–green foliage. Peduncles are short to medium (3–5cm), mid-green and sparsely pubescent. Frequent lateral branching occurs. Spikes are short (1–3cm), mostly truncate or fusiform-conic. Fertile bracts are membranous with strong green veining, and short hair on the margins, becoming finer over the bract. The bract shape is rhombic-cordate and acute. Corollas are dark lavender–violet (92A/B); calyces are finely pubescent and green, with green appendages. Sterile bracts (8–15mm) are elliptic or oblong, with slight to moderately undulating margins. The colour is white with green veining and midribs (illustrated on page 136).

Raised by the McPhersons in New Zealand, 'Clair de Lune' is a low-growing plant of slightly spreading habit which makes a most attractive low hedge, potted plant or ornamental shrub. It is covered in masses of delightful bicoloured spikes over summer.

LAVANDULA 'EVELYN CADZOW'

One of the smallest of the Section *Stoechas* cultivars, growing to just 50cm, with attractive light green to bright green, dense foliage and contrasting light green peduncles. Spikes are short (1–2cm), mostly truncate-conic or occasionally cylindric. Peduncles are thin but medium to long (5–12cm), and finely pubescent. Fertile bracts are obovate and acute or suborbicular, red–purple and finely pubescent. Corollas are dark blue (103A) with prominent yellow stamens. Calyces are pubescent and green, with the upper half red–purple. The appendages are red–purple. Sterile bracts (6–15mm) are linear or narrow-oblong, and red–purple (72A), with slightly undulating margins (illustrated on pages 132 and 136).

Raised by Evelyn Cadzow and named after her by Geoff and Adair Genge, New Zealand, in the early 1990s, this low-growing cultivar is suitable for a pot or hedge, or as an ornamental plant.

TOP LEFT

L. 'Henri Dunont'
L. 'Van Gogh'
L. 'Pippa White'
L. 'Willowbridge White'
L. 'Clair de Lune'

TOP RIGHT

L. 'Clair de Lune'

BELOW

L. 'Evelyn Cadzow'

Lavandula 'Gethsemane'

A large lavender (80cm–1m) with grey–green foliage and a bushy, semi-open habit. Peduncles are very long (18–32cm), broad, rigid and pubescent. Edges of peduncles may be tinged with red–purple. Spikes are medium (2–3.5cm) and mostly cylindric. Fertile bracts are finely pubescent and green, with red–purple on the outer margins. The bract shape is suborbicular to reniform, and occasionally cordate and acute. Corollas are dark violet (86A); calyces are pubescent and mostly green with red–purple tips. Appendages are red–purple. Sterile bracts (15–25mm) are oblong to oblanceolate, red–purple with violet midribs and strongly undulating margins (also illustrated on page 139).

Raised and named in New Zealand by Virginia McNaughton in 1994, 'Gethsemane' has two-toned sterile bracts which make it highly suitable as an ornamental plant.

Lavandula 'Greenwings'

A semi-open, bushy plant of medium size (60–70cm) and mid-green foliage. Peduncles are medium to long (8–10cm), bright green and pubescent. Spikes are medium (2.5–3.5cm) and a mixture of cylindric or truncate and fusiform-conic. Fertile bracts are green, obovate to reniform and acute with fine pubescence. Corollas are vibrant violet (88A); calyces are pubescent and green with tips suffused with brown. Appendages are brown. Sterile bracts (8–15mm) are narrow-oblong or linear, and greenish changing to a pinkish-brown (153A), with moderately undulating margins.

Raised by Geoff Stent in New Zealand in the early 1990s, 'Greenwings' was one of the first green–brown bracted cultivars to be released on the market. Suitable for ornamental purposes. Keep well pruned.

LEFT

L. 'James Compton'
L. 'Wine'
L. 'Marshwood'
L. 'Manakau Village'
L. 'Gethsemane'

RIGHT

L. 'Roselight'
L. 'Pukehou'
L. 'Willowbridge Blueberry'
L. 'Greenwings'
L. 'Pippa'

LAVANDULA 'HELMSDALE'

A bushy, semi-tall plant (70–80cm) with dense mid-green foliage. Peduncles are medium to long (5.5–11cm), and mid-green with medium length hairs. Spikes are medium (2–4cm) and truncate or fusiform-conic, with an occasional base whorl 1–2cm below the main spike. Fertile bracts are red–purple, rhombic-cordate or obovate and acute, and densely hairy. Corollas are dark violet (86A); calyces are densely pubescent and green with purple tips and appendages. Sterile bracts (10–12mm) are elliptic, and rich burgundy (79A/B) with strongly undulating margins (also illustrated on page 132).

Raised by Geoff and Adair Genge, New Zealand, in the late 1980s, 'Helmsdale' is one of the best dark-flowered cultivars available. With its rich burgundy sterile bracts and contrasting dense green foliage, it makes an excellent hedging or ornamental plant. Suitable also for container growing for the first two years.

LAVANDULA 'HENRI DUNONT'

A lower-growing cultivar of spreading habit (50–60cm) with open mid-green foliage. Peduncles are medium (6–9cm), bright green, and covered in long hair. Spikes are medium (2.5–3.5cm) and cylindric. Fertile bracts are membranous with green veining, and pubescent with longer hairs on the margins. The bract shape is obovate to rhombic-cordate and acute. Corollas are dark violet (86A) and large. Calyces are densely pubescent and green, with green appendages. Sterile bracts (8–15mm) are oblanceolate, and white with strongly undulating margins (illustrated on page 136).

Raised in Australia by Neil Richardson and released in the mid-1990s, 'Henri Dunont' is striking in both the contrast of very dark corollas to sterile bracts, and its spikes which appear long and well formed. It requires regular pruning to keep its form but is an attractive ornamental plant. Also known as the 'Red Cross lavender'.

LAVANDULA 'JAMES COMPTON'
(synonyms: **'Butterfly'**, **'Fairy Wings'**)

Habit is upright, bushy and tall (80cm) with semi-open, bright green to grey–green foliage. Peduncles are long (13–23cm), thin but rigid, red–purple and finely pubescent. Occasional branching is present. Spikes are short to medium (1.5–3cm), truncate-conic or sometimes almost cylindric. Fertile bracts are mostly red–purple, with short hairs on the margins and fine pubescence over the bracts. The bract shape is mostly suborbicular and occasionally acute. Corollas are dark violet–blue (93A). Calyces are pubescent with reddish tips and purple appendages. Sterile bracts (20–30mm) are linear or narrow elliptic, and vibrant red–violet (88C) with slight to strongly undulating margins. The number of sterile bracts varies from two to eight (illustrated on pages 130, 137 and 140).

Named by James Compton in the United Kingdom, this is a very different cultivar in habit and form. The spikes borne on long peduncles look like small red butterflies,

LEFT

L. 'Gethsemane', *L. stoechas*
hybrid and *L.* 'Roselight'
in background

RIGHT
L. 'Helmsdale'

hence its synonyms. Suitable as a hedging, ornamental or individual feature plant. Keep this cultivar well pruned to give a more compact shape.

I have found very little difference, if any, between the cultivar known as **'Papillon'** and 'James Compton'.

LAVANDULA 'LUMIERE'

Habit is bushy, semi-open to dense, medium to semi-tall (60–70cm), with grey–green foliage. Peduncles are long (10–19cm), broad, light green and almost tomentose. Spikes are medium to long (3–7cm), almost cylindric with an occasional base whorl 1–2cm below the main spike. Fertile bracts are membranous with green veining, and short hair on the bracts, becoming longer around the margins. The bract shape is broadly obovate, rhombic-cordate and acute or suborbicular. Corollas are rich violet–blue (89A). Calyces are pubescent and green with brownish-green appendages. Sterile bracts (15–30mm) are broadly obovate, oblanceolate or linear, and white with green midribs and moderately undulating margins. The number of sterile bracts varies from four to eight (illustrated on page 134).

Raised by Virginia McNaughton in New Zealand, 'Lumiere' is another cultivar with bicoloured spikes. It also has a number of large semi-double to double-bracted spikes which, coupled with long peduncles, give the bush quite an impressive presence in flower. Use as an ornamental or feature plant.

L. 'James Compton'

LAVANDULA 'MAJOR'

A medium to semi-tall plant of bushy habit (60–70cm) with dense grey–green foliage. Peduncles are medium (6–8cm), bright green and pubescent. Spikes are medium (2.5–4cm) and mostly cylindric. Fertile bracts are obovate or rhombic-cordate and acute, green to red–purple, and finely pubescent. Corollas are dark blue (103A). Calyces are finely pubescent and green with red–purple tips and purple appendages. Sterile bracts (5–20mm) are oblanceolate, and vibrant violet (88A/B) with moderately undulating margins.

Raised in New Zealand and named by Wayne Horrobin and Sarah Hodge in the mid-1980s, 'Major' is one of the best of the violet to purple bracted cultivars and, with its naturally compact form, is very popular as an ornamental or hedging plant.

Another New Zealand–named cultivar **'Merle'** is similar in form to 'Major'.

LAVANDULA 'MANAKAU VILLAGE'

A small to medium plant (50–60cm) of bushy, spreading habit with open bright green to grey–green foliage. Peduncles are medium to long (6–13cm), thin to broad, with short but dense pubescence. There may be reddish tinges to the edges of the peduncles. Spikes are medium to long (3–5cm), truncate to fusiform-conic. Fertile bracts are red–purple, suborbicular or reniform, and finely pubescent. Corollas are dark blue (103A) with prominent white stamens. Calyces are finely pubescent and red–purple with purple appendages. Sterile bracts (15–28mm) are broadly oblong or linear, and number only two (also illustrated on page 137). The colour is vibrant purple–violet (87A/B).

Raised by Geoff Stent, New Zealand, in the mid-1990s, 'Manakau Village' is a most unusual and attractive lavender with large fertile bracts that are shell-like in shape and very striking. The only drawback with this cultivar is that it does not flower a second time during the summer season. Recommended as an ornamental or feature plant. Keep well pruned to promote a more compact bush.

LAVANDULA 'MARSHWOOD'

A large bush (1m) with semi-open, grey–green foliage. Peduncles are dull green, broad, long (12–21cm) and very hairy, being longer immediately under the spike. The spikes are medium (3–4cm), and mostly cylindric or occasionally truncate-conic. Fertile bracts are mostly suborbicular and slightly acute, red–purple and pubescent with longer hair on margins. Corollas are dark blue (103A). Calyces are finely pubescent and green and red–purple, with bright purple appendages. Sterile bracts (20–40mm) are mostly linear to oblong-lanceolate, and vibrant red–violet (88C) with strongly undulating margins (illustrated on pages 100, 137 and 143).

Raised by Geoff and Adair Genge, New Zealand, in the late 1980s, 'Marshwood' is one of the most impressive large lavenders on the market. Suitable for planting en masse, or as an ornamental or back-of-border shrub. It has a tendency to spread as it ages, requiring vigorous pruning to keep its shape.

LAVANDULA 'MORNING MIST'

A small plant (40–50cm) of bushy habit with open, mid-green to grey–green foliage. Peduncles are medium (5–7cm), very finely tomentose and bright green or red–green. Spikes are short (1.5–2cm) and globular truncate-conic to cylindric. Fertile bracts are membranous with green veining, occasionally suffused with purple, and pubescent with longer hair on the margins. The bract shape is mostly rhombic-cordate and acute. Corollas are dark blue (103A). Calyces are quite pubescent and green with the upper half purple, and with faint purple appendages. Sterile bracts (8–15mm) are linear or oblong, vibrant purple–violet (87A) with moderately undulating margins.

Raised by Peter Carter, New Zealand, in 1994, 'Morning Mist' is suitable as an ornamental plant but requires pruning to keep its shape.

LAVANDULA 'OTTO QUAST'

(synonyms: **'Otto Quest'**, **'Quasti'**)

A semi-tall plant (70cm) of bushy habit with dense mid-green to grey–green foliage. Peduncles are medium (6–9cm), reddish and very finely pubescent. Spikes are medium (2.5–4cm), truncate and fusiform-conic or occasionally cylindric. Fertile bracts are very finely pubescent and red–purple with green bases. The bract shape is suborbicular and occasionally acute. Corollas are dark blue (103A) with prominent yellow stamens. Calyces are very finely pubescent and green with the upper half red–purple, and with purple appendages. Sterile bracts (10–20mm) are broadly obovate to spathulate, and vibrant red–violet (88C) with strongly undulating margins (illustrated on page 141).

Raised in the United States, 'Otto Quast' is a compact bushy cultivar with strongly accentuated bracts. Suitable as an ornamental or hedging plant and possibly as a container plant when young.

LAVANDULA 'PASTEL DREAMS'

(synonym: **'Pastel Perfection'**)

A semi-tall, bushy plant (70cm) with dense, bright green foliage. Peduncles are medium to long (8–12cm), light green and pubescent. Spikes are medium to long (3–6cm), and mostly cylindric with an occasional base whorl 1cm below the main spike. Fertile bracts are green, with margins tinged a pale orange–brown, and pubescent with longer hairs on the margins. The bract shape is rhombic-cordate or broadly obovate and acute. Corollas are dark violet (86A). Calyces are densely pubescent and green with a touch of pink at the tips, and with pale pink appendages. Sterile bracts (10–25mm) are elliptic or obovate, with strongly undulating margins. The colour of the bracts ranges from a creamy-white and soft lilac–pink (69B/C) in spring through to a darker muted pink and mauve (84B) over the summer (also illustrated on page 145). Sterile bracts may vary from just four, to four larger bracts and three smaller ones in the centre.

Raised in 1995 by Virginia McNaughton and Dennis Matthews, New Zealand, 'Pastel Dreams' is one of the more unusual lavenders in this range, bearing long narrow flower spikes with variable-coloured sterile bracts. The corollas maintain their rich purple colour against the green fertile bracts particularly well. Like 'Pippa White', the plant tends to flower continually over the long summer period with only the briefest rest periods. Use as an ornamental or hedging plant, for mass planting, or as a container plant for the first two years, when its habit is naturally compact.

LAVANDULA 'PIPPA'

An upright lavender (1m) of bushy habit and moderately dense, bright green foliage. Peduncles are light green, thin, occasionally broader, of medium (5–10cm) length and sparsely pubescent. Spikes are medium (2.5–3.5cm) and truncate-conic. Fertile bracts are pubescent, red–purple or membranous and green-veined in younger spikes.

The bract shape is suborbicular, or broadly obovate and acute. Corollas are rich violet–blue (89A). Calyces are densely pubescent and green with red–purple tips and purple appendages. Sterile bracts (10–25mm) are oblanceolate or obovate, dusky to vibrant violet (88A), with green shading up the centre of the bract. Undulation of the margins is slight (illustrated on page 137).

Bred and named in New Zealand, 'Pippa' is a compact, though large grower, very suitable for hedging or ornamental purposes.

LAVANDULA 'PIPPA PINK'

A medium plant (60cm) of bushy habit and dense, bright green foliage. Peduncles are medium to long (7–11cm), mid-green and almost tomentose. Spikes are medium to long (2.5–5cm), and cylindric to slightly broad conical. Fertile bracts are green, with a slight touch of brown, and very hairy, with longer hairs on the margins. The bract shape is rhombic-cordate and acute or suborbicular. Corollas are lavender–violet (85A); calyces are finely pubescent and green with pinkish appendages. Sterile bracts (8–10mm) are obovate to slightly spathulate, and soft lavender–pink (76A) with slight to moderately undulating margins (illustrated on page 134).

Raised by Peter Carter, New Zealand, in the mid-1990s, 'Pippa Pink' is an unusually coloured cultivar with pinkish sterile bracts. Due to its compact form, it is suitable for hedging or ornamental use and container growing.

LAVANDULA 'PIPPA WHITE'

Habit is bushy to spreading and semi-tall (70–80cm) with open, bright green foliage. Peduncles are medium (6–10cm), broad, light green and densely pubescent. Spikes are long (4–5cm), and cylindric to slightly conical. Fertile bracts are membranous with heavy green veining and finely pubescent with longer hairs on the margins. The bract shape is more obovate to suborbicular and acute. Corollas are dark violet–blue (93A); calyces are densely pubescent and light green, with green appendages. Sterile bracts (15–30mm) are broadly elliptic to oblanceolate, and white with green veining and moderately undulating margins (illustrated on pages 136 and 148).

'Pippa White' was raised in New Zealand by Peter Carter in 1992. The humidity tends to split this plant open, but in colder climates 'Pippa White' grows into the most beautiful bushy form covered in masses of creamy bracted spikes and continues to flower right through the season. Recommended as a hedging or ornamental plant, or grown en masse for effect. Prune well.

LAVANDULA 'PLOUGHMAN'S PURPLE'

Of semi-tall stature (70cm) and bushy habit with mid-green to grey–green foliage. Peduncles are red–purple, long (15–20cm), broad, bright green and sparsely to moderately pubescent. Spikes are medium (2.5–4cm) and cylindric or occasionally truncate-conic. Fertile bracts are rhombic-cordate, obovate and acute or suborbicular. They are green, lightly suffused with red–purple, and sparsely pubescent. Corollas are dark blue (103A). Calyces are slightly pubescent and green, with the upper half red–purple. The appendages are purple. Sterile bracts (15–20mm) are broadly elliptic or oblanceolate, occasionally obovate, and vibrant violet (88A) with strongly undulating margins (illustrated on page 132).

Attractive en masse, this lavender was raised in 1993 by Peter Carter, New Zealand, and named by Clive Larkman, Australia. Another good purple form for ornamental or hedging purposes. Similar to 'Major'.

LAVANDULA 'PLUM'

(synonym: **'Plum Joy'**)

One of the smaller lavenders in this group (60cm). The habit is spreading and open with bright green to grey–green foliage. Peduncles are medium (5–10cm), thin and red–purple for two-thirds the length of the peduncle. Spikes are medium (2–4cm), cylindric to partially broad conical, with the base whorl 1cm below the main spike.

LEFT
L. 'Raycott'
L. 'Willowbridge Calico'
L. 'Pastel Dreams'

RIGHT
L. 'Clair de Lune' in front
with *L. angustifolia* 'Nana
Atropurpurea' Plant A,
L. 'Pastel Dreams'

Fertile bracts are obovate or rhombic cordate and acute, mostly red–purple and finely pubescent. Corollas are dark violet–blue (93A). Calyces are finely pubescent and green, with the upper half red–purple. Appendages are purple. Sterile bracts (10–12mm) are oblong or lanceolate, and vibrant purple–violet (87A/B) with slight to moderately undulating margins (illustrated on pages 134 and 148).

Raised in New Zealand by Terry Hatch, 'Plum' has a ground-hugging habit and can be used to fill gaps in the front-of-border garden. Otherwise it can be generally used as an ornamental plant. Requires hard pruning.

LAVANDULA 'PROVOCATIF'

Habit is bushy, medium to semi-tall (60–70cm), with semi-open, mid-green foliage. Peduncles are short to medium (3–4cm), mid-green and finely pubescent. Spikes are medium (2–4cm) and mostly cylindric. Fertile bracts are membranous with green veining and an occasional tinge of red–purple and very finely pubescent. The bract shape is rhombic-cordate or obovate and acute. Corollas are rich violet–blue (89A); calyces are green with the upper half lightly suffused in purple. The appendages are purple. Sterile bracts (10–20mm) are spathulate or oblanceolate, with moderately undulating margins (illustrated on page 134). The colour begins as a soft lilac to mauve–violet (84A/B) and ranges through to a vibrant red–violet (88C).

'Provocatif' was raised in New Zealand by Virginia McNaughton and Dennis Matthews in 1997. The sterile bracts make quite a statement, being both bold and strikingly coloured. This cultivar tends to stand out from other lavenders in spring because of the translucency of the bracts and is therefore well suited to ornamental uses or planting en masse. Keep well pruned.

LAVANDULA 'PUKEHOU'

Habit is semi-tall (70cm) and bushy, with dense bright green to grey–green foliage. Peduncles are long (10–18cm), with red–purple edges and pubescent. Spikes are medium (2–4cm), almost cylindric in shape, with an occasional base whorl 1–2cm below the main spike. Fertile bracts are red–purple and finely pubescent with longer hair on the margins. The bract shape is obovate and acute or suborbicular. Corollas are royal blue (99A); calyces are finely pubescent and purple, with greenish-brown appendages. Sterile bracts (15–20mm) are narrow-elliptic, purple–violet (86D) with a bluish tinge and strongly undulating margins (illustrated on pages 137 and 148).

Meaning 'Hill of Dedication', 'Pukehou' was named by Mary Robertson, New Zealand. The sterile bracts are a striking blue–purple shade, which is immediately eye-catching, making this cultivar a very appealing addition to any garden. Recommended as a specimen or feature plant, or planted en masse. Suitable for hedging but is probably better shown to perfection as an ornamental plant.

Another New Zealand–named cultivar **'Andrea'** is similar to 'Pukehou' in some respects, but has slightly redder-violet sterile bracts and greener foliage.

LAVANDULA 'PURPLE'
(synonym: **'Purple Joy'**)
A medium plant (60cm) of bushy habit and dense grey–green foliage. Peduncles are short (2–4cm), bright green with a tinge of red to the edges, tomentose and thin. Spikes are medium (3–4cm), and cylindric or fusiform-conic. Fertile bracts are green to red–purple, pubescent and obovate or rhombic-cordate and acute. Corollas are dark violet–purple (83A). Calyces are green with the upper two-thirds red–purple. They are pubescent with green appendages. Sterile bracts (5–15mm) are elliptic to oblanceolate, and rich violet–purple (83A/B) with moderately undulating margins (illustrated on page 141).

Raised by Terry Hatch in New Zealand, 'Purple' is a compact dark-flowered cultivar suitable for hedging, container growing and ornamental purposes.

LAVANDULA 'PURPLE CROWN'

Habit is upright, bushy and semi-tall (70–80cm) with open, bright green foliage. Peduncles are long (12–25cm), broad, dull green with red edges to halfway down the stem and quite tomentose. Spikes are medium to long (3–5cm) and mostly cylindric. Fertile bracts are green, slightly tinged with red–purple, and finely pubescent. The bract shape is cordate, rhombic-cordate and acute or suborbicular. Corollas are dark blue (103A). Calyces are finely pubescent and green, with the upper half purple. The appendages are purple. Sterile bracts (15–25mm) are mostly elliptic, with moderately undulating margins. The colour is dark violet–purple (83B).

Raised in Australia by Andy and Sonja Cameron, 'Purple Crown' is very similar to *L. stoechas* subsp. *pedunculata*. Suitable for ornamental use.

LAVANDULA 'RAYCOTT'

An attractive, semi-tall lavender of bushy habit (70cm) with semi-open, bright green foliage. Peduncles are medium to long (7–13cm), light green and covered in long hair. Some lateral branching is present. Spikes are short (1.5–2.5cm) and truncate-conic. Fertile bracts are green with purple tips and pubescent, more sparsely so on bracts than on margins. The bract shape is cordate to rhombic-cordate and acute. Corollas are dark violet (86A). Calyces are densely pubescent and green with slightly red tips and brown appendages. Sterile bracts (15–25mm) are elliptic, greenish-white changing to soft red–purple with green midribs and slightly undulating margins (illustrated on pages 145 and 151).

'Raycott' was found in an Australian garden called Ray's Cottage in the early 1990s, hence its name. An interesting plant due to the colour changes of the sterile bract, ranging from a pinkish-cream to a mauve–pink. 'Raycott' is suitable as an ornamental plant or for hedging.

LAVANDULA 'REGAL SPLENDOUR'

A semi-tall plant (70cm) of upright, bushy habit with semi-open to dense, bright green foliage. Peduncles are mid-green, short to medium (3–6cm), with medium-length hairs, similar to 'Helmsdale'. Spikes are medium (3–4cm), and broad-conical to cylindric. Frequent lateral branching occurs. Fertile bracts are green, with the upper two-thirds suffused in purple, and pubescent. The bract shape is obovate or rhombic-cordate and acute. Corollas are rich violet–blue (89A). Calyces are densely pubescent and green with the upper half purple. Appendages are purple. Sterile bracts (10–15mm) are very broadly obovate or lanceolate, and vibrant purple–violet (87A) with strongly undulating margins (illustrated on pages 134 and 151).

Raised in the mid-1990s by Marilyn and Ian Wightman, New Zealand, 'Regal Splendour' is the best dark purple-bracted cultivar on the market. However, it needs to be well pruned to maintain its compact shape, as it has a tendency to grow upright. Recommended as an ornamental, hedging or feature plant, or grow en masse for effect.

LAVANDULA 'ROCKY ROAD'

Habit is bushy to spreading and small (50cm) with semi-open to dense, mid-green to grey–green foliage. Peduncles are short to medium (3–5cm), dull green and finely pubescent. Occasional lateral branching occurs. Spikes are short to medium (2–4cm) and truncate or fusiform-conic. Fertile bracts are green and red–purple, obovate or rhombic-cordate and acute. Hair covering is sparse. Corollas are rich violet–blue (89A); calyces are finely pubescent and green, with the upper half red–purple. Appendages are pale purple. Sterile bracts (10–25mm) are linear, oblong or elliptic, with moderately undulating margins (illustrated on pages 141 and 152). The colour is a mixture of soft lavender–purple (76A) and lavender–violet (85A).

Raised about 1994 in New Zealand by Wayne Horrobin and Sarah Hodge, 'Rocky Road' is a small colourful cultivar suitable for container growing, low hedging, as an ornamental plant or as a cheery addition to the front of a border.

LAVANDULA 'ROSELIGHT'

A pretty plant of bushy, semi-open habit and quite tall (70–80cm), with bright green foliage. Peduncles are medium (6–9cm), light green and tomentose. Occasional lateral branching may occur. Spikes are medium (2–4cm) and make a definite statement, being truncate-conic or occasionally fusiform-conic and broader than usual. Fertile bracts are red–purple and pubescent with longer hairs on the margins. The bract shape is broadly obovate or rhombic-cordate, almost reniform and acute. Corollas are rich violet–blue (89A). Calyces are pubescent and green, with the upper half a deep purple. Appendages are red–purple. Sterile bracts (10–20mm) are broadly elliptic or obovate, and red–purple (72A) with moderately undulating margins (illustrated on pages 137 and 152).

Selected from seedlings sourced in Australia and named in New Zealand by Virginia McNaughton in 1995, 'Roselight' is suitable as an ornamental or hedging plant. It is closest to 'Pippa' but a much better form.

LAVANDULA 'ROXLEA PARK'

A compact, medium to semi-tall bush (60–70cm) with dense mid-green foliage. Occasional lateral branching may occur. Peduncles are medium (4–8cm), thin, bright green and pubescent. Spikes are medium (2–4cm), and a mixture of cylindric, truncate and fusiform-conic. Fertile bracts are purple, mostly rhombic-cordate or reniform and acute, with long hair on both bracts and margins. Corollas are dark violet–blue (93B); calyces are pubescent and green with purple tips and appendages. Sterile bracts (10–15mm) are oblong-obovate or slightly spathulate, pinkish-mauve to violet–blue with strongly undulating margins (illustrated on page 132).

Raised by Gil Cayford, New Zealand, in the early 1990s, 'Roxlea Park', with its dense compact form and rose-like inflorescences, makes a fine ornamental or potted plant, or a medium-sized hedge. The sterile bracts are a feature of this plant, forming 'rose-bud' lookalikes prior to opening.

LAVANDULA 'SOMERSET MIST'

A tall plant (1m) of bushy habit and moderately dense, bright green foliage. Peduncles are medium to long (4–12cm), light green to mid-green, tomentose and occasionally broad. Spikes are truncate-conic or cylindric and medium (3–4cm). Fertile bracts are green or red–purple and pubescent. The shape is mostly suborbicular and acute. Corollas are rich violet–blue (89B). Calyces are pubescent, ranging from soft red–purple to greenish-brown, with green appendages. Sterile bracts (10–25mm) are elliptic or linear, and soft pastel pink and green with slightly undulating margins (illustrated on page 132).

Raised at Somerset Downs, New Zealand, in the late 1980s, 'Somerset Mist' was one of the first subtly coloured cultivars to be introduced to the market. Suitable for hedging or ornamental purposes.

LAVANDULA 'SOUTHERN LIGHTS'

Habit is bushy and semi-tall to tall (70–80cm) with semi-open, grey–green foliage. Peduncles are medium to long (9–15cm), broad, dull green and tomentose. Spikes are medium (2–3cm), very broad and truncate-conic. Fertile bracts are membranous with green veining and finely pubescent. The shape is broadly cordate and acute or suborbicular. Corollas are violet–blue (90B). Calyces are finely pubescent and light green, with brownish-green appendages. Sterile bracts (15–30mm) are elliptic, with strongly undulating margins. There are generally four large and four smaller sterile bracts, and their colour ranges from creamy-white through to mauve–pink (75B) (illustrated on page 134).

Raised by Geoff and Adair Genge, New Zealand, in the early 1990s, 'Southern Lights' is a splendid double-bracted specimen with broad impressive spikes. Suitable for ornamental planting or as a feature plant. Keep well pruned.

LAVANDULA 'SUGAR PLUM'

A medium plant (60–70cm) of spreading habit with open, bright green foliage. Peduncles are long (8–19cm), light green, broad and rigid with medium hair cover. Spikes are medium (3–4cm) and truncate-conic. Fertile bracts are green with red–purple veining and pubescent with longer hair on the margins. The bract shape is cordate and acute or obovate. Corollas are dark blue (103A). Calyces are pubescent, two-thirds green with red–purple tips and purple appendages. Sterile bracts (15–25mm) are green, heavily suffused in red–violet, oblong or elliptic, with slightly undulating margins.

LEFT
L. 'Raycott'

RIGHT
L. 'Regal Splendour'

Named by Wayne Horrobin and Sarah Hodge, New Zealand, and released in the mid-1990s, 'Sugar Plum' is a more prostrate lavender with almost dark red sterile bracts. It may be used as a front-of-border or an ornamental plant. Keep well pruned.

LAVANDULA 'SWAN RIVER PINK'

(synonym: **'Magenta Aurora'**)
A small bushy to spreading plant (40–50cm) with open mid-green to grey–green foliage. Peduncles are short to medium (3–4cm), red–purple or bright green and very finely pubescent. Spikes are short (1.5–2.5cm) and mostly cylindric. Fertile bracts are red–purple, and obovate or rhombic-cordate and acute or almost reniform in shape. They are finely pubescent with longer hairs on the margins. Corollas are red–purple (72A). Calyces are finely pubescent and green suffused with red–purple. Appendages are purple. Sterile bracts (5–12mm) are elliptic, obovate or slightly spathulate with strongly undulating margins (illustrated on page 132). The colour is lavender–pink (69C) with patches of red–purple (61A).

Discovered and named in Australia by K. and G. Napier, 'Swan River Pink' is a very attractive pink-flowered lavender suitable as a front-of-border or general ornamental plant. Because of its spreading open nature, it requires regular pruning.

LAVANDULA 'SWEET CAROLINE'

Habit is bushy and medium (60–70cm) with dense grey–green foliage. Peduncles are medium (5–7cm), dull green, occasionally broad and tomentose. Spikes are medium (2.5–3cm), fusiform-conic or cylindric. Fertile bracts are membranous with green veins and finely pubescent with longer dense hair on the margins. The bract shape is obovate

and acute. Corollas are rich violet–blue (89A), though a slightly different shade from 'Lumiere'. Calyces are pubescent and pale green with green appendages. Sterile bracts (15–25mm) are white (155B), oblanceolate or oblong, with slightly undulating margins. There are usually four sterile bracts with an occasional eight-bracted spike.

Raised by Jeff Elliott, New Zealand, in the late 1990s, 'Sweet Caroline' is an attractive compact cultivar with bicoloured spikes, suitable for hedging, ornamental or container culture.

LAVANDULA 'TICKLED PINK'

An upright bushy plant of medium to semi-tall proportions (70cm) with semi-open to dense, grey–green foliage. Peduncles are short (0.5–3.5cm) and bright green. Spikes are medium (2–4cm), mostly cylindric or fusiform-conic. Fertile bracts are membranous with green veining suffused with red–purple around the edges and almost glabrous. The bract shape is cordate and acute or suborbicular. Corollas are dark blue (103A). Calyces are pubescent and green, or green with red–purple ribbing and appendages. Sterile bracts (15–25mm) are broadly obovate or spathulate, with moderately undulating margins (illustrated on pages 132 and 154). The colour is a mixture of vibrant pink–violet (82C) to purple–violet (87C).

Raised by Virginia McNaughton in New Zealand about 1991, 'Tickled Pink' is a vivid pinkish-violet, sterile-bracted cultivar with an unusual growth habit due to its *L. stoechas* subsp. *luisieri* parent. Suitable for ornamental or hedging purposes, or for mass planting.

LAVANDULA 'VAN GOGH'

An upright bushy plant of medium height (60–70cm) with semi-open, bright green foliage. Peduncles are medium to long (4–12cm), occasionally broad, light green and covered in medium-length but sparse hair. Spikes are medium (2–4cm) and mostly cylindric. Occasional lateral branching occurs. Fertile bracts are green, mostly obovate or rhombic-cordate and acute, and finely pubescent with longer hair on the margins. Corollas are lavender–blue (91A); calyces are finely pubescent and green, with olive-green appendages. Sterile bracts (10–20mm) are oblanceolate or obovate, greenish-white with green midribs and veining, and moderately undulating margins (illustrated on pages 136 and 155).

'Van Gogh' was bred in New Zealand and released about 1996. The lighter blue corollas are a striking contrast to the sterile bracts. Suitable for hedging or ornamental purposes.

LAVANDULA 'VERY WHITE FORM'

Habit is bushy to spherical and medium (60cm) with dense bright green to grey–green foliage. Peduncles are short (1.5–3cm), thin, bright green and finely pubescent. Frequent short lateral branching occurs. Spikes are short (1–3cm) and truncate-conic. Fertile bracts are pale green, rhombic-cordate or broadly obovate and acute, and finely pubescent. Corollas are white; calyces are pubescent and membranous with green veining and green appendages. Sterile bracts (7–11mm) are very white with green bases, midribs and veining and broadly obovate, with slightly undulating margins (illustrated on pages 155 and 156).

Discovered by Phil Brown, New Zealand, this cultivar may also be known as 'Alba'. It is one of the whitest sterile-bracted small cultivars. Suitable for pot growing, ornamental use or as a small hedge.

LAVANDULA 'WHITE FORM'
(synonym: **'Alba'**)
A semi-tall plant (70cm), of bushy habit with dense bright green to grey–green foliage. Peduncles are short to medium (4–5cm), bright green and pubescent. Spikes are medium (2.5–4cm) and truncate to fusiform-conic. Fertile bracts are rhombic-cordate and acute and membranous with very strong green veining and longer hairs on the margins. Corollas are white; calyces are green and pubescent with green appendages. Sterile bracts (5–10mm) are creamy-white and narrow-obovate or slightly elliptic, with strongly undulating margins (illustrated on page 155).

This cultivar was raised in New Zealand in the late 1980s and incorrectly known as 'Alba'. (Latinised names such as 'Alba' have been banned from use in cultivar names for some years now.) With its naturally compact shape, this white form is suitable for ornamental or hedging purposes.

LAVANDULA 'WILLOWBRIDGE BLUEBERRY'

Habit is medium (60cm) and bushy with semi-open, bright green foliage. Peduncles are short to medium (3–6cm), thin, bright green and tomentose. Spikes are medium (2.5–3.5cm) and mostly cylindric. Fertile bracts are membranous with green veining, and pubescent. The bract shape is obovate and acute. Corollas are deep purple (79A); calyces are densely pubescent and light green, with green appendages. Sterile bracts (5–15mm) are elliptic and dark blueberry–violet (86B) with slightly undulating margins (illustrated on page 137).

Raised in New Zealand by Leone and Rex Young and released in the mid- to late 1990s, 'Willowbridge Blueberry' is best used as an ornamental plant, but dislikes being pruned back too hard.

LAVANDULA 'WILLOWBRIDGE CALICO'

A semi-tall plant (70cm) of bushy habit with dense, bright green foliage. Peduncles are short (3–4.5cm), bright green and pubescent. Spikes are short to medium (1.5–3cm) and truncate-conic. Fertile bracts are membranous, with strong green veining, rhombic-cordate or obovate and acute, with slight pubescence. Corollas are very light violet–blue (97B). Calyces are densely pubescent and green, with green appendages. Sterile bracts (8–10mm) are obovate, linear or elliptic, and orange or calico (159) with a slight pinkish tinge and green veining. There may also be occasional green shading in the centre of the bracts (illustrated on pages 145 and 157).

Raised in the early 1990s by Leone and Rex Young, New Zealand, this is an attractive cultivar with appealing and different coloured sterile bracts. Suitable for hedging or ornamental purposes, and can be container grown when young.

LAVANDULA 'WILLOWBRIDGE SNOW'

Habit is bushy and semi-tall (70–80cm) with dense mid-green foliage. Peduncles are short to medium (3–6cm), thin and bright green, with a sparse covering of medium-length hair. Occasional lateral branching occurs. Spikes are medium (2.5–4cm), truncate to fusiform-conic. Fertile bracts are membranous with green veining and very finely pubescent. The bract shape is rhombic-cordate or cordate and mostly acute. Corollas are white; calyces are green and pubescent with green appendages. Sterile bracts (10–15mm) are creamy-white (155B) with green midribs and veining, mostly oblong to oblanceolate, with slight to moderately undulating margins.

'Willowbridge Snow' is another in the Willowbridge series released in the mid-1990s. As a young plant it is not much different from other white-flowered lavenders but, when mature, it becomes a very attractive specimen plant. Use for hedging or other ornamental purposes; its compact form also makes it suitable as a potted plant for the first two years.

LAVANDULA 'WILLOWBRIDGE WHITE'
(synonym: **'Willowbridge Joy'**)

The habit is medium (60–70cm) and bushy with dense bright green to grey–green foliage. Peduncles are short (2–4cm), bright green, thin and finely pubescent. Frequent lateral branching occurs. Spikes are medium (2–3cm), truncate-conic or cylindric. Fertile bracts are membranous with green veining, deltoid or rhombic-cordate and acute, and finely pubescent. Corollas are bright violet–blue (90A); calyces are pubescent and light green, with green appendages. Sterile bracts (10–20mm) are oblanceolate or oblong-obovate, white with green midribs and slightly undulating margins (illustrated on page 136).

OPPOSITE
L. 'Tickled Pink'

LEFT
L. 'Very White Form'
L. stoechas forma *leucantha*
L. 'White Form'
L. 'Willowbridge Snow'

RIGHT
L. 'Van Gogh'

Another cultivar in the Willowbridge series released in the mid-1990s, 'Willowbridge White' resembles *L. stoechas* subsp. *stoechas* in habit and is suitable for low hedging, ornamental use or container growing.

LAVANDULA 'WILLOWBRIDGE WINGS'

A spreading plant to 70cm with open grey foliage. Peduncles are medium to long (8–12cm), broad and dull green with long hair. Spikes are medium (2–3cm), very broadly truncate-conic, with an infrequent base whorl 1–2cm below the main spike.

L. 'Very White Form'

Fertile bracts are membranous with green veining and long hairs on margins, shorter on the bracts. The bract shape is very broadly cordate or obovate and acute. Corollas are bright violet–blue (90A). Calyces are densely pubescent and light green, with green appendages. Sterile bracts (20–40mm) are mostly oblanceolate to elliptic, creamy-white with thick green midribs and green veining changing to a soft pinkish shade in hot sun. There are usually four large sterile bracts and up to ten shorter narrower bracts. The first spikes for the season may have only four sterile bracts (illustrated on page 134).

'Willowbridge Wings' is a most unusual and attractive lavender with its double-bracted spikes. Very suitable as an ornamental, collector's item or feature plant but possibly too open in habit for hedging. A recent release in the Willowbridge series and one of the best for the combination of spike, sterile bract and foliage.

LAVANDULA 'WINE'
(synonym: **'Wine Red'**)
Habit is bushy and semi-tall (70–80cm) with semi-open, bright green foliage. Peduncles are medium to long (7–15cm), bright green with short to medium pubescence. Spikes are medium (2–3cm), truncate-conic to cylindric. Fertile bracts are green with red–purple veining and densely pubescent with longer hairs on the margins. The bract shape is obovate or rhombic-cordate and acute, and occasionally suborbicular and acute. Corollas are dark violet (86A). Calyces are pubescent and green with red–purple veining and appendages. Sterile bracts (5–20mm) are elliptic or oblong, with slightly undulating margins, varying in number from two to five (illustrated on page 137). Their colour is mauve–violet (84A).

Raised by Gary and Linda Winter, New Zealand, in the early 1990s, 'Wine' looks similar to *L. stoechas* subsp. *pedunculata* except that the sterile bracts are a different colour. Use as an ornamental plant.

LAVANDULA VIRIDIS 'SILVER GHOST'

Not a cultivar of *L. stoechas* but of *L. viridis*. A semi-tall plant (60–70cm) of upright bushy habit with semi-open, variegated foliage. Leaves have mostly green centres with cream margins and tips. Peduncles are medium (5–8cm), bright green and strongly hairy. Spikes are medium (2–4cm). Fertile bracts are white with green margins, broadly obovate and slightly pubescent. Corollas and calyces are white. The calyces are densely pubescent and have white appendages. Sterile bracts (10–15mm) are elliptic, and white with green bases and occasional green spotting around the margins; veining is white. Undulation of margins is only slight.

Raised around 1991 in New Zealand from a sport of *L. viridis* by Wayne Horrobin and Sarah Hodge, 'Silver Ghost' is a very stable, attractively variegated cultivar with slightly curling leaves — the only cultivar with white fertile bracts. 'Silver Ghost' has an upright growth habit, so it can be used in the middle or the back of a border. Quite distinctive from a distance, it can therefore be used for effect, or as a general ornamental plant.

OTHER LAVENDERS

SECTION *DENTATA* CULTIVARS

The following five cultivars belong to Section *Dentata* and are hybrids. While not as fragrant as other lavenders, the spikes are very colourful and may be used fresh or dried for arrangements or coloured crafts. All cultivars will flower year-round in warmer climates but need to be planted in a sunny spot in frost-prone areas. The peduncles do not have lateral branching and there are no bracteoles present.

L. 'Sidonie' and Thalictrum sp.

LAVANDULA 'ALLWOOD'

A bushy shrub to 1m with dense, light green foliage. Peduncles are long (10–30cm), grey–green and tomentose. All leaves are narrow. Spikes are medium (3–6cm), loosely compact and broad-conical, with the base whorl 1–2cm below the main spike. Fertile bracts are green and violet. Corollas are pale violet–blue (97C), and calyces are either green or half-green and half-violet. The sterile bracts are dark lavender (94C) (illustrated on pages 60 and 62).

This cultivar was raised about or before 1950 and donated to the Adelaide Botanic Gardens; subsequently named by Clive Larkman, Australia. An attractive smaller-growing cultivar, which appears hardier than the species *L. dentata*, 'Allwood' is suitable for ornamental use or topiary work, as well as for large container growing. Commonly known as the 'Mount Lofty lavender'.

LAVANDULA 'LAMBIKINS'

'Lambikins' is similar in some characteristics to 'Ploughman's Blue'. It has very broad but lighter-green leaves and the bush has a tendency to be more open and spreading, with a height of 60–70cm. Peduncles and spikes are a similar length. Corollas are soft violet–blue (92A) and sterile bracts lavender–violet (91A).

Raised in the United States of America, 'Lambikins' has a tendency to be difficult to grow and dislikes frost. Suitable for ornamental purposes.

LAVANDULA 'LINDA LIGON'

L. 'Linda Ligon'

A variegated, semi-tall cultivar (70–80cm) of bushy habit with semi-open, green and creamy-yellow foliage. Peduncles are medium to long (10–25cm), compact and broad-conical, with an occasional base whorl 1cm below the main spike. Spikes are medium (3–5cm), compact and broad-conical. Fertile bracts are green suffused with purple. Corollas are dark lavender–violet (92A), and calyces green with dark violet tips. Sterile bracts are bright violet–blue (90B).

Raised in the United States by Tom DeBaggio, 'Linda Ligon' is not as well or evenly variegated as some of the other variegated cultivars. The variegation is quite patchy and some cuttings will display more colour than others. However, it is a novelty plant suitable for hedging or topiary, as an ornamental shrub or for large container growing. It will tolerate light frosts only.

LAVANDULA 'PLOUGHMAN'S BLUE'

A smaller-growing plant (60–70cm) of bushy to spreading habit with semi-open, grey–green foliage. Leaves are darker green and broader than many other cultivars; peduncles are medium to long (10–25cm), very broad, grey–green and tomentose. Spikes are medium (3–5cm), compact and broad-conical. Fertile bracts are suffused with violet giving the spike a much darker appearance. Corollas are lavender–violet (91A); calyces are green with the upper half violet. Sterile bracts are bright violet–blue (90A) (illustrated on page 60).

Raised in 1991 by Peter Carter, New Zealand, 'Ploughman's Blue' seems to perform well only in certain areas and dislikes too much humidity. Best grown in a frost-free area as an ornamental plant.

LAVANDULA 'PURE HARMONY'

A medium shrub to over 1m with dense grey–green foliage. Peduncles are 10–25cm, green and tomentose; spikes are medium (2–5cm), compact and broad-conical. Fertile bracts and calyces are green, and sterile bracts and corollas white.

An exciting, new white-flowered cultivar on the market, 'Pure Harmony' is suitable for hedging or topiary, or as a feature, ornamental or container plant.

The following three cultivars are hybrids within Section *Pterostoechas*. Corollas are two-toned in colour, making it difficult to match against a colour chart. The fragrance is unusual and pleasant but not the scent normally associated with lavender. They are generally grown as ornamental plants but are very frost-tender.

LAVANDULA 'BLUE CANARIES'

A tall cultivar to over 1m with semi-open, bright green foliage similar to its *L. canariensis* parent. Leaves are bipinnate, and peduncles are very long (30–60cm), green, finely pubescent and only branched near the base of the peduncle. Spikes are long (8–12cm), arranged singly or in groups of six (illustrated on page 64). The corollas are vibrant blue–purple and smaller than those of 'Sidonie', but nonetheless striking. Raised by Ruth Bookman, New Zealand, in the mid-1990s, 'Blue Canaries' is a stunning ornamental plant, especially en masse.

LAVANDULA 'SIDONIE'

A tall shrub to over 1m with semi-open, grey–green foliage. Leaves are large and bipinnate. Peduncles are very long (30–60cm), grey–green, finely pubescent and frequently branched. Spikes are either single or arranged in threes (6–12cm). Corollas are a deep vibrant blue–purple (illustrated on pages 64 and 158). One of its parents is probably *L. pinnata*.

L. 'Pure Harmony'

Raised in Australia by Sidonie Barton and Ian Cunliffe in the early 1990s, 'Sidonie' is a beautiful, elegant cultivar grown for ornamental purposes in warmer areas. It needs only light pruning over summer. The spikes can be carefully dried and used in pot pourri for their colour.

Another cultivar **'Silver Feather'** is very similar to 'Sidonie' but differs in having a smaller, less-divided leaf area and more bushy, denser habit. Corollas are also more purple than 'Sidonie'. It was raised by the University of Sydney, Australia.

LAVANDULA 'GOODWIN CREEK GREY'

'Goodwin Creek Grey' is reputed to be a hybrid between *L.* x *heterophylla* and *L. lanata*, but is more likely to have *L. dentata* as a parent rather than *L.* x *heterophylla,* as the latter appears to be sterile. With partly dentate, silver–grey leaves and long spikes, the bush is semi-open to dense and quite large (60–80cm). Peduncles are long (19–35cm), grey–green and tomentose. Spikes are long (6–14cm) and narrow-conical. Fertile bracts are suffused with violet. Bracteoles are broad (2–3mm), corollas are rich violet–blue (89B) and calyces green and violet. Sterile bracts are a fluorescent violet–blue (90A/B) (illustrated on page 63). Raised at Goodwin Creek Gardens in Oregon, United States, this cultivar is a wonderful addition to any garden. Try planting it against a sunny wall.

LAVENDER GROWING AROUND THE WORLD

AUSTRALIA

Lavender farming began in Australia as early as 1894, when a government perfume farm was established in central Victoria, with the perfume industry promoted as a viable adjunct to farming. At the time the asking price for lavender cuttings was four shillings per thousand plants; small numbers of cuttings (up to 100) were given away without charge. The venture, however, did not progress, apparently due to bureaucratic problems.

In 1912 a number of 'Mother Patches' of lavender were established in Victoria, with the Labour Colony in Gippsland in south-east Victoria selling bundles of 1000 cuttings for three shillings and nine pence. However, despite liberal government assistance there was little interest at the time in farming this aromatic herb.

Bridestowe Lavender Estate, Tasmania, Australia

The only early venture to succeed is now Australia's oldest and best-known lavender farm, the Bridestowe Lavender Estate in north-east Tasmania. Established in 1921, Bridestowe has been growing lavender for over 75 years, farming in particular for quality oil production.

In mainland Australia, however, serious commercial interest in growing lavender for the retail and wholesale markets only emerged in the last 20 years. Rural recession, the decline in traditional farming enterprises, higher costs and fluctuating world markets forced farmers to consider alternative enterprises and crops.

Yuulong Lavender Estate was established in Victoria in 1980, and was growing 14 different varieties of lavender by 1988, when it was asked by the newly formed Ornamental Plant

Collections Association at the Royal Botanic Gardens in Melbourne to hold the National Collection of *Lavandula*.

Subsequent interest in growing lavender for its diverse uses developed quickly around Australia and hundreds of people visited Yuulong to study lavender farming. Names and addresses of interested persons were added to a growing mailing list. By 1990 several other commercial lavender farms had been established.

Discussions about the formation of an Australian Lavender Association commenced in late 1994, with formal meetings initiated in 1995. By September 1995 the first Australian lavender conference was held in Bombala, New South Wales, at which The Australian Lavender Growers' Association (TALGA) was launched. Just over a year later, in November 1996, the first International Lavender Conference was held in Australia at Ballarat, Victoria. Henry Head, owner of Norfolk Lavender in England, was a guest speaker and delegates came from across Australia and New Zealand. Since then national conferences have been held each year and the membership of TALGA continues to grow.

Yuulong Lavender Estate now grows 84 different varieties of lavenders, having trialled them in the ground for several years to check the best varieties for fresh or dried flowers and for oil production. Drought conditions during the 1990s have shown that Section *Lavandula* varieties grow particularly well in dry areas.

Some *L. angustifolia* cultivars are flourishing in warmer climates in the north of the country. Among these the *L. angustifolia* cultivars 'Egerton Blue' and 'Bosisto' and the *L.* x *intermedia* cultivars 'Grosso', 'Seal', 'Yuulong' and 'Miss Donnington' are being cultivated for fresh and dried flowers as well as for oil production.

> *Rosemary Holmes*
> *General Manager, Yuulong Lavender Estate*
> *Australia*

'Lavandula' near Daylesford, Victoria, Australia

FRANCE

For many centuries lavender has grown wild on the sunny, stony soils of the mountains and hills of Provence, where it was traditionally gathered and used as an antiseptic for wounds and as a perfuming agent.

Over time a more formal cosmetic and perfumery industry developed and lavender was an obvious choice for use in this industry, especially as it grew abundantly. During the nineteenth century, a more organised system of lavender collection began and portable stills (alembics) were used to distil lavender oil in the fields.

Commercial crops of lavandins were planted in the 1920s. Until that time, mixed plantings of wild lavender had mainly been harvested and used for distillation and this practice continued into the 1950s when clonal selection of *L. angustifolia* began. The larger lavandins, often referred to as 'big lavender' or 'bastard lavender', had the advantage of increased spike production and a much higher yield of oil — four to eight times the amount extracted from lavender.

The first lavandin to be found growing in the wild was simply called 'Ordinary'. The cultivar known as *L.* x *intermedia* 'Abrialii' was developed by Professor Abrial in the 1930s and was used for most of the planting at that time. Unfortunately, yellow decline had a disastrous effect on these plants and on lavender farming generally. Hence the development of *L.* x *intermedia* 'Super' in the 1950s and 1960s and *L.* x *intermedia* 'Grosso' in the 1970s, both of which were resistant to yellow decline. *Lavandula* x *intermedia* 'Sumian' was another cultivar used for oil, but to a lesser extent.

In recent times, lavandin oil production has mostly superseded lavender oil production in France due to the lavandins' ability to produce more oil and their easier adaptation to mechanical harvesting compared to lavender. The main areas of production are in Drome, Vaucluse and the Alpes de haute, Provence. Lavender production has mostly been abandoned in the highest regions — Hautes-Alpes.

The primary lavandin used commercially is *L.* x *intermedia* 'Grosso' and one of the few lavenders still in production is *L. angustifolia* 'Maillette'.

Today the stills are very large and no longer transportable, and much of the harvesting is done by machine. Plants in commercial production may be replaced at eight-year intervals.

A collection of lavender is kept at INRA, a French government department, and another is held by Catherine Couttolenc in Sault, Provence.

The annual Sault Festival is one of the highlights of the French lavender season and there is a well-marked and popular lavender route that delights visitors not only with vistas of lavender and other flower crops, but also with its wine tasting and delicious cuisine opportunities.

JAPAN

Japanese lavender history began in 1937 when the late Mr Seiji Soda, a founder of Soda Perfumery, brought 5kg of lavender seeds from Marseilles, France, for the purpose of growing lavender for cosmetic perfumery.

After various agricultural experiments with lavenders, full cultivation of lavender began around 1948 in the Furano district of Hokkaido, located at latitude 43 degrees north. At that time the late Mr Ueda Yoshikazu, pioneer of lavender growing in the Furano district, was assigned by Soda Perfumery to cultivate lavender.

Representative of Farm Tomita, Mr Tadao Tomita at the age of 21 was captivated by the blue lavender fields tended by Mr Ueda, and by the sweet fragrance and beauty of the flowers, and started lavender cultivation seven years later in 1958.

Subsequently, the Japanese Government supported lavender growers, with numbers increasing to around 250 farmers engaged in the cultivation of 200 hectares of lavender. Essential oil production reached over 5 tons at its peak, around 1970.

However the rapid improvement of the synthetic perfume industry and less expensive imported perfumery affected the lavender farmers in the Furano district so severely that most of the lavender fields disappeared. Similarly affected, Mr Tomita thought he could not survive without abandoning his fields of lavender, as had other farmers. In later years, Mr Tomita recalled: 'When I got on a tractor and started to crush them, I stopped immediately, hearing the scream of the lavender flowers, and I could not step on the accelerator further.'

In 1975, lavender fields were featured in a Japanese National Railway's calendar, triggering a flood of interest from all over Japan. Perhaps it was the appeal of the fairies of the lavenders bringing 'peace of mind' and 'satisfaction' through the calendar's spectacular images.

Farm Tomita has introduced many visitors to the charm of lavender, with 800,000 people touring their lavender fields during 1998. Farm Tomita claims that a first encounter with lavender will leave a lasting impression on its many visitors.

In June 1998, Mr Tomita established the Lavender Club as a network aiming to conserve and promote lavenders. By April 1999, the club had 1800 members from all over Japan and also from abroad.

The blossom time for lavender in Furano extends for a whole month from the beginning of July.

Four *L. angustifolia* cultivars named 'Hayasaki', 'Youtei', 'Hanamoiwa' and 'Okamurasaki' have been selected as superior cultivars, which, due to their different blooming periods, bring continuing enjoyment to visitors throughout the season.

> *Public Relations Office of Farm Tomita*
> *Japan*

In northern Japan in the Koshinetstu area where the Japan Alps are located, covered with heavy snow during winter, mainly *L. angustifolia* cultivars and sometimes *L.* x *intermedia* cultivars are planted.

In southern Japan including the Kanto area where Tokyo is located, climatic conditions are not suitable for growing *L. angustifolia* due to high temperatures and humidity. With mid-summer temperatures exceeding 30°C, a town in the Kanto plain cultivates *L.* x *intermedia* on the riverbanks, attracting many tourists during flowering time in June.

At Kawaguchi Lake, nestled at the foot of Mount Fuji, *L. angustifolia* cultivars are planted throughout the parks. The purple lavenders bloom beautifully against the scenic backdrop of Mount Fuji.

A range of lavenders — *L. dentata*, *L. multifida* or *L. pinnata*, and *Stoechas*-group lavenders — are sold by city florists in the southern Kanto area.

In downtown Tokyo, lavender is as popular with Japanese people for their gardens as are tulips and pansies.

> *Noriko Iwao*
> *Japan*

NEW ZEALAND

Lavender has been grown in New Zealand since the arrival of English settlers in the 1800s. Presumably most plants would have been brought in as seed. However, serious importation of lavender plants did not commence until the late 1950s. A very keen herb enthusiast, Avice Hill, always particular about the authenticity of her plants, started to import lavender from the United Kingdom in the late 1950s and early 1960s, thus providing the basis for the two large collections held in New Zealand. One is held in the North Island by Peter Carter and one in the South Island by Virginia McNaughton, and they are overseen by the Herb Federation of New Zealand. Both collections hold over 250 different lavenders from New Zealand, Australia, United Kingdom, Japan, United States of America, South Africa, France, Hungary, Germany and Austria. Such diversity has created an opportunity for serious, ongoing research into the *Lavandula* genus.

Over the years the dried lavender industry, both locally and for export, has been developed. Likewise small lavender farms have attracted tourists and furthered interest in lavender in general. Government departments took an active interest in lavender oil production and imported plants from France in 1983 to conduct field trials. These trials proved very successful and lavender growing on a larger scale was initiated. In October 1995, the New Zealand Lavender Oil Producers' Association (NZLOPA) was formally incorporated and an enthusiastic group of people pooled their knowledge with worthwhile results.

New Zealand is fortunate to have an ideal climate for growing lavender and there are few places where lavender cannot grow. However, the more tender plants are better suited to warmer parts of the North Island and frost-free areas of the South Island. Cultivars from Sections *Lavandula* and *Stoechas* are hardy enough to be grown throughout New Zealand and do not need to be overwintered inside. The diversity and range of recent new cultivars are exciting, with New Zealand producing a number of its own good-quality cultivars over the years. Some of the more notable plants are *L.* 'Pukehou', *L.* 'Marshwood', *L.* 'Helmsdale' and *L.* 'Pippa White'. More recent introductions include *L.* 'Regal Splendour', *L.* 'Rocky Road', *L.* 'Roxlea Park', *L.* 'Tickled Pink' and some of the smaller-growing *L. angustifolia* cultivars such as 'Lavenite Petite' and 'Crystal Lights'.

The lavender industry continues to grow rapidly in New Zealand, where the climate and soils favour this versatile and aromatic herb.

UNITED KINGDOM

They say that lavender was brought to England by the Romans, but I have a strong suspicion that it may well have arrived before then. After all, the Phoenicians who came from the Mediterranean, the origin of many lavenders, traded with Cornwall and may have used lavender as part of their medicine chest.

However once it arrived, it stayed. After the Romans left, it was cultivated by monks, principally the Benedictines in their monasteries as part of their physick garden, a fact that is much supported by mediaeval manuscripts.

With the end of the Wars of the Roses and generally more settled conditions in England, gardens were laid out and lavender became an essential feature of the Tudor knot garden. It was also a very important culinary herb. Queen Elizabeth I is known to have preferred lavender conserve with lamb above all others.

The commercial growing of lavender in England developed on the south-facing chalk downs surrounding London — Wallington, Carshalton to the south, and Hitchin to the north. They were within easy reach of Covent Garden and it is said that, in the reign of Charles I, Charles Yardley was able to scent soap with lavender oil. Until then, soap had smelled only of its basic ingredient — boiled fat.

The use of fragrance in England became widespread in the eighteenth and nineteenth centuries and the House of Yardley was founded in 1770. During the nineteenth century other illustrious names like Perks at Hitchin and Potter and Moore at Carshalton sprang up but have now, like the once-illustrious Yardleys, passed away.

After the First World War, lavender growing in England went into decline because of the change of fashion, disease in the lavender fields and the spread of London, which meant it was more profitable to 'farm' houses than it was to farm lavender.

However, in the nick of time, Linn Chilvers founded Norfolk Lavender Ltd in 1932 and so kept alive the great tradition of lavender growing in England. Until recently there were no other lavender farms in England. Norfolk Lavender Ltd is still by far the largest and best known, welcoming almost 150,000 visitors a year. Its products are also exported all round the world. Norfolk Lavender held one of the early National Collections — that of *Lavandula* of course, and has been responsible for breeding or introducing some of the cultivars now commonly grown in gardens: *L. angustifolia* 'Imperial Gem', *L. angustifolia* 'Princess Blue', *L. angustifolia* 'Royal Purple', *L. angustifolia* 'Miss Katherine' and *L.* 'Sawyers'.

Henry Head
Managing Director, Norfolk Lavender
United Kingdom

UNITED STATES OF AMERICA

Modern-day appreciation and popularity of lavender began as long ago as 1933 when the Herb Society of America was formed. This society — made up of both keen amateur and professional nurseryman alike — embarked on a mission to rekindle a national interest in herbs. Its adopted motto 'Herbs — for use and delight' became its mission statement. In 1981, Nancy Howard (HSA member, Philadelphia) imported a collection of lavenders and lavandins from both the RHS gardens at Wisley, England, and the Syon Garden Centre, England. (The lavandins had originally come from the garden of the Vicomte de Noailles in France.) Another HSA member, Joyce Douglas, also imported lavender cultivars (namely, *L. angustifolia* 'Maillette') at this time. Each contributed live specimen material to Dr Arthur O. Tucker for proper identification through analysis of their essential oil make-up. From their essential oil 'fingerprints', he was able to correctly identify and confirm several cultivars of both lavender and lavandin clones. Lavender growers in North America owe a large debt of gratitude to the quest of these two women for proper identification of lavender, and to Dr Tucker's contagious enthusiasm for public education and dissemination of lavender and its clones.

In the past 15 years, the popularity of lavender has steadily increased along with consumer awareness. Major trends of commercial lavender production have been basically twofold: to increase public awareness of the staggering number of lavender species and cultivars commercially available as well as educating the public in their many uses; and to propagate and disseminate lavender species and cultivars to an ever-desirous populace.

Growers of lavenders have responded in various ways to the ensuing public demand and in a uniquely regional way. In Virginia, Thomas DeBaggio selected and introduced *L. angustifolia* cultivars for both dark-flowered characteristics (*L. angustifolia* 'Tucker's Early Purple', *L. angustifolia* 'Dark Supreme') and for strong repeat bloomers (*L. angustifolia* 'Two Seasons'). He is also credited with introducing the first commercially available variegated lavender, *L.* 'Linda Ligon'. In Oregon, Jim Becker (Goodwin Creek Gardens) introduced a unique silver-foliaged lavender from a *L. dentata* cross, *L.* 'Goodwin Creek Grey'. Dr Don Roberts (Premier Botanicals Ltd), also of Oregon, bred and selected *L. angustifolia* cultivars originally for essential oil quality, but later released them for horticultural landscape use. He introduced *L. angustifolia* 'Sharon Roberts' and, later, *L. angustifolia* 'Buena Vista', *L. angustifolia* 'Sachet' and *L. angustifolia* 'Premier'. Andrew and Melissa Van Hevelingen (Van Hevelingen Herbs) began with *L. angustifolia* selections for flower characteristics, *L. angustifolia* 'Melissa' (pink-flowered), and *L. angustifolia* 'Royal Velvet'. Since then, they have selected from *L. angustifolia* x *L. lanata* crosses for year-round silver foliage characteristics. These selections include *L.* 'Silver Frost' and *L.* 'Ana Luisa'.

California has also played an integral part in promoting new cultivars. Foremost in their introductions have been *L. stoechas* cultivars such as *L.* 'Otto Quast' (synonyms:

L. 'Quasti' = *L*. 'Otto Quest') and *L*. 'Atlas' — which are now widely circulated along the West Coast of the United States. More recently selected cultivars for superb silver foliage are *L*. x *intermedia* 'Fred Boutin' (Huntington Botanical Gardens) and *L*. x *intermedia* 'Lisa Marie'. Selected for a tight compact growth habit was the cultivar *L. angustifolia* 'Martha Roderick'.

Especially unique to California has been the increasing trend of wineries to employ lavender not only as a secondary cash crop but as a tourist attraction and medium for advertising. The popular choice for these large plantings has been lavandins, especially the cultivars *L*. x *intermedia* 'Grosso' and *L*. x *intermedia* 'Super', not only for their fresh cut and dried flowers but for their distillation value in oils for aromatherapy use. There has been some minor experimentation with the *L. angustifolia* cultivar, especially *L. angustifolia* 'Maillette' for possible commercial oil extraction. In Sequim, Washington, a lavender cooperative made up of several growers has developed its own local market ranging from u-pick fresh flowers to dried lavender products and oil distillation.

It is not too surprising that the forefront of major lavender production is located in the West Coast States as the climate is much more similar to Mediterranean conditions, allowing for a larger number of both species and cultivars of lavender to be grown successfully. Large areas of arable land are still available and hand labour is plentiful.

Harsh winter temperatures in the northern United States limit lavender growing there to only some of the hardier *L. angustifolia* cultivars. The East Coast States are affected by either cold winter temperatures or high summer humidity, which causes fungal infection.

Due to the ever-increasing number of lavender species and clones appearing in the United States, the Herb Society of America has embarked on a national collection scheme similar to England's, and two national lavender collections are presently located in Oregon and Washington respectively.

Andrew Van Hevelingen
Van Hevelingen Herbs
United States of America

The Lavender Bag

The Lavender Bag is a newsletter for lavender enthusiasts. It had its beginnings in a study day, held in 1993 at Norfolk Lavender in the United Kingdom, organised by the British Herb Trades Association. At this meeting it was agreed that there was much confusion in the naming of lavenders, with different plants bearing the same cultivar name and different names being given to plants that are extremely alike. Basic differences between species were highlighted (in particular, botanical features of *L. angustifolia, L. latifolia* and the hybrid *L.* x *intermedia*) and anomalies in plant labels circulated in the nursery trade were discussed. As a result, a newsletter was suggested, to keep lavender growers, sellers and gardeners abreast of developments in research, particularly nomenclature issues.

Research on the genus *Lavandula* is still in progress: new species are being described and reclassification of existing species is under consideration. The newsletter aims to bring forward the results of this research to encourage accurate identification and labelling of lavender plants and to foster discussion. Experienced growers comment on propagation and cultivation techniques and amateur gardeners share their experiences of growing lavender and incorporating it in planting schemes. Botanists contribute articles on their observations and findings; accounts of their field trips are written up and their expertise passed on to readers.

The five National Collection holders of the genus *Lavandula* in the United Kingdom and parallel collection holders in Australia and New Zealand are among the subscribers; thus the newsletter provides a unique link between lavender enthusiasts many thousands of miles apart. The United States, New Zealand and Australia are well represented among the subscribers; mainland Europe puts in an appearance with France, Italy, Holland and Belgium. In the past year, we have also welcomed subscribers from South Africa and Japan. The burgeoning of interest in lavender is indeed worldwide.

Joan Head
Editor, **The Lavender Bag**
United Kingdom

APPENDICES

Section *Lavandula* cultivars,
by general corolla colour
or other distinctive features

White-flowered cultivars
L. angustifolia 'Alba'
L. angustifolia 'Celestial Star'
L. angustifolia 'Crystal Lights'
L. angustifolia 'Nana Alba'
L. x *intermedia* 'Alba'
L. x *intermedia* 'Dutch White'

Lilac–pink/pink-flowered cultivars
L. angustifolia 'Coconut Ice'
L. angustifolia 'Hidcote Pink'
L. angustifolia 'Jean Davis'
L. angustifolia 'Loddon Pink'
L. angustifolia 'Lullaby'
L. angustifolia 'Melissa'
L. angustifolia 'Miss Katherine'
L. angustifolia 'Pacific Pink'
L. angustifolia 'Rosea'

Dark blue/purple-flowered cultivars
L. angustifolia 'Blue Mountain'
L. angustifolia 'Foveaux Storm'
L. angustifolia 'Gray Lady'
L. angustifolia 'Hidcote'
L. angustifolia 'Imperial Gem'
L. angustifolia 'Mitcham Gray'
L. angustifolia 'Nana Atropurpurea'
  (Plant A)
L. angustifolia 'The Colour Purple'
L. angustifolia 'Tom Garbutt'
L. x *intermedia* 'Grosso'
L. x *intermedia* 'Hidcote Giant'
L. x *intermedia* 'Impress Purple'

Mid-blue-flowered cultivars
L. angustifolia 'Avice Hill'
L. angustifolia 'Backhouse Purple'
L. angustifolia 'Common'
L. angustifolia 'Fiona English'
L. angustifolia 'Folgate'

L. angustifolia 'Irene Doyle'
L. angustifolia 'Loddon Blue'
L. angustifolia 'Lullaby Blue'
L. angustifolia 'Mausen Dwarf'
L. angustifolia 'Munstead'
L. angustifolia 'Tarras'
L. angustifolia 'Trolla'
L. angustifolia 'Waller's Munstead'
L. angustifolia 'Winton'
L. x *intermedia* 'Dutch'
L. x *intermedia* 'Margaret'

Bright or vivid blue-flowered cultivars
L. angustifolia 'Ashdown Forest'
L. angustifolia 'Beechwood Blue'
L. angustifolia 'Blue Bun'
L. angustifolia 'Blue Cushion'
L. angustifolia 'Bowles Early'
L. angustifolia 'Budakalaszi'
L. angustifolia 'Egerton Blue'
L. angustifolia 'Fring'
L. angustifolia 'Granny's Bouquet'
L. angustifolia 'Heacham Blue'
L. angustifolia 'Helen Batchelder'
L. angustifolia 'Lavenite Petite'
L. angustifolia 'Little Lady'
L. angustifolia 'Martha Roderick'
L. angustifolia 'Mystique'
L. angustifolia 'Nana Atropurpurea'
  (Plant B)
L. angustifolia 'Okamurasaki'
L. angustifolia 'Pacific Blue'
L. angustifolia 'Princess Blue'
L. angustifolia 'Purple Pixie'
L. angustifolia 'Royal Velvet'
L. angustifolia 'Sachet'
L. angustifolia 'Sarah'
L. angustifolia 'Susan Belsinger'
L. angustifolia 'Tucker's Early Purple'
L. x *intermedia* 'Abrialii'
L. x *intermedia* 'Bogong'/
  'Miss Donnington'
L. x *intermedia* 'Seal'
L. x *intermedia* 'Sumian'

Light blue-flowered cultivars
L. angustifolia 'Bosisto'
L. angustifolia 'Lullaby Blue'
L. angustifolia 'Midhall'
L. angustifolia 'Otago Haze'
L. angustifolia 'South Pole'
L. x *intermedia* 'Fragrant Memories'
L. x *intermedia* 'Fred Boutin'
L. x *intermedia* 'Grappenhall'
L. x *intermedia* 'Lullingstone Castle'
L. x *intermedia* 'Nicoleii'
L. x *intermedia* 'Old English'
L. x *intermedia* 'Super'
L. x *intermedia* 'Yuulong'

Short-headed cultivars
L. angustifolia 'Cedar Blue'
L. angustifolia 'Lady'
L. angustifolia 'Thumbelina Leigh'
L. 'Richard Gray'

Long-headed cultivars
L. angustifolia 'Amanda Carter'
L. angustifolia 'Buena Vista'
L. angustifolia 'Maillette'
L. angustifolia 'Royal Purple'
L. angustifolia 'Sharon Roberts'
L. angustifolia 'Tasm'
L. angustifolia 'Twickel Purple'
L. angustifolia 'Violet Intrigue'
L. x *intermedia* 'Jaubert'

Foliage plants
L. x *intermedia* 'Chaix'
L. x *intermedia* 'Grey Hedge'
L. x *intermedia* 'Walberton's
  Silver Edge'
L. 'Andreas'
L. 'Joan Head'
L. 'Molten Silver'
L. 'Sawyers'
L. 'Silver Frost'

Lavender suitable for container growing

Listed here is a limited selection of lavenders suitable for container growing. Many others may also be grown in this way providing they are well pruned and adequately fed.

Small plants suitable for long-term container growing

Section *Stoechas*
'Clair de Lune'
'Evelyn Cadzow'
'Rocky Road'
L. stoechas forma *leucantha*
   ('Snowman')

Section *Lavandula* —
Lavandula angustifolia cultivars
'Blue Bun'
'Blue Cushion'
'Cedar Blue'
'Coconut Ice'
'Crystal Lights'
'Granny's Bouquet'
'Irene Doyle'
'Lavenite Petite'
'Little Lady'
'Little Lottie'
'Martha Roderick'
'Nana Alba'
'Otago Haze'
'Susan Belsinger'
'Thumbelina Leigh'
'Trolla'

Larger plants suitable for container growing for at least two years

Section *Lavandula* —
Lavandula angustifolia and
Lavandula x *intermedia* cultivars
'Alba'
'Ashdown Forest'
'Beechwood Blue'
'Blue Mountain'
'Bowles Early'
'Hidcote Pink'
'Loddon Blue'
'Lullaby Blue'
'Miss Katherine'
'Pacific Pink'
'Princess Blue'
'Violet Intrigue'
L. x *intermedia* 'Grosso'

Other cultivars not mentioned elsewhere in this book

Section *Lavandula*
Lavandula angustifolia cultivars —
numbered cultivars that are not
generally available
'338/8'   New Zealand
'M4'   New Zealand
'Lang2'   New Zealand
'DMAW'   New Zealand
'No. 9'   United Kingdom
'J2'   United Kingdom

Other *Lavandula angustifolia* **cultivars**
'Baby Pink'
'Betty's Blue'
'Carroll'
'Compacta'/'Nana Compacta'
   (similar to 'Munstead')
'Croxton's Wild'
'Dark Supreme'
'Dwarf Blue'/'Baby Blue' (dark blue)
'Edelweiss'
'Fragrance'
'Graves' (dark aster violet)
'Gwendolyn Anley'
'Hardstoft Pink'
'Lumiere des Alpes'

'Middachten' (dark blue)
'Pastor's Pride'
'Premier'
'Summerland Supreme'
   (soft lilac–lavender)
'W.K. Doyle'
'Waltham'
'Warburton Gem'
'Wilderness'
'Wycoff'/'Wyckoff'

Lavandula angustifolia
cultivars mentioned
on the Internet
'Eastgrove Nana'
'Gravetye'
'Hyemal Silver'
'Jackman's Dwarf'
'Maiden Blush'
'Nizza'
'Norfolk'
'Purpurzwerg'
'Resenfreund'
'Shakespeare'
'Silver Blue'
'Skylark'
'Snow Cap'
'Staudenhochzeit'
'Stratford-on-Avon'

Lavandula x *intermedia* cultivars
'Dutch Mill'
'Provencal'
'Provence'
'Silver Grey'
'Waltham' (deep purple)

Lavandula x *intermedia* cultivars
mentioned on the Internet
'Emeric'
'Mitcham Blue'
'White Spikes'

Lavandula lanata x *Lavandula
angustifolia* cultivars
'Ana Luisa'
'Lisa Marie'

Section *Stoechas*
'Fathead'
'Hazel'
'Kew Red'
'St Brelade'
'Willow Vale'
'Wings of Night'

Section *Dentata*
L. dentata var. *candicans* (pink form)
L. dentata var. *dentata* forma *rosea*
'Royal Crown'

GLOSSARY

accuminate
in lavender, refers to the tip of the leaf tapering gradually to a point

acute
having a sharp point

alternate
one leaf or bract at each node of the stem, or arrangement of pairs of leaves in an alternating pattern up the stem

angustifolia
narrow-leaved

apiculate
possessing a short, sharp point which terminates a leaf or bract

appendage
in lavender, refers to an attachment of a secondary part to the upper tooth of the calyx covering the bud before it opens

appendiculate
having appendages

areole
a small area or space

axil
the upper angle formed by the union of a leaf with the stem

bipinnate
a pinnate leaf with the primary leaflets divided in a pinnate manner

bract
a modified protective leaf which subtends or partially subtends the buds of the inflorescence (termed fertile bract in lavenders)

bracteole
small leaf-like organ occurring between the subtending fertile bract and the calyx

calyx
a term for all the sepals of a flower; in the case of lavender, the sepals are fused together

coma
a tuft of leaves or bracts terminating an inflorescence (seen in Section *Stoechas* lavenders) and referred to in lavenders as sterile bracts

cordate
heart-shaped

corolla
all the petals of the flower; in the case of lavender, the petals are fused together

crenate
with shallow, rounded teeth; scalloped

cylindric
elongated and more or less circular in cross-section

deltoid
an equilateral triangle which is attached by the broad end rather than the point

elliptic
oval-shaped with narrow ends

entire
margins of leaf, not toothed or lobed but uninterrupted; continuous

forma
below subspecies and variety in the taxonomic hierarchy — usually distinguished by characteristics such as habit, flower colour, leaf division, etc.

fusiform
shaped like a diamond with rounded edges

glabrous
smooth, hairless

hirsute
with long hairs, usually rather coarse and distinct

imbricate
bracts or leaves overlapping, usually in a regular pattern

interrupted
noticeable gaps, either even or uneven, between whorls in a lavender spike

lanate
woolly, possessing long densely matted and curling hairs

lanceolate
narrow like a lance with tapering ends; broadest point below the middle and the apex shaped like the end of a spear

latifolia
broad-leaved

linear
elongated with parallel sides

lobe
curved or rounded part

lobed leaves
leaves with curved or rounded edges

membranous
clear, transparent

nerved
ribs or veins

nucellus
the central nutritive tissue of the ovule containing the embryo sac

nutlet
a small nut or stone similar to a fruit but with a harder and thicker outer covering

obcordate
with the heart-shaped part at the apex rather than the base

oblanceolate
with the broadest part more towards the top than the base

oblong
two to three times long as broad with parallel sides and rounded ends

obovate
egg-shaped with the broadest point above the middle and attached at the narrowest end

opposite
arrangement of a pair of bracts or leaves opposite each other on a stem

orbicular
perfectly circular, or nearly so

ovate
egg-shaped with the narrow end above the middle and both ends rounded

pedicel
stalk supporting an individual flower

pedicellate
borne or growing on a pedicel

peduncle
the stalk of an inflorescence

pinnate
a compound leaf (feather-like arrangement) of the leaflets in pairs on opposite sides of the midrib

pubescent
generally hairy or, more specifically, covered with short, fine, soft hair

reniform
kidney-shaped with the concave base of the shape as the attachment point

revolute
leaf margins rolled under

rhomboid
diamond-shaped with acute ends and both sides forming obtuse angles

ribbed
possessing one or more prominent veins

sessile
without a stalk, i.e. a leaf without a stalk

simple
plain leaf

spathulate/spatulate
spatula-shaped with rounded portion towards the apex

species
class of individuals; in this case, plants that have common characteristics; taxonomically placed between genus and subspecies

spicate
spike-like or borne on a spike-like inflorescence

spinose
spiny

spiral
referring to the arrangement of bracts around a stem

stalked
in lavender, refers to the stalk (petiole) of a leaf

stamen
the male floral organ that produces pollen

stellate
star-shaped

sterile bract
see coma

sub
a prefix meaning more or less, or somewhat

subspecies
taxonomically between species and variety; a population that differs slightly from the species and is mostly isolated geographically

subtend
to be inserted directly below an organ or structure often sheathing or enclosing it; in lavender, subtend may be used to describe the fertile bract covering or partly covering the flower

tomentose
densely woolly, short, rigid hairs able to be felt by the finger

truncate
cut off sharply at base and apex

variety/varietas (var.)
intermediate between subspecies and forma

vertical
one on top of another in tiers

whorl
refers in lavender to the arrangement of flowers at the same level and same axis in an encircling ring around the peduncle

PHOTOGRAPHY CREDITS

Hal Tapley: 5 (top two photographs), 24, 26, 28, 30, 33, 34, 35, 36, 38, 39, 48, 49, 50, 52, 60, 63, 64, 69, 70, 71 (right-hand photograph), 72, 73, 74, 75, 76, 77, 78 ('Celestial Star'), 80, 81 (right-hand photograph), 84 ('Heacham Blue'), 85 ('Hidcote Pink'), 86, 88, 90, 91, 92, 95 ('Munstead'), 96 ('Nana Atropurpurea' Plant A), 100, 102, 103, 105, 109, 110 (left-hand photograph), 111, 112 (left-hand photograph), 115 ('Grosso'), 116 (right-hand photograph), 117 ('Jaubert'), 121 (left-hand photograph), 122, 127 (left-hand photograph), 128 (right-hand photograph), 132, 134 (bottom two photographs), 136 (top left photograph, 'Evelyn Cadzow'),

137, 141 (left-hand photograph), 145 (left-hand photograph), 157 ('Silver Ghost'), 160

Deborah Ward: i, ii, vi, viii, ix, xii, 5 (bottom photograph), 9, 12, 16, 21, 22, 42, 54, 57, 62, 66, 68, 71 (centre photograph), 78 ('Crystal Lights'), 79, 81 ('Egerton Blue'), 82, 84 ('Hidcote' Plant A), 85 ('Hidcote' Plant B), 95 ('Mystique'), 96 ('Nana Alba'), 106, 108, 110 ('Bogong'), 112 (right-hand photograph), 115 ('Grappenhall', 'Grey Hedge'), 116 ('Hidcote Giant'), 117 ('Impress Purple'), 118, 119, 120, 121 (right-hand photograph), 123, 124, 127 ('Molten Silver'),

128 ('Molten Silver'), 130, 134 (top photograph), 136 ('Clair de Lune'), 139, 140, 141 ('Manakau Village'), 143, 145 (right-hand photograph), 148, 151, 152, 154, 155, 156, 157 ('Willowbridge Calico'), 158

Other photographs supplied by:
Bridestowe Lavender Estate, Tasmania, Australia: 162
Farm Tomita, Japan: 98, 166, 167
Lavandula, Daylesford, Victoria, Australia: 10, 164
Plant Growers Australia: 161

BIBLIOGRAPHY

Pamela Allardice, *Lavender*
Hill of Content, 1990
ISBN 0-85572-197-9

Patti Barrett, *Growing and Using Lavender*
Storey Books, 1996
ISBN 0-8826-6475-1

Olive Dunn, *Delights of Lavender*
Random House NZ, 1993
ISBN 1-86941-175-7

Tessa Evelegh, *Lavender*
Anness Publishing, 1996
ISBN 1-85967-206-X

Jackie French, *Book of Lavender*
Collins, Angus & Robertson, 1993
ISBN 0-207-17959-X

Robert Kurik and Deborah Jones
The Lavender Garden
Chronicle Books, 1998
ISBN 0-8118-1570-6

Julia Lawless, *Lavender Oil*
Thorsons, 1994
ISBN 0-7225-3031-5

Judyth A. McLeod, *Lavender, Sweet Lavender*
Kangaroo Press, 1989
ISBN 0-86417-139-0

Virginia McNaughton, *The Essential Lavender*
Penguin Books NZ, 1994
ISBN 0-670-85713-0

Deborah Schneebeli-Morrell
The Victorian Book of Lavender and Old Lace
Coombe Books, 1996
ISBN 1-85833-501-9

Joanna Sheen, *Lavender*
Dorling Kindersley, 1991
ISBN 0-86318-562-2

Hans Silvester and Christine Meunier
Lavender Country of Provence
Thames and Hudson, 1995
ISBN 0-500-01678-X

Hans Silvester, Christine Meunier
and Alexandra Campbell
Lavender: Fragrance of Provence
Harry N. Abrams, 1996
ISBN 0-8109-3576-7

Ellen Spector Platt, *Lavender*
Kitchen Keepsakes, 1999
ISBN 0-8117-2849-8

Maggie Tisserand and Monika Junemann
The Magic and Power of Lavender
Windpferd Verlagsgesellschaft, 1994
ISBN 0-941524-88-4

Lois Vickers, *The Scented Lavender Book*
Edbury Press, 1991
ISBN 0-7126-4702-3

Philippa Waring, *Lavender*
I.P.G. Chicag, 1997
ISBN 0-2856-3370-8

INDEX